HOLDING FAST/
PRESSING ON

HOLDING FAST/ PRESSING ON

Religion in America in the 1980s

ERLING JORSTAD

New York
Westport, Connecticut
London

Library of Congress Cataloging-in-Publication Data

Jorstad, Erling
    Holding fast/pressing on :   religion in America in the 1980s   /
Erling Jorstad.
      p.   cm.
    Includes bibliographical references.
    ISBN 0-275-93607-4 (alk. paper)
    1. United States—Religion—1960–   I. Title.
BL2525.J674   1990a
291'.0973'09048—dc20   90-6717

A hardcover edition of *Holding Fast/Pressing On* is available
from Greenwood Press (Contributions to the study of religion,
no. 26; ISBN 0-313-26599-2).

Library of Congress Catalog Card Number: 90-6717
ISBN: 0-275-93607-4

First published in 1990

Praeger Publishers, One Madison Avenue, New York, NY 10010
An imprint of Greenwood Publishing Group, Inc.

Printed in the United States of America

The paper used in this book complies with the
Permanent Paper Standard issued by the National
Information Standards Organization (Z39.48—1984).

10 9 8 7 6 5 4 3 2 1

Copyright Acknowledgments

Grateful acknowledgment is given for permission to reprint from the following: Robert
Bellah et al., *Habits of the Heart* © 1985 The Regents of the University of California,
pp. 98–99; Joseph W. Trigg and William L. Sachs, *Of One Body: Renewal Movements
in the Church* (Atlanta, Ga.: John Knox Press, 1986); reprinted by permission from *The
Emerging New Class: Implications for Church and Society* by Barbara Hargrove. The
Pilgrim Press, copyright 1986, New York, New York.

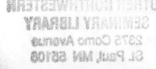

To Ruth

Contents

Preface

As the United States lurches into the last decade before the millennium, the transition calls for a sustained look at its recent religious past. Should the human race be alive for that magical moment of entrance into A.D. 2000, Americans, among others, will be able to ponder in the most profound terms their past, their present, and especially their future. After all, none of us will be around for the same event in 3000, so our reflections will be of great import.

The occasion may well inspire such sentiments as awe, fear, hope, gratitude, judgment, and commitment. These also are cornerstones for what we call religion, especially "religious faith."[1] Both those who profess faith and those who study it (and the two often intertwine) will have the opportunity on December 31, 1999, to ponder again one of the most deep-reaching of all questions: Should people of religious faith hold fast to those truths and organizations they believe to have come from the eternal, from the permanent, from God? Will personal conviction and social expression of faith be strong enough to withstand the awesome, as yet unknown forces of the new millennium? Or should people of faith press on in this world of ceaseless scientific and social change to absorb and create new insights, new truths, new social expressions, and new ways to survive in the 2000s?

Holding fast or pressing on?[2] The question is as ancient as recorded time itself. That question also defines for us the boundaries of this study. Aware of the "fallacy of the undivided middle" (that the truth about such polarizing questions is found somewhere between its extremes), we use the impending millennium as our signal that it is time to take stock of where we have just been. Students of all ages traditionally turn to theology or religion or astrology (especially now with the New Age religion) to answer our blockbuster question. In this book, however, we examine the historical record. As a source of illumination, history needs no apologia from this author or anyone else. For all its ambiguity and methodological limitations, it has no worthy competitors as an integrative, critical discipline to elucidate that ever-elusive "human condition."

History is best briefly defined as "change over time." In this study we attempt to mark out what in religious life did change over the years of the 1980s, why those changes occurred, and what they portend for this premillenium decade of ours. We are aware that the conventional wisdom (also known as CW) among historians writing on the 1980s will conclude that (1) the New Christian Right was the most important and certainly the most energetic religious movement of the decade; (2) the mainline churches certainly became the oldline or sideline churches during that period; (3) the privatization of religious faith expanded at an unparalleled (and immeasurable) rate of growth; (4) secularization made significant inroads but failed to eliminate basic religious outreach; and (5) both public and private moral behavior underwent profound transformations.

Conventionally speaking, that wisdom is somewhat close to what did occur. But CW, by definition, lacks both perspective and synthesis. It falls short of telling us how events of the previous decades shaped current events, and it makes little attempt to weave together in a meaningful pattern an interpretation of what it all means.

This book brings together not all but surely the most illuminating information about the religious expressions of the 1980s. It attempts to show that the decade coheres into a meaningful pattern when its religious expression is seen in a threefold design: (1) mainline moves into frontline; (2) evangelicalism moves toward popular religion; and (3) privatization moves into New Age religion. In more traditional analytic terms, the threefold pattern appears as denominational, transdenominational, and nondenominational religion, with profound changes in each. Of course, overlaps abound among the three, as will be evident. The pattern is anything but logically tidy. It has repetitions, ambiguities, and idiosyncrasies. But then so does that human record we call history.

What appears documentably clear by the end of the 1980s is that (1) the fundamentalist-evangelical dominance of the religious and moral energies of the 1980s has been overrated; (2) the mainline churches are in far deeper trouble than even their critics acknowledge; and (3) individualistic privatization, so convincingly documented in *Habits of the Heart*, is as of now the most visible and plausible wave of the future.[3]

Why should this book be written at this time? These three developments have great import for students of American religious history. They call for interpretation, for finding the pattern in the carpet. The students who turn for understanding to the widely influential concept of secularization in the field of the sociology of religion discover something very surprising. That concept, so influential for so many years among social historians and sociologists, actually falls short of explaining the inner dynamics of the religious energy of the 1980s.[4]

However, students may well conclude, as did this author, that an understanding of the process of modernization clearly describes how those forces that created religious change during the 1980s became intertwined with the energies of religious outreach.[5] Religious faith and modernization somehow attempted to come to terms with one another. Finally, students may see that the sum total of the verifiable evidence and the social indices available to them for discerning the future strongly indicates that the new wave of privatization will somehow find a way to accommodate itself to the new technological and sociopolitical forces of the 1990s by means that we cannot yet anticipate.[6]

These reasons in themselves would be adequate to warrant writing a work such as this. However, the case for such a book is even more compelling when we carry out the mandate of scholars who now write "religious history" rather than "church history."[7] Rather than focus exclusively on the specific activities and teachings of formal social organizations, denominations, sects, and cults, the "top" or the elites, we start rather from the bottom and work up. Further, we accept the vastly broadened definition of our age of what "religious faith" means.[8] In brief, we recognize here the primacy of looking at popular expressions of religion, and as historians we incorporate the more recently utilized tools of analysis, such as those from sociology of religion, social psychology, popular culture and popular religion, and communication theory, into our existing collection of historical and theological instruments.[9]

In addition, we have for our probes a highly impressive list of new secondary interpretations made available in the last few years. These include works by Robert Wuthnow, Martin E. Marty, Wade Clark Roof and James McKinney, James Davison Hunter, George Marsden, Jeffrey Hadden, and Charles Lippy, among others. The immensely learned multivolume encyclopedias edited by Mircea Eliade and by Charles Lippy and Peter Williams add greatly to our resources. Further, in the 1980s we witnessed the rising importance of high-quality editors of religion news in national newspapers, such as Peter Steinfels in the *New York Times*, John Dart and Russell Chandler in the *Los Angeles Times* and Clark Morphew in the *St. Paul Pioneer Press Dispatch*, as well as the continuing great work of the George Cornells and Wilfred Thorkelsons. We now have an increasingly large number of periodicals such as *Religion Watch, National and International Religion Report, National Christian Reporter,* and the *National Catholic Reporter*, among others. We still have available such old stalwarts as *Christian Century, Christianity Today,* and *Christianity and Crisis.* Add to this the proliferating number of thoughtful and responsible journals from the seminaries and divinity schools, and one clearly has more material than her or his files can handle. Beyond that, some two to four dozen graduate-school–level research dissertations in this field appear every year.

But the rationale for this book goes beyond the writing of religious history. In the 1980s, more than in earlier decades, religious news became front-page news, not only because of the televangelist scandals and eyebrow-raising fund-raising schemes, but because fundamentalist and evangelical preachers were consulted by the highest officials in the Oval Office. Major news developments were also made by devout religionists taking to the streets, to the hospitals, to the military installations, and to the courtrooms to demonstrate their convictions for or against abortion, capital punishment, arms proliferation, and related causes. Finally, we are only now faintly becoming aware of just how decisive the media, especially television, have become in shaping all our sensibilities, including those qualities that we believe are religious. We stand in need of much deeper understanding here.

Now historians have at their disposal the ubiquitous, consciousness-transforming power of word processing to speed and simplify their researches. Hopefully, scholars are now at work to help us find a firmer handle on understanding than we now have available. What is computing doing to understanding? We are just now beginning to see the first light through that tunnel.

For all these reasons we have good cause to set out a book such as this for an early guide to the next millennium. Like every historian, this one would have appreciated about 800 more pages from his editor for inclusion. Such quantity, plus the fact that some important communities have their own integral history waiting to be written or updated, explains why the black evangelicals, Jehovah's Witnesses, Seventh-Day Adventists, and Mormons, as well as the hundreds of smaller "new religions" and traditional non-Western religions, cannot be included in these all-too-few pages.[10]

I chose the rationale of chronology to establish the placement of the three major groupings in the order that follows. Since the mainline has been the oldest and most influential of all Protestant traditions in the United States, its history in the 1980s is set down first. In that decade the fundamentalists/evangelicals came into greater national prominence than ever before; hence their record occupies the middle position chronologically. Finally, privatization and New Age developments are, in this writer's estimate, the transition to the new "mainstream" religious life of the future; hence they are placed at the end of the threefold division.

To each of the three clusters analyzed here, I try to send a personal message. To mainliners: If growth is what will keep you from going under, what models of growth do you want to follow? Can any model outside your denominational characteristics be effective? To fundamentalists/evangelicals: Will your growth continue to be modeled at least in part on the secular standards of success in the 1980s? To privatizers: What might probably emerge amid your commendable individualism as some very dysfunctional damage to the integrative features of religious tradition and community?

It is a pleasure to acknowledge the many courtesies and downright direct first aid shown me by the following. Brother Curtis, son Eric, and daughters Laura and Becky Myrick were family anchors as well as sources of materials and ideas. Emily and Jim White continued their long-standing tradition of friendship and reflection. Once again, the whole staff at Rolvaag Memorial Library went far beyond regular support in meeting my many requests: Forrest Brown, Edna Harmer, Kris Huber, Jean Parker, Connie Gunderson, Judy Holt, J.R. Cox, and especially Gretchen Hardgrove and Betsy Boyum Busa, who cordially put up with my frequent idiosyncrasies. The editors at Greenwood Publishing Group made many important improvements. Among colleagues, my history confreres gave me steady help and constructive criticisms at several key points. Mary Jane Smith deserves extra stars in her crown for frequent direct help. Within the faculty Stu Hendrickson, Michael Leming, and Susan Lindley were always available for consultation and advice. Good friends, also editors, Ron Klug and Mary Nasby Lohre gave freely of their skills. Lois Wilkens again prepared the manuscript superbly. Dean Jon Moline provided financial support at key junctures. And to Ruth, who never let me take myself as seriously as I thought I should, I dedicate this book.

NOTES

1. I follow the definition of Clifford Geertz of religion as (1) a system of symbols that act to (2) establish powerful, pervasive, and long-lasting moods and motivations in men by (3) formulating conceptions of a general order of existence and (4) clothing these conceptions with such an aura of factuality that (5) the moods and motivations seem uniquely realistic. Clifford Geertz, "Religion as a Cultural System," in Donald Cutler, ed., *The Religious Situation: 1968* (Boston: Beacon Press, 1968), p. 643.

2. See my *Evangelicals in the White House: The Cultural Maturation of Born Again Christianity, 1960-1981* (New York: Edwin Mellen Press, 1981), pp. 3-5.

3. See Robert Bellah et al., *Habits of the Heart: Individualism and Commitment in American Life* (Berkeley: University of California Press, 1985).

4. Peter Berger defines secularization as "the process by which sectors of society are removed from the domination of religious institutions and symbols." That is, as quoted by Phillip E. Hammond, "Not only do churches lose clout but also do people generally think less about religion." "Secularization . . . not only involves the removal of domination by 'religious institutions and symbols' over society-at-large; it also involves the decline of the sacred *within* those religious institutions and symbols." Hammond, "Religion in the Modern World," in James Davison Hunter and Stephen C. Ainlay, eds., *Making Sense of Modern Times: Peter L. Berger and the Vision of Interpretive Sociology* (New York: Routledge and Kegan Paul, 1986), pp. 146-57; see Berger, "Some Second Thoughts on the Substantive versus the Functional Definitions of Religion," *Journal for the Scientific Study of Religion* 13, 2 (June 1974): 125-32.

5. "Modernization" can be defined in various ways; see James Davison Hunter, *American Evangelicalism: Conservative Religion and the Quandary of Modernity* (New Brunswick, N.J.: Rutgers University Press, 1983), chaps. 1-2. I follow Barbara Hargrove, who states that it is a term close to "rationalization," a process "which seeks to ignore such human elements as mystery and wonder as well as to organize social groups along the lines of rational principles. . . . There is an underlying assumption in rationality, and in the modernization process, that it is possible to organize all life in ways that make sense, at least to persons with sufficient expertise to understand what is going on." See Barbara Hargrove, *The Emerging New Class: Implications for Church and Society* (New York: Pilgrim Press, 1986), pp. 31-32ff.

6. "Privatization" within religion is defined by John F. Wilson as the movement to "maximize self-realization and personal growth and reward primary relationships. Divine commandments are transformed into instrumental strategies for achieving personal satisfaction. . . . it is more preoccupied with the emotional and psychological dimensions of human experience and with individual problems such as anxiety, stress, depression, and tension." See John F. Wilson, "The Sociological Study of American Religion," in Charles H. Lippy and Peter W. Williams, eds., *Encyclopedia of the American Religious Experience*, Vol. 1 (New York: Scribner, 1988), p. 28. See also the discussion of privatization in Robert

Wuthnow, "The Social Significance of Religious Television," *Review of Religious Research* 29, 2 (December 1987): 125–27.

7. See David W. Lotz, "A Changing Historiography: From Church History to Religious History," in David Lotz, Donald W. Shriver, Jr., and John F. Wilson, eds., *Altered Landscapes: Christianity in America, 1935–1985* (Grand Rapids, Mich.: Wm. B. Eerdmans, 1989), pp. 312–39.

8. See Martin E. Marty, "The Religious Situation in 1969," in Donald R. Cutler, ed., *The Religious Situation: 1969* (Boston: Beacon Press, 1969), pp. 25–43.

9. For instance, see David G. Hackett, "Sociology of Religion and American Religious History: Retrospect and Prospect," *Journal for the Scientific Study of Religion* 27, 4 (1988): 461–74.

10. For instance, see the bibliographic materials in William C. Turner, Jr., "Black Evangelicalism: Theology, Politics, and Race," *Journal of Religious Thought* 45, 2 (Winter/Spring 1989): 40–56.

HOLDING FAST/
PRESSING ON

Introduction: The Great Awakening, 1960-1979

In the next several pages we review briefly the major forces in American religious life that gave the events of the 1980s their unique configurations. As highly selective and interpretive as our discussion of these episodes is, it nonetheless stands as the essential foundation for Chapter 1.

The first major evidence of the hold-fast/press-on struggle of the 1980s came into clear public view as early as 1960. Prior to then, most Americans seemed publicly satisfied to conduct the politics of consensus, concentrating on unified public policy at home and militant anticommunism overseas. Best known as the era of the cold war (1945-1960), these years were times of rapid economic growth and celebration of all things American in light of the threat of world Communist expansionism.

Underneath the signs of unity, however, specific interest groups were in the first stages of what would become one of the most transforming of all epochs in the nation's history. Not the implementation of any utopian theorist, this upheaval rather emerged from grass roots rebellion and demands by disempowered minorities for redesign of the social, economic, and moral landscape itself. It embraced racial minorities long held in second-class citizenship; it attracted women and men demanding gender equality in every phase of public life. It aroused a large cross section of the populace determined to preserve the delicate ecological balance of humankind and the natural world. Finally, it awoke across the country the largest citizen-based antiwar crusade in the nation's history.

Beginning with a black college student sit-in to protest segregation in North Carolina, and given heretofore unprecedented coverage through the new medium of television, the civil rights movement convinced citizens of the need to demand greater decision-making participation for themselves ("power to the people"). They concluded that for too long such power had been the domain of white, upper middle-class males, given to overpriced, high-tech armaments programs and overseas military intervention in the name of anitcommunism. In the eyes of the newly empowered activists, these same elites (the buzzword was "the establishment")

1

were also helping economic developers despoil the environment and squander priceless natural resources. Soon underclass Americans, Hispanics, Native Americans, civil rights advocates, antiwar activists, feminists, and nontraditional communalists, among others, were demanding that public policy, as well as consciousness itself, be transformed to meet their agenda for what became known as "peace and justice" or "liberation" issues.

Much of their energy and vision emerged out of the negative despair and disillusionment over an assassinated president, over pervasive white resistance to black demands for equality, over increasingly strong demands from womens' rights advocates for implementation of the feminist agenda for equality, and from outrage that the physical environment was being despoiled in the name of economic growth. Crowning the new protestation was an escalating antiwar movement, the first of its scope in American history, over the growing military involvement of the United States in the Vietnamese civil war. As events unfolded, Americans became increasingly aware of that participation as constituting more a defense of the old, imperialistic regime of Western capitalism than a recognition of traditional American dedication to the aspirations of underclass people for self-rule.[1]

Students of the 1960s have come to interpret this upheaval as one of the great transformations in American history. They see it as a "seismic shift," a quickening, a cultural revolution, a time of national travail, a point of no return, a "greening," or a rebirth. Perhaps William F. McLoughlin best encapsulates in a phrase the enormity of the forces for change at work. He concludes that this was an age of "awakening" in the great American tradition of such religious outbursts. His definition is worth quoting at some length:

Awakenings—the most vital and yet most mysterious of all folk arts—are periods of cultural revitalization that begin in a general crisis of beliefs and values and extend over a period of a generation or so, during which time a profound reorientation in beliefs and values takes place. Revivals alter the lives of individuals; awakenings alter the world view of a whole people or culture.

He goes on to explain that although awakenings emerge in times of cultural disorientation and grave personal stress, "they are therapeutic and cathartic, not pathological. They restore our cultural verve and our self-confidence, helping us to maintain faith in ourselves, our ideals, and our 'covenant with God' even while they compel us to reinterpret that convenant in the light of new experience."[2]

This awakening emerged from the cultural disorientation and grave personal stress of the 1960s. Many Americans came to decide that they could cope with the anguish of the civil rights movement, the women's liberation movement, the peace movement, and the environmental movement only by transforming their most cherished values and convictions.

The all-embracing unifying theme to all this upheaval was the conviction that America must make good the promises of the Declaration of Independence: liberty and justice for all. So powerful was this demand for drastic change and so strong was the distrust that existing governing institutions such as education, business, government, church, and the traditional family could bring about a new society that a major "values shift" (as sociologists call it) burst out across generations, regions, classes, and ethnic groups.

This shift embraced a rejection of traditional moral standards, especially in the areas of sexuality, family values, and personal life-styles, and "an affirmation of personal autonomy and tolerance for personal differences."[3] Some observers started calling this a "counterculture," a transformation of consciousness and the first steps toward a society freed from class oppression and exploitation. Experimental communities eschewing traditional family morality and the capitalistic work ethic and reward system soon appeared as statements of the new consciousness. Fueled partly by a growing drug culture, by Asian-inspired religious insights, and often by increasingly influential rock singers of protest and new consciousness music, this culture in its myriad forms became evidence of the new awakening.

In addition, the basic social institutions that held American society together came under deep suspicion. How could a people respect a government that supported racial separation or unequal rights (pay, education, promotion, physical abuse, and so on) for women or allowed business to foul the environment? How could people trust educational institutions that championed the stratified class society or subsidized clandestine military research? How could they honor the military that was killing unarmed civilians overseas? How could they respect corporations motivated only by the profit motive and not by a sense of social responsibility?[4]

As the holders and pressers came into the scene, how could the churches and synagogues support any institutions that were not condemning such outrages? With speed rarely shown by such slow-moving institutions as churches, many members and leaders responded to the awakening by joining one or several of the crusades. Motivated at first by the stirring religious and moral idealism of Dr. Martin Luther King, Jr., church people carried the dream of a racially integrated society into their communities and churches. That same quickening propelled others into joining antiwar programs and movements opposed to the arms race buildup, complete with counseling and protection for young men who believed that participation in the military was immoral. Still others entered into the several environmental preservation programs, inspired by their hopes to help preserve God's creation. In building on earlier demands for achieving their agenda, feminists demanded that churches give far greater policy-making authority, including the right of ordination, to women. In brief, these became known as "peace and justice" issues.[5]

The awakening, however, reached beyond the activists' public agendas. In a curious, even self-contradictory way, the activists' suspicion of the existing governing social institutions led them both to work for improving (even transforming) those institutions and to explore the very consciousness that had created such a society. In this, the "age of Aquarius," people came to believe that perhaps a new age and a new level of reality had dawned, and that transformation of the old, egotistical self and of materialistic society could be turned into a world of peace and justice. From a variety of sources such as Asian religions, the human potential movement, the drug culture, and experimental Christian spirituality came the call for "celebration," a favorite word of the 1960s. The seeker, in or out of organized religion, should accentuate her or his own uniqueness and the capacity to love one another, to share, and to indulge in fantasy and inner renewal. From such sources of power could come the energy to renew life and hope on this old, tired planet. For these believers this truly would be an awakening, a liberation from old capitalist values and old, competitive, task-oriented roles, and the creation instead of a totally new consciousness, a new way of understanding reality. This is well described by Joseph W. Trigg and William L. Sachs:

The counterculture opposed privatization and recast self-interest as self-fulfillment. It assumed an organic view of society in which life is one. Love, however vaguely understood, became the supreme norm. For personal fulfillment, love meant honest, total self-expression at any given moment. The counterculture prized affectivity: immediate, direct experience (being there) and expression (letting it all hang out); knowing oneself fully (being in touch with feelings); and participating directly in the experience of others (knowing where they are coming from).[6]

Such a transformation, enhanced vividly by mass-media exposure, quickly flowed into the churches. The impact was almost immediate; some (the pressers on) called for a totally new way of understanding what faith was all about, including the possibility of not needing organized religion to do so, while the holders called for fidelity to the great truths and practices that had brought Christianity through many earlier crises and would be able to do the same again in this new challenge to its authority.

Already by the late 1960s, as the peace and justice agendas came to dominate the outreach programs of many churches, the beginnings of a major backlash against them came into view. From the early 1960s onward, substantial numbers of clergy and laity across the country opposed the speed and often the goals of the King-led civil rights movement. Laity and clergy flatly opposed any ordination of women. Others believed that the churches had no business trying to tell American industry how to develop its resources; was not humankind to have dominion over the earth, including its economic utilization? A sizeable portion of Christendom in America believed that the White House should be given the public support it said it needed to help it win the war over the Communists in Asia.[7]

Furthermore, the awakening started leading some seekers to find direction, authority, and community outside the familiar structures of organized religion, the churches and synagogues. Observers such as Martin E. Marty and Thomas Luckmann detected a quickly expanding tendency toward what they called "privatization." In a world where trust in institutions that supported the status quo seemed so misplaced, where community among people could disappear in high-rise apartments and in front of television sets, people could easily generate their own self-styled searches for spiritual bliss. As denominational loyalty for many started to fade, as peace and justice issues began to transcend theological and doctrinal controversies, people came to find in their own private set of convictions or immediate circle of fellow activists the nurture and meaning that once had been the purview of organized faith.

Privatization, known by a variety of names, tended to maximize self-realization and personal growth and reward primary relationships. As John Wilson suggested, divine commandments were "transformed into instrumental strategies for achieving personal satisfaction."[8] That movement blended nicely with the growing human potential movement, which offered ways of finding such desirable goals as self-respect, self-esteem, integrity, and authenticity in the name of religious or spiritual growth. The personal growth qualities it offered were obviously qualities that could be learned from agencies other than the churches, or so the promotions for EST, transcendental meditation, Arica Mind Control, scientology, and others were advertising.[9]

This transformation seemed to some observers to be turning into a weird or contradictory kind of awakening. On the one hand they could see the outburst of the new spirituality, created both by disgust with status quo institutions and by hope that Aquarius just might be within reach. Yet at the same time Americans, like people in all industrialized societies, were living out their lives within the social process of modernization. That process differed sharply from the new spirituality in that it took its energy from the technology generated economic growth of society. That is, the new culture in its values and culture adapted to the "rapidly changing attitudes, realities, and values that place a premium on rationality, objectivity, relativity, novelty, science and technology, social action, organization, differentiation and distributive justice."[10] How, critics asked, could one balance the new spirituality and yet hold confidence in rationalization?

A major critic, Leonard I. Sweet, finds that in the 1960s and 1970s modernization found full expression and great influence among the mainline churches.[11] Hence the paradox: the existence of a church-related constituency, largely white, middle-class, and urban, searching for peace and justice causes while probing the luxuries of a privatized, nonecclesial church in a society dominated by modernist values and culture. This is another way of saying that the awakening was at work in such a way that older institutions, such as the churches, could never survive in the next decades in their existing form. It was a matter of holding on to some features here, pressing on for other features there. The old patterns that had for so long in American history kept the lines between holding and pressing were now for many fast disappearing as the decade closed.

Just as eras in history often have vaguely defined beginnings, they may conclude with equal vagueness. For the 1960s, however, such was not the case. After an alarmingly rapid increase in urban rioting, campus violence, the assassinations in the spring of 1968 of two of the dominant heroes of the "greening" of America (Dr. King and Senator Robert F. Kennedy), and the riot of the Chicago police against demonstrators at the Democratic National Convention in August of that year, the era collapsed one fine spring morning in Kent, Ohio. The date of May 4, 1970, is well considered the end of the age of Aquarius with the death of four unarmed civilians during a riotous Ohio National Guard put-down of a major campus upheaval at Kent State University.

As though given a cue from an invisible national leader, campuses simply closed, or colleges gave passing grades to departing students. The black community, already depleted of unifying leadership by King's death, divided itself even further into hostile, competing factions, each with its own agenda, and thus lost more national influence. Feminists collided with highly effective, tightly organized political opposition from both women and men to their demand for the Equal Rights Amendment (ERA). The children of the counterculture, the hippies and the straights, all watched in horror as their attempt in 1970 to duplicate the communal bliss of the Woodstock rock music festival of 1969 ended with the murder of spectators at an Altamont, California, concert. Meanwhile, the violence in Vietnam continued, with the news media each Thursday presenting the latest body count of American fatalities. No visible peacemaking initiatives were forthcoming from the White House or its political opposition. Yet, in an anomalous expression of modernization during this time of distress, the United States in 1969 started sending explorers to the moon, a triumph for rationalistic mentality.

Despite the violence and the setbacks, activists carried on their militant crusading into the early 1970s. Those within the churches, the pressers on, concluded that their demands for the liberal agenda of the 1960s, even though far from being a reality, still needed their full support. That meant continuing the battles for ERA, putting an end to the war and the arms race, working for environmental safeguards, and the advancement of civil rights.

But in the early 1970s several major crises emerged within the mainline churches to stymie their programs. These crises arose largely from the profound transformations created by the many-sided awakening. What many pressers on during the 1960s had neglected was the continuation of an ongoing ministry for a deeper, more nurturing experience of spiritual faith. For many seekers such renewal must come from within, not from reformist activism. For them Aquarius had not yet dawned; they continued, as they had always done, to find religion a source of comfort and personal renewal. In addition, many of them concluded that the goals of the pressers on were not, as the latter seemed to claim, the will of God; rather, holders fast decided that such goals were in reality the political agenda of the liberal Democrats.[12]

This struggle seemed only to encourage both sides to work even harder for the implementation of their programs. Mainline pressers on added new items, such as arms control, the elimination of nuclear weaponry, and major educational programs for pursuing peacemaking, starting at the parish level. They expanded their agenda in certain locales to help the homeless, the poor, and the semiliterate. They also launched major programs to expand the decision-making power of women within the churches, including ordination in those denominations still led by males. Mainline activists added to these programs the call for adoption of inclusive, nonsexist language in the liturgy, in traditional hymnody ("Rise Up, O Men of God"), and in Scripture.[13]

Again, holders fast held their ground. By the late 1960s and into the 1970s the privatization and politicization processes already at work helped produce what became a major crisis, what Wade Clark Roof and William McKinney have called a "serious religious depression." Mainline churches (Episcopal, Methodist, United Church of Christ, Disciples of Christ, Presbyterian, liberal Baptist, and some Lutheran bodies) started losing startlingly large numbers of members, financial support and program vitality. For a variety of reasons, significant drops in membership, attendance, and stewardship swept over the mainline churches. Compared to the heyday growth years of the 1950s, by 1980 the United Methodists had lost 11.4 percent, the United Presbyterians had dropped some 23 percent, the Episcopalians some 16.9 percent, the Christian Church (Disciples of Christ) over 22.6 percent, and the United Church of Christ just under 11 percent.[14]

To some analysts the drops were not so startling. The declines seemed to mirror a trend showing that the lack of American public confidence in church impact on American life was widespread in other areas of life also. That impact had dropped from its high point in 1958 of 69 percent to a low point in 1970 of 14 percent. Pollsters suggested that the drastic sag was "no more or less than the erosion of confidence found for most of our major social institutions."[15]

Such a drastic turnabout, however, sent religion watchers a clear message that something in the awakening had turned some of its energy in an unfamiliar direction. Awakenings traditionally had led converts and revitalized believers back into more clearly church-related programs of worship and outreach. However, such results in the 1970s failed to materialize among many mainliners. Some experts found verifiable demographic evidence as the chief explanation of the decline. Mainliner parents, mostly college educated and upwardly mobile, were having smaller families; hence fewer eligible children were available to join the church. Also, the number of new members started to be overshadowed by dropouts and deaths of existing church folk. Further, some mainliners came to prefer the more politically conservative ministries now beginning to flourish among evangelicals.[16]

Finally, sizeable numbers of young adults, more often single than married, expressed in the values shift of the 1960s their distaste for and suspicion of organized religion. Privatization and modernization were beginning to reap their inexorable harvest: Who needed a church when one's own values and interests furnished the spiritual nourishment they decided was adequate for this new age?[17]

However, other mainline observers, such as Leonard I. Sweet, reached far different, more foreboding conclusions as to the reasons for the decline in members and vitality. Himself a mainline leader, he argued vigorously that the mainline in the 1970s deserved its decline; it had brought on its own crises. In "its attempt to express spiritual realities in ways beyond the reach of, or at flagrant odds with popular piety," it had failed in its mission.[18]

Specifically, Sweet argued, the decline came from the mainliners' inability to bring together in a meaningful, shared way a common understanding of faith.

The educated clergy elite were ignoring or insensitive to the needs and agendas of the laity. Second, there developed within member families a major falloff from such devotional expressions as regular Bible reading, family worship, and prayer. This, Sweet and others argued, created a major void in their spiritual nourishment.[19]

Finally, over the years the role of the minister had changed drastically from pastor and counselor to expert in increasingly specialized religious scholarship, including liberal theology and left-wing political activism. Professional church leadership staffs had modeled themselves after efficient corporate leadership at the expense of one-to-one personal communication. In brief, they simply lost touch with the people. The latter, in turn, either dropped out, swtiched to other churches, or cut back on their involvement in their local churches. Thus the decline was due to the clergy and related staffs simply joining in the modernist mode of seeing all truths, including the ancient truth claims of the faith, as relative to the time and situation and spirit of the age.[20]

Beyond the collapse in religious vitality during these years, mainline churches found themselves sharply divided over the growing charismatic renewal movement first seen among Episcopalians and Lutherans in 1960. Drawing from the classical Pentecostal church emphasis on the "spiritual gifts of the Holy Spirit" and a "second baptism," church people in the mainline were starting to conduct prayer meetings, devotional studies, and related renewal movements within the parent churches. For many this was the kind of personal, highly experiential form of spirituality they had not found in the more politicized mainline peace and justice churches. As a result, the influence of this movement grew quickly where an attractive program or leader within the mainline started a charismatic ministry.[21]

Additional problems for mainline identity continued to grow through the 1960s. With the speed of social change accelerating at a pace often too difficult for either leadership or laity to understand, the awakening of the 1960s found new expression in at least three additional major movements. First, the human potential movement, with its attractively packaged offer of self-help, improved self-esteem, and self-fulfillment, started to find a surprisingly large, enthusiastic number of seekers. Those looking for something new, something enriching, or simply for keeping up with the latest trends could find anything from a one-hour to a weekend or even longer program offering self-actualization, inner harmony, self-empowerment, and comparable benefits. What seemed to be at work here was the inclusion by mainline, evangelical, and charismatic leaders of many of the insights, teachings, and techniques of secular, humanistic psychology, especially the works of Carl Rodgers, Abraham Maslow, and Fritz Perls. All of these embraced some loosely defined spirituality dimensions, thus making themselves popular to those in and out of the organized churches seeking something more than the old fare of preawakening years.[22]

Second, the awakening also helped bring out otherwise latent growth potential in the evangelical and fundamentalist communities of the country. From the outset of the awakening, their leaders and members held a distinct advantage over mainline churchfolk in the dynamics for membership and program growth. Most if not all of the evangelicals' church-related work—evangelism, education, social outreach, worship, and public-policy involvement—had from the earliest years of their history been conducted through parachurch institutions rather than through specific denominational channels. As such, evangelicals found far more freedom, informality, and flexibility for expansion compared to mainliners, who were by definition required to remain within their specific denominational loyalties and disciplines. During the 1970s a vast array of networking parachurch groups helped enormously by skilled media promotion came to rival the mainline and to attract its members and resources to switch into their ranks.

Further, the evangelicals had the advantage of offering a very clearly understood popular culture version of religious faith as contrasted to the centuries-old confessions and liturgies of most mainliners. For example, they identified directly with the more secular culture of the American entertainment world to promote interest in Christian professional athletes and coaches, Christian beauty queens, Christian luxury cruises, Christian romantic novels, and large amounts of Christian contemporary music.[23]

The growing popularity took clear visible form in several other areas of religious growth. Evangelicals gave more financial support to their churches than before, including funds for foreign missions. This factor ranks high as an index of religious vitality because none of those funds are utilized to improve the local parish. Second, in both Christian day schools and post–high-school educational institutions (including Bible schools), evangelicals showed remarkable growth: there was a 47 percent increase between 1971 and 1978 in the number of such schools, a 113 percent increase in the number of teachers, and a 95 percent increase in the number of students. This meant some 66,080 teachers and 1,068,000 students.[24]

Third, evangelical leaders found the 1970s to be the most prosperous time in their history for expansion through use of the electronic media. In those years the expenditures for religious broadcasting grew from about $50 million to over $600 million annually; each of the four most famous celebrity preachers, Jerry Falwell, Oral Roberts, Jim Bakker, and Pat Robertson, by 1980 was receiving over $50 million annually for his programs.[25]

Thus the awakening, true to the larger trends that produced enormously rapid change in American life, had by the decade's end simply remade much of the religious landscape. Some of the force behind this transformation clearly had centered on the growing theological rivalry between pressers and holders. Some seekers chose with their feet (switching membership) which community of faith they would support.[26]

But the inner dynamics of change revolved around more than doctrine, Biblical teachings, and related cognitive appeals. That is, doctrinal competition was not the dominant force within the awakening that led to the transformations of these two decades. Other, arguably deeper, currents of change moved through American religious life. The most important, as documented by Robert Wuthnow, were such social processes as the expansion of science, technology, and higher education.

Over the two decades the number of Americans who had completed college-level education increased dramatically. By 1980 some 32 percent of adults (those over twenty-five) had completed at least some college education, contrasted with 21 percent ten years earlier. The total enrollments in higher education rose from 8.6 million in 1970 to 12.1 million in 1980. Those between eighteen and twenty-four attending college increased from 35 to 40 percent in that decade, this after equally strong increases in higher-education enrollment during the 1960s.[27]

What seemed to be emerging was a new class of college-educated professionals, deeply influenced by modernist rationality and determined to maintain individual choice in their personal lives. Those who did join a church enrolled with the mainline far more than in evangelical bodies.[28] They had, observers noted, accepted a fundamental outgrowth of the awakening, as discussed by Barbara Hargrove: "As the functions of economics, government, family, education, and religion have come to be associated with specialized institutions, religion has come to occupy only one sphere of many in human life, rather than permeating all its structures. Thus it loses much of its influence over human life."[29] In sum, the society itself became transformed from an industrial to a postindustrial status—where education, including the cultural orientations, professionalized occupations, and access to mobility and power that were dependent on education, came to be a major new basis of social order.[30]

Of course, such movements were hardly absolute in their cleavages; young college-educated adults became evangelicals; mainliners without new-class college degrees remained in their home churches. But on the whole, the social transformation by 1980 was undeniably apparent in the religious scene. Trends hardly noticeable in the 1960s such as privatization, modernization, and secularization now served as convincing explanations as to how this awakening had worked out its own expression, contrasting sharply with the earlier awakenings in American life. Pressing on or holding fast: the 1980s would see the next chapter of that ancient battle.

NOTES

1. See, for instance, Neil Sheehan, *A Bright, Shining Lie: John Paul Vann and America in Vietnam* (New York: Random House, 1988); Stanley Karnow, *Vietnam: A History* (New York: Viking Press, 1983).

2. William F. McLoughlin, *Revivals, Awakenings, and Reform: An Essay on Religion and Social Change in America, 1607–1977* (Chicago: University of Chicago Press, 1978), pp. xiii, 2; Sydney E. Ahlstrom, *A Religious History of the American People* (New Haven: Yale University Press, 1972), p. 1079. See the documentation of this interpretation in Dick Anthony et al., eds., *Spiritual Choices: The Problem of Recognizing Authentic Paths to Spiritual Transformation* (New York: Paragon House Publishers, 1987), pp. 27–29 nn. 11–12; Wade Clark Roof and William McKinney, *American Mainline Religion: Its Changing Shape and Future* (New Brunswick, N.J.: Rutgers University Press, 1987), pp. 11–13.

3. Benton Johnson, "Liberal Protestantism: End of the Road?" in Wade Clark Roof, ed., *Religion in America Today*, Annals of the American Academy of Political and Social Science, Vol. 480 (Beverly Hills, Calif.: Sage Publications, 1985), p. 43.

4. Mark Silk, *Spiritual Politics: Religion and America since 1945* (New York: Simon and Schuster, 1988), pp. 146–55; Robert Wuthnow, "Religious Movements and Counter-movements in North America," In James Beckford, ed., *New Religious Movements and Rapid Social Change* (Beverly Hills, Calif.: Sage Publications, 1986), pp. 11–12; William P. Mahedy, "It Don't Mean Nothin': The Vietnam Experience," in Kenneth Aman, ed., *Border Regions of Faith* (New York: Orbis Books, 1987), pp. 123–33; John D'Emilio and Estelle B. Freedman, *Intimate Matters: A History of Sexuality in America* (New York: Perennial Library, Harper and Row, 1988), pp. 306–11; *Religion in America: 50 Years, 1935–1985*, The Gallup Report no. 236, (Princeton: Gallup Poll, 1985), passim.

5. Roderick Frazier Nash, *The Rights of Nature: A History of Environmental Ethics* (Madison: University of Wisconsin Press, 1989), pp. 87–120; Silk, *Spiritual Politics*, pp. 146–55; Aman, *Border Regions of Faith*, pts. 1 and 3.

6. Joseph W. Trigg and William L. Sachs, *Of One Body: Renewal Movements in the Church* (Atlanta, Ga.: John Knox Press, 1986), pp. 48–49. See the data in Daniel Yankelovich, *New Rules: Searching for Self-Fulfillment in a World Turned Upside Down* (New York: Random House, 1981), pp. 83–103; R. Stephen Warner, *New Wine in Old Wineskins: Evangelicals in a Small-Town Church* (Berkeley: University of California Press, 1988), pp. 14–17.

7. Wuthnow, "Religious Movements," pp. 9–15; Robert Wuthnow, *The Restructuring of American Religion: Society and Faith since World War II* (Princeton: Princeton University Press, 1988), pp. 154–67; Jeffrey K. Hadden, *The Gathering Storm in the Churches* (Garden City, N.Y.: Doubleday, 1969), passim.

8. John F. Wilson, "The Sociological Study of American Religion," in Charles H. Lippy and Peter N. Williams, eds., *Encyclopedia of the American Religious Experience*, Vol. 1 (New York: Scribner, 1988), p. 28; Martin E. Marty, "Transpositions: American Religion in the 1980s," in Roof, *Religion in America Today*, pp. 20–21; Wuthnow, *Restructuring*, pp. 145–57, 224–25, 235–36; Johnson, "Liberal Protestantism," pp. 47–48; Roof and McKinney, *American Mainline Religion*, pp. 11–39.

9. See the insightful personal journey of David Toolan, *Facing West from California's Shores: A Jesuit's Journey into New Age Consciousness* (New York: Crossroad, 1988); Edwin Schur, *The Awareness Trap: Self-Absorption Instead of Social Change* (New York: Quadrangle Books, 1976); Leonard I. Sweet, "The 1960s: The Crisis of Liberal Christianity and the Public Emergence of Evangelicalism," in George Marsden, ed., *Evangelicalism and Modern America* (Grand Rapids, Mich.: Wm. B. Eerdmans, 1984), pp. 38–43.

10. Leonard I. Sweet, "The Modernization of Protestant Religion in America," in David Lotz, Donald W. Shriver, Jr., and John F. Wilson, eds., *Altered Landscapes: Christianity in America, 1935–1985* (Grand Rapids, Mich.: Wm. B. Eerdmans, 1989), p. 21.

11. Ibid., pp. 31–37.

12. See Donald W. Shriver, Jr., "The Biblical Life in America: Which Past Fits Us for the Future?" in Lotz, Shriver, and Wilson, *Altered Landscapes*, pp. 343–61.

13. Ibid.

14. Harold E. Quinley, "The Dilemma of an Activist Church: Protestant Religion in the Sixties and Seventies," *Journal for the Scientific Study of Religion* 13, 1 (March 1974): 1–22; Jackson W. Carroll et al., *Religion in America, 1950 to the Present* (San Francisco: Harper and Row, 1979), pp. 8–45; Constant Jacquet, ed., *Yearbook of American and Canadian Churches 1984* (Nashville, Tenn.: Abingdon Press, 1985), pp. 246–47, 273–84; Wade Clark Roof and William McKinney, "Denominational America and the New Religious

Pluralism,'' in Roof, *Religion in America Today*, p. 29; Cullen Murphy, ''Protestantism and the Evangelicals,'' *Wilson Quarterly*, Autumn 1987, p. 107. Other important data are in Wuthnow, ''Religious Movements,'' pp. 15–16; James R. Wood, *Leadership in Voluntary Organizations: The Controversy over Social Action in Protestant Churches* (New Brunswick, N.J.: Rutgers University Press, 1981); Wuthnow, *Restructuring*, p. 164.

15. See Gallup Report, *Religion in America*, pp. 7–9; David Roozen, ''What Hath the 70s Wrought?'' in Jacquet, *Yearbook, 1984*, p. 280; Dean R. Hoge et al., ''Theology as a Source of Disagreement about Protestant Church Goals and Priorities,'' *Review of Religious Research* 19, 2 (Winter 1978): 116–38.

16. This is spelled out in Robert Bellah et al., *Habits of the Heart: Individualism and Commitment in American Life* (Berkeley: University of California Press, 1985), pp. 221, 235; James Davison Hunter, ''American Protestantism: Sorting Out the Present; Looking toward the Future,'' *This World*, no. 17 (Spring 1987): 64; R. Stephen Warner, ''Research Note,'' *Sociological Analysis* 44 (1983): 243–54. A helpful summary of the research is Robert Booth Fowler, *Unconventional Partners: Religion and Liberal Culture in the United States* (Grand Rapids, Mich.: Wm. B. Eerdmans, 1989), pp. 22–24 and notes.

17. See especially Bellah, *Habits of the Heart*, pp. 221, 235.

18. Sweet, ''Modernization,'' pp. 27–41.

19. Ibid.; James H. Smylie, '' 'Of Secret and Family Worship:' Historical Meditations, 1875–1975,'' *Journal of Presbyterian History* 58 (Summer 1980): 95–115.

20. Sweet, *Modernization*; Wade Clark Roof, *Community and Commitment: Religious Plausibility in a Liberal Protestant Church* (New York: Elsevier, 1978), pp. 209–17.

21. See several excellent articles, including that by C.P. Wagner, ''Church Growth,'' in Stanley M. Burgess and Gary B. McGee, eds., *Dictionary of Pentecostal and Charismatic Movements* (Grand Rapids, Mich.: Zondervan Publishing House, 1988), pp. 181–95; Margaret Poloma, *The Charismatic Movement* (Boston: Twayne Publishers, 1982).

22. Schur, *Awareness Trap*; Paul C. Vitz, *Psychology as Religion: The Cult of Self Worship* (Grand Rapids, Mich.: W. B. Eerdmans, 1977); Tom Wolfe, ''The Me Decade and the Third Great Awakening,'' in *The Purple Decades: A Reader* (New York: Farrar, Straus, Giroux, 1982), pp. 265–93.

23. See Richard Quebedeaux, *By What Authority: The Rise of Personality Cults in American Christianity* (San Francisco: Harper and Row, 1982).

24. Hunter, '' American Protestantism,'' pp. 53–76; Wuthnow, *Restructuring*, pp. 164–72.

25. Hunter, ''American Protestantism,'' pp. 53–76; Peter G. Horsfield, *Religious Television: The American Experience* (New York: Longman, 1984), pp. 101–10.

26. See Wade Clark Roof and Christopher Kirk Hadaway, ''Denominational Switching in the Seventies: Going beyond Glock and Stark,'' *Journal for the Scientific Study of Religion* 18, 4 (1979): 363–79; Frank Newport, ''The Religious Switcher in the United States,'' *American Sociological Review* 44 (August 1979): 528–52.

27. Wuthnow, *Restructuring*, pp. 154–64.

28. Warner, *New Wine*, pp. 11–32; Wuthnow, ''Religious Movements,'' pp. 20–21; Barbara Hargrove, *The Emerging New Class: Implications for Church and Society* (New York: Pilgrim Press, 1986), pp. 117–39.

29. Hargrove, *Emerging New Class*, p. 119.

30. Wuthnow, *Restructuring*, p. 163; idem, ''Religious Movements,'' p. 15.

PART I

FROM MAINLINE TO FRONTLINE

INTRODUCTION

For most of its history, the United States has claimed the mainline Protestant church tradition as the most representative expression of its public faith. For all its pride in embracing such widely varying faiths as Roman Catholicism, the main strands of Judaism, various Asian groups, and the evangelicals, the mainline churches have occupied center stage when Americans express what the core of their national faith represents. To give one example, from the first election for the presidency until 1960 (with the election of Senator John F. Kennedy, a Roman Catholic) every American president represented the mainline. It revolved around the immigrant churches from the British Isles: Congregational, Episcopal, Methodist, and Presbyterian, and added in the twentieth century the ecumenical Lutheran and national Baptist bodies to that constituency.

However, during the 1980s all of this changed and changed dramatically. The forces of secularization and privatization, long just under the surface of mainline involvement in public issues, came to reshape the very core of those bodies. Unable to respond rapidly or flexibly to the impact of the 1960s awakening, the mainline churches found themselves caught up in continued decline in membership and internal bickering. Their uniqueness within the larger family of religious bodies had always depended on the ability of each to hold fast to its respective denominational heritage. Each understood clearly that it must maintain fidelity to what it meant to be Lutheran or Episcopalian or Methodist. By contrast, evangelicals had little such loyalty to denominationalism and could more easily move during the decade into new pressing on kinds of religious expressions.

The differences between these two groupings, mainline and evangelical, reached crisis proportions for the former during the 1980s. Not only would membership and financial support continue to decline, but other disruptive controversies would increase; these included the proper way to interpret the Bible, loyalty to older church traditions, and the incorporation of modern wisdom and scholarship.

Thus, it was the old contending against the new as each mainline body attempted to stay loyal to its heritage in a rapidly changing world.

Each came to face these questions: Should it press forward with full rights for women? Should it embrace gay and lesbian candidates for the ministry? Should it incorporate inclusive language in its liturgy? Should it involve its social outreach programs with the secular special purpose groups involved in environmental, gender, peace, and social justice issues? How should it respond to the growing attractiveness of privatized religion? How to react to the expanding number of parishioners pursuing their personal agendas for psychological well being as informed by secular wisdom?

During this decade those issues dominated the holding fast/pressing on controversies within the rapidly changing mainline. By decade's end it was clear that the major transformation came to be the shift from mainline to frontline; from holding fast for its own sake, to direct involvement in frontline issues such as peace, justice, gender, race, and environment. This transformation exacted a very heavy price, one which in the early 1990s is now becoming visible.

1

The Decline of Mainline Leadership

The enormous religious energy generated by the awakening of the 1960s, filtered and redirected as it was during the 1970s, burst out across the nation again during the 1980s, and in typically unpredictable ways. In 1980 religionists were fearing matters such as the disappearance of the local parish or a deepening of tensions over charismatic renewal or the born-again revival, but by decade's end they had turned to an entirely different agenda: New Age spirituality, permanent cleavage over the right to abortion, and the ordination of homosexuals, to name but a few of the headline grabbers. Underneath this volatility the pressers and holders would continue their combat, but during the 1980s they would fashion new weapons for use in new arenas. Part I examines in some detail how this unfolded in the mainline church bodies.

Of the most immediate importance for these churches, the heirs to the dominant religious tradition of the American past, stood the question of survival itself. In the late 1960s membership, financial support, and program vitality started to decline, then declined some more, leaving many wondering if their church had any future.[1]

Briefly summarized, in the 1970s the United Presbyterian Church lost some 19 percent of its members, the Disciples of Christ (Christian Church) 23 percent, Episcopalians 17 percent, United Church of Christ (UCC, largely Congregationalists) 11 percent, the United Methodist Church more than 11 percent, and Lutherans some 11 percent. By the end of 1987 (the last year for which data are available), the numbers read as follows: the UCC down a total over twenty years of 20 percent, the Presbyterians down 25 percent, the Episcopalians down 28 percent, the United Methodists down 18 percent, and the Christian Church down 43 percent (after a de facto schism). These five bodies lost a total of 5.2 million members during a period in which the national population rose 47 million people, and black Protestants and Roman Catholics showed impressive membership growth.[2] Along with the decline came necessary cutbacks in professional staff, social outreach programs, and regional support personnel and, in less measurable terms, a marked decline in morale and confidence in the future of these bodies.[3]

The severity of the decline led specialists in church growth to study in extensive detail what was occurring. Some causes were demographic, such as the well-established move of millions of Americans away from the Frostbelt and into the Sunbelt states, there either to join more lively evangelical congregations or simply to drop out. Further, the awakening of the 1960s had clearly convinced the children, now becoming young adults, that they did not need the church, caught up as it was in angry internal battles. In addition, mainline churches appeared ineffectual or cumbersome agents for producing significant social change.[4]

Others, notably Dean Kelley of the mainline National Council of Churches, argued vigorously that the mainline bodies were failing because they did not provide the discipline, authority, and meaning for life supplied by the expanding evangelical and conservative bodies. Throughout the 1960s and 1970s and well into the 1980s, those churches attracting new members were largely nondenominational, precise in teaching orthodox doctrine and ethics, traditional in gender roles, largely antiabortion, and featuring high-profile preachers and mass-media education programs for families.[5] Kelley's clear message was that mainliners should find resources from the evangelicals to keep their programs alive.[6]

Throughout the 1980s, however, mainline bodies chose to move in directions other than aggressive proselytization. Much energy was spent in tending to their own internal matters or moving toward what would become "a new social gospel" of peace and justice activism. Mainliners also became embroiled in a series of other issues, largely in the realm of public relations, which added to the general sense of turmoil and decline. For instance, a new conservative think tank, the Institute for Religion and Democracy (IRD), in 1983 convinced the highly prestigious CBS "Sixty Minutes" news magazine to devote a double segment (forty minutes) to its charge that the National Council of Churches and World Council of Churches were "soft on communism." Interestingly, CBS itself was perceived by the general public as being politically liberal and open to ecumenical movements such as those these councils represented. In this particular case the indictment by the IRD was accepted by a sizeable portion of the viewing public, creating serious financial and morale setbacks for the mainline cause.[7]

Signs of decline and confusion also emerged as the National Council of Churches, the service organization providing coordination and leadership for ecumenical ministry, fell into bitter quarreling over much of its outreach. Best known to the public as a New York City–based agency consisting (in 1989) of thirty-two denominations with a total membership of 42 million, it had provided since its appearance in 1950 a wide variety of ministries for Americans and overseas partners.[8]

Out of its headquarters at 475 Riverside Drive in Manhattan, it came to represent for many the best hope among mainline Protestants and some Orthodox Christians for coordinating and advancing the many programs in its jurisdiction, including inner-city missions, programs for the illiterate and homeless, housing, social welfare, education, theology, public advocacy for legislation, specialized ministries for special-purpose groups, translations of the Bible (it has the copyright for the Revised Standard Version), foreign-policy information, leadership to unite constitutionally several of its mainline members (in the Consultation on Church Union), and continuing dialogue with Roman Catholics, Jews, Muslims, and members of other faiths, this in conjunction with the World Council of Churches.[9]

With so impressive a record, the question may well be asked by 1990 why the NCC came on such difficult times. In brief, its leadership problems paralleled those of its members: declining membership and attendant loss of revenue, ongoing conflict between clergy and laity over social outreach involvement, and personality conflicts within its own ranks. For example, by 1989 over 100 of its program directors had been released, a decline from 187 to 61. It could not, or would not, attempt to duplicate the evangelizing prowess of evangelicals and fundamentalists who became masters of the mass media in the 1980s. Perhaps most serious of all was its lack of ongoing trust with the laity. Its leaders often alienated the rank and file by giving extended discussion to the ordination of homosexuals or controversial pronouncements on a variety of foreign-policy matters, such as Israel, Nicaragua, and South Africa. It became in the minds of many an elitist, religion-from-the-top-down bureaucracy in an age when broad, ground-swell support from the bottom up seemed more the general trend; it seemed to press on while many wanted to hold fast.[10]

Hopeful signs for renewal came in late 1989 when the newly merged Evangelical Lutheran Church in America (ELCA) with some 5.2 million members voted enthusiastically to join the National Council. On a more local level, NCC affiliates started utilizing computer-powered telemarketing to reach potential new members, adding a variety of word-processor technologies.[11]

At the national leadership level, however, long-standing conflicts over budget, program priorities, allocation of resources, and conflicting styles of executive management led to a fierce struggle throughout early 1989. After several "tumultuous" meetings, the official governing board voted to restructure the entire organization. Its controversial and embattled director, the Reverend Arie R. Brouwer, resigned. The decade ended with members determined to find some means of recovery.[12]

NOTES

1. Benton Johnson, "Liberal Protestantism: End of the Road?" in Wade Clark Roof, ed., *Religion in America Today*, Annals of the American Academy of Political and Social Science, Vol. 480 (Beverly Hills, Calif.: Sage Publications, 1985), p. 29.

2. *Time*, May 22, 1989, p. 94; by late 1987, the last date for which data are available, this had leveled off. See the news story in the *Washington Post*, August 19, 1989, p. C11; *Christian Century*, September 6, 1989, pp. 775–76; see the helpful survey, Robbin D. Perrin and Armand L. Mauss, "The Great Protestant Puzzle: Retreat, Renewal, or

Reshuffle?'' in Thomas Robbins and Dick Anthony, eds., *In Gods We Trust: New Patterns of Religious Pluralism in America*, 2nd ed., (New Brunswick, N.J.: Transaction Books, 1990), pp. 153–66.

3. A. James Reichley, *Religion in American Public Life* (Washington, D.C.: Brookings Institution, 1985), pp. 278–80; William R. Hutchison, ''Past Imperfect: History and the Prospect for Liberalism,'' in Robert S. Michaelsen and Wade Clark Roof, eds., *Liberal Protestantism: Realities and Possibilities* (New York: Pilgrim Press, 1986), pp. 65–82.

4. The most extensive demographic research is in Dean R. Hoge and David A. Roozen, eds., *Understanding Church Growth and Decline, 1950–1979* (New York: Pilgrim Press, 1979), passim.

5. See, for example, Randall Balmer, *Mine Eyes Have Seen the Glory: A Journey into the Evangelical Subculture in America* (New York: Oxford University Press, 1989); news story in *Religious Broadcasting*, March 1988, pp. 20–22; editorial, *Lutheran*, June 14, 1989, p. 50.

6. Dean Kelley, *Why Conservative Churches Are Growing* (New York: Harper and Row, 1972; rev. ed., 1977; rev. ed., Macon, Ga.: Mercer University Press, 1986). This author is preparing an extended critique of the Kelley thesis.

7. The news departments of *Christian Century, Christianity Today,* and *Christianity and Crisis* for 1983 have many stories, too numerous to mention here. See Michael Parenti, ''Red Baiting the Peace Movement,'' in *Inventing Reality: The Politics of the Mass Media* (New York: St. Martin's Press, 1986), pp. 102–6.

8. Linda-Marie Deloff, ''The NCC in a New Time,'' *Christianity and Crisis*, January 9, 1989, p. 467; see the lists of ministries contained in Constant Jacquet, ed., *Yearbook of American and Canadian Churches* (Nashville, Tenn.: Abingdon Press, annual).

9. George E. Todd, ''Ecumenism Where Church Members Live,'' *Christianity and Crisis*, February 6, 1989, pp. 15–16.

10. Robert Wuthnow, ''Struggle in One Denomination,'' *The Struggle for America's Soul: Evangelicals, Liberals and Secularism* (Grand Rapids, Mich.: Wm. B. Eerdmans Press, 1989), pp. 68–94; news story in *Reformed Journal*, August 1989, pp. 14–21; *Minneapolis Star Tribune*, February 12, 1989, p. 21B; *Tucson Citizen*, February 12, 1989, p. 1; *National and International Religion Report*, February 13, 1989, p. 5.

11. Kittredge Chery and James Mitulski, ''Raising Lazarus: Can Liberal Churches Grow?'' *Witness*, March 1989, pp. 12–15; news story, *Miami Herald*, March 28, 1988, p. 1E. See also the catalog of publications for the Alban Institute, Washington, D.C.

12. *New York Times*, May 22, 1989, p. 8; *Los Angeles Times*, May 20, 1989, sec. 2, p. 6; *Washington Post*, January 7, 1989, p. G12; *Christianity Today*, September 18, 1989, p. 44; *National Christian Reporter*, July 28, 1989, p. 1.

2

Denominational Warfare

During the 1980s mainline denominations, traditionally agencies for conciliation and moderation, became battlegrounds for internal warfare. Their characteristic irenic temper, previously a force to find middle ground among feuding members, failed in that decade to sustain itself on a variety of divisive issues. Although this struggle was not for these people the dominant motif of the decade, it clearly required an enormous amount of time, energy, and resources.

For instance, by late 1987 some five new denominations each week were appearing across the American religious landscape, adding regularly to the 22,190 separate ones already flourishing by then.[1] Although most of these were numerically minuscule, their continuing appearance reflected how deeply the pressers/holders battle was felt by participants. For many, new problems demanded new forms of organization; hence the proliferation of new groups. For others, new problems could only be faced by standing on the ground occupied since the earliest days of Christianity. The appearance of these new bodies simply proved how easy it was to slip into error.

Within the mainline tradition, by contrast to evangelicalism, members (both lay and clerical) historically have taken their identity and sense of public mission very strongly from their specific denomination. Evangelicals, by contrast, are less denomination-intensive, able to move more easily from one organized body to another.[2] As this pattern continued in the 1980s, mainliners found it necessary to define and redefine over and over what it meant to be Episcopalian or Presbyterian or a member of any of these groups. Lacking the public-relations and fund-raising skills of their evangelical competitors, and pitted in identity battles (over polity, for example) that often had little attractiveness to potential new members, mainliners found themselves often stymied from responding to the rapidly changing needs of potential members.[3]

Throughout the decade holders and pressers came often to dispute, sometimes reaching stalemate over a variety of theological and administrative questions, of which only the more visible can be outlined here. Two kinds of issues stood out:

those remaining within each mainline body, and those shared in common by most if not all such denominations. The latter included the ordination and leadership of women and feminist theology, the inerrancy and infallibility of the Scriptures, and the charismatic movement. This chapter looks at these.

All of these issues, however, emerged from an extremely intertwined, often illogically arranged set of causes. Outsiders may well wonder, for instance why in the 1980s, by contrast to earlier times, old animosities and pitched battles, such as those between Protestant groups and the Roman Catholic church, had virtually disappeared. If those issues causing bitterness had been real in earlier days, they should still be real in the 1980s. But in those years the most bitter battles were carried out within each of the respective mainline bodies.[4] Holding to the old identity, or pressing on to embrace the rapidly changing culture of the present—Christians could not agree.

Within the mainline the question of the inerrancy of the Bible surfaced with some regularity during the 1980s. Basically a doctrinal issue going back at least 150 years in Protestant scholarly circles, "inerrancy" stood for the extent to which the norms, teachings, and historical accuracy of the Bible (in geology, history, geography, and the like) were "without error." If it were inerrant, then its standards and teachings must prevail over any possibly countervailing human wisdom or factual record. But if it were errant, then perhaps all of the Bible stood merely as a collection of early Jewish literature. In brief, that was the claim of the inerrantists.

Most mainline bodies officially had resolved this issue some decades back, standing apart from strict inerrancy. Now, by contrast to the openly bitter warfare among other groups such as the Southern Baptist Convention, mainline struggles seemed mild.[5] Yet within most of those bodies there emerged well-organized dissenter groups calling on the parent church to restore loyalty to their particular interpretation of scriptural truth. Inspired largely by fear that their cherished denominational identity was being destroyed by the modernists, and worried about identity in this age of do-it-yourself religion, they emerged within groups such as the Methodist Good News, Episcopalian Fellowship of Witness, Lutheran Fellowship of Laity and Pastors, and Presbyterians for Democracy and Religious Freedom.[6]

Although identifying with their respective denominational creeds such as the Augsburg or Westminster confessions, these movements shared much in common. They were determined to repeal the legacy of the awakening of the 1960s that embraced what they determined were anti-Biblical teachings in central areas of church life: child and youth programs, liturgy, social outreach, and evangelism. These groups served as public forums to help mobilize the protest sentiments of the holders and to call the general public's attention to their cause. They found little or no support among their respective denominational seminary faculties or at the large prestige seminaries on the East Coast. At these institutions seminarians studied the Bible during the 1980s in much the same manner as had been done in the last half century, academically in the classroom and devotionally in one's personal life. Such a procedure gave the noninerrantists a distinct advantage; their cause was presented in an orderly, rational manner, while inerrantists often seemed to be holding on to indefensible relics of earlier scholarship.[7] In the larger setting of interdenominational battles the inerrancy question helped keep conflict, mistrust, and disputation alive at a time when the denominations were also facing other major upheavals.

The continuing controversy over inerrancy reflected deeper conflicts among mainliners. With the pressures of privatization and secularization mounting during the 1980s, members would find themselves in the midst of a complexity not of their own making. These bodies had emerged within American history as denominations, recognizing that diversity within the ranks was healthy, discussion a sign of strength, and openness a symptom of growth. Denominations consciously had set themselves off from the more sectarian discipline and uniformity of such bodies as the Jehovah's Witnesses or Seventh-Day Adventists. In the 1980s that openness came under fresh criticism.

The dangers of privatization were obvious: if one could believe just about anything, of what value or importance was denominational membership or identity? If secularization continued to challenge the revealed and supernatural dimensions of religious faith, was not the church headed to be simply one more special-purpose group? In that setting the denominational battles we explore here take on a high degree of significance. Not clearly understood by outsiders, those within these respective bodies—American Baptist, Episcopal, Evangelical Lutheran (ELCA), United Methodist, Presbyterian, and United Church of Christ—chose these years to affirm vigorously: This is what it means to be Methodist, or Presbyterian, or any of the others. The bodies considered here are representative of the larger mainline picture.

AMERICAN BAPTISTS

Among the dozens of Baptist groups, the largest of the mainline bodies is the American Baptist Convention. In 1986 it numbered some 1,576,483 members. It has survived many of the tensions plaguing other mainline groups because its heritage, as is true with all Baptists, allows it to keep most of the major decision-making power in the local congregations. Thus, when highly emotional issues such as abortion or ordination of women or foreign-policy issues came before the convention delegates in annual meetings, members gave each position a hearing with careful attention to maximum participation and minimum attention to reaching uniform consensus. For a brief time a spiritual renewal group, the American Baptist Fellowship, made efforts at increasing awareness of personal piety, inner spirituality, and conservative Biblical teachings. However, as signs of cleavage surfaced, the fellowship leaders, rather than risk serious dissension, stated in 1987 that they had achieved their goals. They disbanded their program.[8]

EPISCOPALIANS

By sharp contrast, the Episcopal church by decade's end faced a highly serious internal crisis. Faced with the need for defining a distinctive denominational ethos within the swirling currents of pluralism, Episcopalians chose to hang on to their identity rather than accommodate to compromise with more popular trends. The problem was: Who represented pure Episcopalianism? Even as this book is published, the contestants remain in deadlock over that central issue.

Over the 450 years of its existence, this body slowly divided itself, at least in the United States, into three distinct groups: Anglo-Catholic, evangelical, and charismatic. Each claims the mantle of legitimacy of loyalty to the ancient traditions, but each also insists that its claims must be fully acknowledged by the others; that has proven to be a very complex matter.

The Anglo-Catholics, those with the oldest ties to the Anglican parentage in Great Britain and to Roman Catholicism, chose in the 1980s that foundation to lodge their protest against perceived modernist transformations within the denomination. Anglo-Catholics especially objected to the ordination of women and to the use of the updated Book of Common Prayer, with its inclusive language. They also deplored the discussion by some high-ranking officials over Episcopal recognition of homosexual marriages and ministries established to minister to the gay and lesbian communities. The Anglo-Catholics also objected to the strong emphasis among many Episcopalians on peace and justice issues and on more contemporary understanding of traditional interpretations of Biblical teachings.[9]

Evangelicals, meanwhile, were attempting to keep the priorities not so strongly with Rome but centered on stronger commitment to prayer, Bible study, inner renewal, and personal piety. They also showed little enthusiasm for contemporary recasting of Biblical doctrine, but at the same time they stood aside from the Anglo-Catholic devotion to high-church liturgy and meticulous attention to the traditional observation of the church year. The evangelicals' most visible presence appeared through the Fellowship of Witness, publishing the magazine *Kerygma*, and its seminary for clericals and laity, Trinity Episcopal School for Ministry.[10] Their specific activist organization has been the Episcopalians United for Revelation, Renewal, and Reformation, a clear example of the movement for making clear what Episcopalian identity must be.

The third major grouping has been that of the charismatic renewal. Starting in 1960, it spread rapidly throughout many parts of the country, reflecting a growing interest among Episcopalians in a more experiential and, often, more privatized kind of spirituality. The charismatic populace joined with comparable groups within the Lutheran and Roman Catholic faiths to sponsor various kinds of renewal programs: Bible study, journals, weekend retreats, and congregational education programs to enable seekers to share the ''spiritual gifts.'' The charismatics, however, chose to remain outside of the battles within the denomination over peace and justice issues.[11]

After some years of internecine conflict, both over church practices and out of personality conflicts, the turmoil boiled over when a woman, the Reverend

Barbara Harris, was nominated to be suffragan bishop for eastern Massachusetts. She was the first female to be named to that office, although just under 1,000 were already ordained as priests. In the Episcopal church the bishops of a geographic area determine who will be named to their ranks. The Massachusetts bishops chose her with the full support of the national headquarters leadership. The event was celebrated joyously by those in attendance and supporters across the nation. It was also criticized bitterly by the dissenters, especially the Anglo-Catholic wing.[12]

Out of that and some evangelical sources came a major, organized protest movement in June 1989. After months of planning, some 2,000 traditionalists met in Fort Worth, Texas, in hopes of creating a church freed from what the host bishop called "secular ideals of equality and liberation." Bishop Clarence Pope made the case for preserving traditional identity. The church had become "subject to the shifting sands of the present age," which had "taken a heavy toll on family and life and done [their] best to undermine revealed religion." He and supportive bishops and laity planned to create an independent synod, consisting of sympathetic parishes.[13]

But as the months wore on after the conference, the forces making for unity gradually prevented any major schism from developing out of the Fort Worth consultation. Little visible sentiment for improving relations among the three major branches was forthcoming, but the issues, divisive as they were, found themselves on hold.

LUTHERANS

Although the details differed, that same struggle for maintaining a true identity also characterized much of internal American Lutheranism in the 1980s. The four major bodies within this tradition by decade's end were the Evangelical Lutheran Church in America (5.2 million members), the Lutheran Church–Missouri Synod (some 2.7 million members), the Wisconsin Evangelical Lutheran Synod (some 420,000 members), and a variety of separated, independent groups (none larger than 20,000).[14] In this discussion we consider the ELCA as representative of Lutheran mainliners. Space limitations prevent consideration of the others, none of whom would want to be considered mainline.

The ELCA itself was a product of the 1980s, a merger of three smaller bodies into what became the largest Lutheran denomination in the United States on January 1, 1988. The merger, some ten years in preparation, indicated that the older ethnic loyalties once so dominant in Lutheranism had given way to a more ecumenical sense of identity.

Yet disputations did emerge, mostly over the strong Lutheran emphasis on maintaining pure doctrine as its central feature of identity with Christendom. The merger meetings and talks with the Missouri and Wisconsin bodies also brought into public view long-held differences over doctrine, inerrancy, and related interpretations of the Bible. As the merger developed, some fifty congregations officially resigned to join one of the other nonmainstream bodies.[15] Identity, the dissenters insisted, could be maintained only by maintaining fidelity to what they understood that the core of Lutheran pure doctrine represented, the holders-fast position in clear form.

Battles also erupted over the traditional dispute within Protestantism over evangelism versus social outreach. The more conservative elements insisted that the saving of souls was paramount, while the more liberal argued that evangelism need not weaken their interest in expanding Lutheran concern for peace and justice matters.

Beneath these battles, as was true among most mainliners, stood the issue of the extent to which homosexuals should be considered for ordination or given attention with ministries aimed at their concerns. As with other mainline bodies, gay and lesbian Lutherans had formed special-purpose groups for mutual support, for educating others, and for acceptance. Given all of the deep emotional anguish of the issue, Lutherans found themselves squarely facing a central issue of the 1980s. The critics argued that the Bible clearly forbade the kind of lifestyle of this group; supporters argued that all believers must be affirmed and reconciled within the ministry of the church.

In California several ministers attempted to create a special-purpose group, demanding that the ELCA change its traditional ban on ordaining practicing homosexuals. This produced extremely sharp discussion across the country, with many fearing that Lutheranism would lose its identity in the name of this form of social outreach. The national leadership gave its Commission for Church in Society a mandate to study the issue from the standpoint of Scripture, church teachings, and contemporary scholarship. The commission was also asked to study and bring to the national body recommendations on a large number of sexuality issues: AIDS, reproductive technologies, nonmarital sex, pornography, and the like.[16] Clearly the issue that had for so long been either ignored or deflected by Lutherans (as well as by most mainline bodies) could no longer be put aside. Although not central to the church's sense of mission and identity in the world, the sexuality questions came to occupy center stage for many Lutherans. Holders preferred the older ethnic loyalties; pressers found that the church was moving unsteadily into the 1990s.

METHODISTS

With the second-largest membership of any Protestant body (some 9,192,117), the United Methodist church mirrored in many ways the same internal problems of the other mainline bodies.[17] It too found sharp, internal battles over identity occupying much of its energy and resources during the 1980s. Historically more pluralistic in doctrine than Lutherans or Episcopalians, it, like the American Baptists, continued to emphasize the value of diversity.

Where the 1980s and Methodism collided showed up early in the issue of inclusive language, especially the wording of hymns. Feminists called for rewording lyrics that reflected male sexist preferences; they would replace "men" with "all," "mankind" with "people," and, where possible, "His" with "God's." After considerable debate the 1988 national convention approved several far-reaching changes. Despite a group of some fifty conservative United Methodist ministers who had asked for no change in "traditional doctrines and liturgical language," the church moved ahead with a new, more inclusive hymnal. It also reached out for the growing number of racial minorities involved with Methodism.[18]

The question of homosexuality also appeared in the 1988 conference. Most delegates, acting with the force of making national policy for all United Methodist members, made clear their objections to ordaining gay or lesbian people. On the equally complex issue of abortion, the delegates voted 805 to 130 for a position of reluctance to approve such a procedure, but they added, "We are equally bound to respect the sacredness of the life of the mother, for whom devastating damage may result from unacceptable pregnancy." As did the Lutherans, the United Methodists also created a task force to continue studying both issues, plus a range of other sexuality matters.[19]

Beneath the surface lay the long-standing dispute within this denomination over the extent to which it should involve itself in social outreach ministry. For several decades Methodism had been at the forefront of such activity, with strong programs for the poor and homeless, labor union organization, ecological and environmental issues, mental health programs, control of alcohol and related substances, in national foreign policy, and in almost every similar public-policy issue. The impact of the awakening of the 1960s quickened even further this movement, centered as it was around the journal *Engage/Social Action*, published by the Board of Church and Society.

While not deploring the intentions of the activists, more evangelical-minded Methodists started organizing a renewal movement around a new magazine, entitled *Good News*. Founded by Charles Keysor in 1967, the program called for more Biblically based Sunday school materials, more conservative theology to be taught in Methodist seminaries, and increased world missionary activity. It claimed to represent authentic Methodism, a claim also made by the social activists.[20]

Much of the dynamics underlying the 1988 convention disputation emerged from this continuing tension. In part, it was fueled also by the strong presence of religious Right bodies such as the Moral Majority, who were attracting considerable national attention with demands for restrictions on homosexuals, inclusive language, and abortion. By contrast to Lutherans and Episcopalians, however, Methodists did not break up into exclusive, separated factions. Decades earlier they had chosen to remain open to a variety of emphases. Hence the battle of the late 1980s intensified older contests and renewed the debate over identity but did not lead to separated splinter groups.[21]

PRESBYTERIANS

Much the same pattern of identity crisis and disputation over sexuality matters came to dominate internal Presbyterian struggles in the late 1980s. The largest of several bodies, with a membership in 1986 of 3,007,322, the United Presbyterian church (UPC) stood as a major contributor to mainline life.[22] Over the years it had come, like the Methodists, to support considerable differences of viewpoints among its laity and clerical members. But as was true of all mainliner bodies, the UPC had suffered serious membership and financial losses since the mid-1960s.

Symptomatic of the internal struggles were the reasons given for this decline by the leadership and by the conservative "lay" or "concerned" members. The former attributed the slump to demographic causes. The conservatives, however, as was true in the other mainline bodies, located the cause in the polarization between grass roots laity and highly educated clergy elites and in resentment over the liberal politics of the latter at the expense of the preference of the former, especially during the controversial Reagan administration years.

One expert, Robert Wuthnow, locates the causes of Presbyterian conflict at a deeper level. On the demographic side, Presbyterians who married outside that church tended to join the spouse's organization, thus leading to membership decline. About 50 percent of all ordained Presbyterian ministers had attended nondenominational seminaries, thus perhaps coming into that ministry with something less than full loyalty to the parent church.

Furthermore, the Presbyterians attracted extensive debate over peace and justice battles, foreign policy, sexuality matters, and public-policy debates—the full range of national disputation. What happened repeatedly were battles between differing factions over which would be able to dominate the statements and educational programs of the national headquarters on these matters. This tended to sap energy and resources away from support for grass roots and strictly Presbyterian programs.[23]

The trend in the late 1980s seemed to be in favor of the conservative programs becoming more popular within the parishes. Wuthnow found a gradual increase of their priorities for more Bible study groups, more emphasis on Christian education at all age levels, more prayer fellowships, and more conventional liturgies. Liberal pastors were seen as losing their programs for the ordination of gay and lesbian candidates. On the other hand, the female ministers almost unanimously were more liberal politically, more activist in social outreach, and more ready to defend the kind of vision they had gained during the awakening of the 1960s.[24]

UNITED CHURCH OF CHRIST

Finally, in alphabetical order, the last major voice for the mainline was the United Church of Christ, whose membership in 1986 stood at 1,613,618.[25] Being the product of mergers of smaller groups with strong traditions for local autonomy, the UCC found the struggle for identity less critical during these years. It had a long-standing tradition of ordaining women; it was not stymied over discussions of pure doctrine; its stand on matters such as abortion were clearly supported by the rank and file. In 1989, in fact, its national convention made a strong reaffirmation of the prochoice position.[26]

Within the ranks during this decade a small but energetic spiritual renewal group made known its presence. Named the Biblical Witness Fellowship (BWF), it concentrated on increasing overseas missionary programs. Its members gave their funds directly to missionaries not necessarily connected with the UCC. The official United Church Board for World Ministries disputed the BWF claim that it was not sufficiently evangelism-oriented; it claimed that it emphasized the propagation of the gospel everywhere.[27] Some sharp exchanges of charges were made over priorities on social activist policies, but beyond that, no deep-rooted liberal/conservative polarization seemed evident.[28]

In sum, the mainline during the 1980s spent considerable energy establishing workable programs within the boundaries of each group. Aggravating and demoralizing as many of these contests became, they did not overshadow such other areas as those we explore next, feminist theology and women's leadership, the charismatic movement, and the change from mainline to frontline in "the new social gospel."

WOMEN'S ISSUES

Deeply intertwined in the struggles of the mainline churches to maintain their many-sided ministries has been the enormous impact made by the women's movement. Emerging out of the awakening of the 1960s, it quickly entered into the churches and synagogues, agencies dedicated to the goals of love, understanding, reconciliation, justice, and mercy. Over the last three decades the entire range of such religious issues had been scrutinized in minute detail by both supporters and opponents of the demands of women for carrying out their several agendas. The struggle has been and continues to be a compelling example of the differences between pressers on and holders fast. It also illustrates well that in this area the important differences between mainliners and evangelicals fade into obscurity. In both camps the issues are basically the same; hence some overlapping here and at other pertinent areas does occur. Here we look at the decisive trends, especially in the 1980s: the problems and rewards of ordination of women; the many-sided world of feminist spirituality and theology; and the specific issue of inclusive language.

Starting in the 1960s, a dramatic rise occurred in the number of women graduating from colleges and universities and moving into professions once the exclusive domain of men. More women ran for political office at all levels; strong support for an Equal Rights Amendment came to unite large numbers across social and economic class lines. Although considerable resistance to such change occurred among both females and males from the outset, it became clear that a major social revolution, a transformation of consciousness, was under way. This would strike the religious communities with full force.[29]

At least four specific sources for creating such energy can be identified. Within the churches, evangelical and mainline, scholars and laity alike started examining the scriptural basis for what the women's movement labeled oppression by patriarchy. The women would do almost all of the necessary domestic work; the men would make the decisions and keep the women subordinate. Women, whose talent for ordained ministry, for example, was clearly evident, were told that their gender made them unsatisfactory for ordination and leadership.

The Bible came under very close scrutiny for a fresh understanding of this age-old dilemma. What an increasing number of investigators found was a clear, defendable case for full equality between the sexes, and for clear feminine as well as masculine teachings about the nature of the Godhead and religious faith. The opponents countered that the older, traditionally patriarchal texts were not gender-free; that God indeed was a father and Jesus indeed was a male, and that Paul indeed laid down very clear rules about the place of each gender in the churches. But by the late 1970s the cause for equality had taken too deep root to be deflected; scholars had continued their reinterpretations and found increasing support among both mainline and evangelical groups.

Second, the physical and social changes occurring in the lives of women made a strong impact. Women were living longer, expecting (by 1986 research findings) to live past eighty on the average. Coupled with the trend toward smaller families and improved housekeeping technology, that meant that women who had been busy as mothers for some twenty years now found long years of children-free living ahead. In addition, an enormous increase occurred in the number of women becoming part- or full-time wage earners. Only 21 percent of women considered themselves full-time homemakers; well over 50 percent were gainfully employed. Many went on to higher-education degrees. All this added up to evidence that they were qualified to have careers both as homemakers and as wage earners; they were prepared to serve the churches in a wider capacity than the old hierarchical patterns had allowed.

Third, the rapidly growing and diversifying feminist movement furnished much of the energy, rationale, and organization needed for transforming so slow-moving an institution as the church. The feminist movement burst out among religious-minded women and men in a variety of ways, leading to an expanding number of options as to how this transformation should best serve humankind. Despite its diversity, it became clear by the 1980s that it would not go away.[30]

Finally, personal experience contributed strongly to the movement. Among the deepest emotions and convictions are those centered around parental and family experiences, such as matters of love, sacrifice, devotion, fidelity, and trust. From these, as well as from experiences in the working world and from the world of ideas, came personal experiences and convictions among church people (as well as everyone else) as to what the role of parent, child, spouse, mentor, and leaders should be. The churches, of course, revolve around such experiences. They organize and direct such energies. Women now started to say more directly than ever before that they were at least as well qualified as males for making such decisions and carrying them out.[31]

This mosaic started to impact the churches directly in the form of changing policies on ordination. Between 1956 and 1977 five large denominations—Presbyterians, Methodists, Lutherans, Episcopalians, and national Baptists—approved the ordination of women. By 1990 only a handful of the major bodies did not ordain women: the Roman Catholic church, eight U.S. Orthodox churches, the Lutheran Church–Missouri Synod, and the Church of God in Christ. In 1972 women constituted only 10.2 percent of the total student population in the seminaries accredited by the American Theological Society; by 1987 this had grown to 27 percent. The average annual increase from 1980 to 1987 was 4.6 percent. Even as seminary enrollments declined slightly at the decade's end, women's enrollment continued to grow. By 1990 some 21,000 women served as ministers.[32]

With such growth has come considerable turmoil within mainline ranks at every level over female leadership. This has contributed in both obvious and subtle ways to the crises they have faced in the past decade. But ordination has also removed an enormous source of conflict and anguish within the mainline churches, and it has contributed directly to the opportunities and challenges feminists (of both sexes) see ahead for mainline renewal in the 1990s.

Supporters point out that ordination has made more visible in the liturgy the full human relationship with the Godhead, enhancing through symbol the qualities of feeding, healing, and nurturing. In the teaching ministry, older stories have been reinterpreted through the eyes of women's experiences, leading to fresh expressions of older truths. Ordination of women has increased church members' understandings of the deeper meanings of everyday experience. In sum, it has made a more human and serviceable institution of a traditionally austere and formalistic establishment.[33] All this has constituted hope for the survival of mainline faith into the future.

At the same time, women clergy encountered enormous problems, contributing to their own and their denomination's confusions. Some were seen by parishioners automatically as "radicals," as women refusing to accept their divinely appointed place in life, and hence to be suspected, even rejected. Tales, often exaggerated about just how "radical" and "antimale" some feminist religionists really were, followed women ministers. Single women clergy were often assumed, by their situation, to be lesbian or prolesbian. Where avowed lesbian clergy made clear their choice, the congregations or synods often reacted by withdrawal of support.[34]

In another category, women clergy found strong criticism from laywomen at the local level. The latter often resented other women having power over men or asked "why this woman could not be satisfied by serving a congregation in a lay capacity." Men and women had trouble adjusting to hearing a woman's voice delivering the sermon or leading the liturgy. Men had trouble relating personal problems to women clergy in counseling situations. The latter also found that few head pastorships were open for them; they would be hired and kept at the associate level, and these positions were usually in smaller congregations with lower salaries. Many found that parishioners had great trouble when the pastor became pregnant; in front of a congregation it was distracting, and when time for delivery came, the parish often had not worked out plans for maternity leave. Finally, many of the old stereotypical convictions regarding masculinity and femininity seemed to increase among parishioners and critical observers as the number of women clergy increased and their influence widened.[35]

As a means of support, women clergy organized a variety of networks. Some created informal associations within their denominations or geographical locations. They and others joined such national organizations as the National Church Women, the Daughters of Sarah, or the Evangelical Women's Caucus. The EWC, however, clearly showed the tensions of internal conflict when in 1986 it became bitterly divided. Some members called for a resolution showing EWC support for the lesbian sisters and civil rights for homosexuals. That blew apart the organization; within a year the antilesbian faction reorganized a new group, Christians for Biblical Equality.[36] Others found support in more academic settings such as the Women's Theological Center in Boston or its counterpart in Berkeley, California.

Such centers also served a highly important function for the widespread, often diffuse energies of the women's movement. They worked with the academic communities (and parishes also) to provide more formal structured analyses of theology, Scripture, doctrine, ethics, and related subjects. Across the nation interested women had little other direct access to the kind of informed, articulate arguments being made by feminists.[37]

At that point, however, mainliners found probably more questions raised and puzzles defined than answers given. Feminist theology (to use one term rather than the traditional list of specific religious studies subjects) offered a very wide variety of schools of thought, methodologies of research, and challenges to even the most foundational ideas of traditional Christianity. As part of a new, highly charged discipline, with the stakes involved being placed at very high levels, the participants found themselves exhilarated by the challenge and importance of its potential, yet baffled over the failure of a scholarly consensus to emerge. Some scholars in the field of religious studies rejected Christianity and the Bible altogether; others identified the feminist tradition with goddess ideas, ancient fertility rites, and similar variations.

Scholars of the movement took this diversity to be more a sign of strength than of weakness. The dissonant voices were all making their contribution; in the long run the diversity could only help break down the powerful domination patriarchal theology had exercised since earliest times.[38]

The academic world reflected throughout the decade this kind of tension. Scholars would often hold in suspension new or revisionist ideas just emerging from the academy. Laity, however, could not help but be puzzled over the vast diversity and conflicting interpretations of a message that for so many centuries had seemed so secure. Why should gender, the objections went, be able to transform the truth-giving symbols, language, and texts of the faith?[39] Feminists could reply with the answer of Sandra Schneiders, a Catholic nun and scholar in Berkeley:

The Gospel portrays Jesus as nonaggressive, noncompetitive, meek and humble of heart, a nurturer of the weak and a friend of the outcast. By becoming a human person, becoming flesh as a male rather than a female, Jesus assumed the sin of "belonging to the oppressor class" which he then subverted. Today, we would call Jesus a feminist, that is, a person who believes in the full personhood and equality of women and who acts to bring that belief to the realization of society and church.[40]

The movement also attracted those more interested in exploring the implications of spirituality. Among the several groups to organize has been the Women-Church movement. At first this attracted women moving out of Roman Catholicism. Then came others starting to probe the full range of feminist insight into the spiritual realm through the lenses of psychology, ritual, folk wisdom, and world religion.[41]

Such explorations both helped and hindered mainline church life in the 1980s. The irenic temper attracted feminists who might elsewhere have left organized church life altogether. It also posed very direct, often confrontational situations within local parish life as well as at state and national levels. Questions kept emerging over requiring fixed quotas of women and ethnic minorities on governance and policy-making boards. Disagreements arose over the degree to which goddess and spirituality insights were actually more inspired by wicca (white witchcraft) sources than by Christian faith.

Finally, since the feminist movement touched so directly on personal experience, its demands for inclusive language in liturgy and hymnology produced several enormously sharp and divisive debates. The issue for some mainliners seemed trivial; after all, the hymns were sung to the same God; the meanings of the words were familiar to all; many felt comfortable with singing the old verses. Some wondered why the creeds and formal statements, so much a part of the lifelong experience of church people, should be changed so drastically so quickly.

These were some of the questions faced by proponents of inclusive or gender-free language. Proponents insisted that Christians try to portray in words the "transcendent realities of a living faith." They argued that such truths have been expressed in art, music, movement, and metaphor; such features have held strong power over people's understanding and faith. But this was not the case when the feminists explored the riches of language. There they found, for instance, that when "mankind" was stated as "man," the women had disappeared. As stated by Barbara Brown Zikmund, "Psychological studies on language confirmed that people considered human and male attributes equivalent, whereas women and feminine characteristics remained secondary. So, if in Christ there is neither male nor female, the use of generic male language in the church was counterproductive."[42]

Further, the growth of faith among younger girls could not avoid being distorted by the male bias of the language. Where the Bible was often gender-neutral, certain translations of it were sex-specific. God, who in theology stands above human attributes, had been portrayed in human gender terms. Feminists pointed out that to insure that faith would survive into the future required people to infuse its meaning now with inclusive symbols.[43]

Critics such as Roland Mushat Frye countered these arguments by insisting that if Christians changed these symbols and the language, they were in fact changing the very essence of the message itself. "The fundamental literary principle is that figures cannot be abandoned, symbols cannot be substituted, images cannot be altered without changing the meaning they convey. That literary principle is even more pertinent to the Bible, where figurative expressions far more often operate as figures of thought than as ornamental figures of speech.[44]

Everyone involved agreed that church people have not agreed at all about the best solution to the controversy. The issue, however, illustrates a major dilemma at work in the mainline: some members would leave if one language policy were followed; others would leave if such a policy were prohibited. In sum, pressers and holders, caught up in making the message of faith understandable to people living in an increasingly secularized, modernist world, were forced to face the women's issues controversy head on.

CHARISMATICS

Just as the women's movement brought both new strength and new complications to mainline growth in the 1980s, so too the charismatic movement involved much the same two-sided experience. Like the women's movement, it had emerged during the awakening of the 1960s to meet specific needs. But contrary to the former movement, the charismatic outpouring in the 1980s eventually found its place within the status quo. In this section we examine its definition, its unfolding story, its numerical strength, its expression within the mainline, and some important variations alongside that entity.

Although its origins had little to do with the sociopolitical turmoil of the awakening of the 1960s, the charismatic renewal first came into public view then. Appearing first among Episcopalians, then among Lutherans and other mainline bodies, and moving into Roman Catholic circles in 1967, this spiritual renewal movement soon came to understand itself clearly. It was made up of Christians who had undergone a "second" or "Holy Spirit" baptism wherein the believer received the power and the gifts (charisms) of the Holy Spirit. These included speaking in tongues (glossolalia), prophecy, healing, miracles, "and an acceptance of other biblical paranormal phenomena . . . as valid contemporary religious experiences."[45]

Central to this renewal is the commitment to remain within the parent church after the baptism. Older or "classical" Pentecostalists who had undergone the same experience had separated themselves into specific Pentecostal bodies. Not so with charismatics. As they unfolded, the two movements developed clear distinctions, with charismatics generally emphasizing (as well defined by Elaine Lawless) "the quiet, intellectual nature of their evening meetings, held perforce in homes rather than in the church proper. The Holy Spirit is gently wooed through quiet individual prayer and testimony." The more energetic, public meetings of Pentecostalists who had been separated out for a more pure witness were generally discouraged.[46]

As the renewal moved into the 1980s within mainline boundaries, it faced a considerable number of difficulties. Often national leaders and local church members suspected it of wanting not only to dominate the spiritual life of the church, but actually to take control of its governance. Second, its way of interpreting the Bible often led spokespersons to affiliate strongly with very conservative, more secular political causes such as the crusade against "secular humanism," led by the Moral Majority. Finally, it could not find the means by which it could hold what became a considerable number of dropouts who simply lost interest, or keep within the ranks those who wanted an even stronger witness, such as that being made by the Pentecostalists.[47]

With such pressures close by, the movement itself tended more toward consolidation of earlier influences rather than exploration into new, unmapped territories. That consolidation involved more emphasis on local Bible study, and small-sized spiritual retreats and renewal experiences, and finding theological answers to the critics who charged that the movement was almost entirely based on personal experience and emotional insights rather than fidelity to older truths. Greater sophistication of understanding was reached among charismatics over various healing ministries, with the emphasis now being placed more on healings related to inner renewal and personal relationships. Yet participants would join or drop out with some frequency. This was almost unavoidable because charismatics chose to work through informal settings. Small group study and prayer associations would attract some of the curious who, having considered the possibilities, would move on. Or there would be burnouts, those who had gone through an intensive second baptism and had found that little if anything had changed in their lives. They came to wonder what had gone wrong.[48]

During the 1980s new energies and new priorities penetrated the movement. Considerable overlapping among denominational members occurred, especially as fresh faces among the leaders and new teachings attracted the attention of the faithful. At the core was the holding/pressing problem. Since, as the participants believed, the Holy Spirit was leading them where church people had not walked before, how far should they journey? How could they be sure that theirs was an authentic understanding?

From California came one new way, entitled the "signs and wonders movement," led by John Wimber of the Vineyard Christian Fellowship. It accented a ministry of healings, deliverance, and exorcisms from perceived demonic spirits, prophecies, foretellings, and the like. Followers believed that since God at Pentecost had promised signs and wonders, then they, the faithful, must claim those promises and show the world what could be done.[49] Sometimes this emphasis, which spread slowly but steadily eastward, is classified by observers as part of a new ''third wave'' in Holy Spirit renewal. That means that a new phase that could rival the first wave, the classical Pentecostal movement, or the second wave, the charismatic mainline renewal, was now witnessing a surge of growth.

Within this form of religious expression, attractive spokespersons (mostly men, although women do lead in Pentecostal circles) launched new ministries, emphasizing what each believed was divine superintendence in the troubled years of the 1980s. Among these, briefly, have been the ''dominion theology'' group, calling on the renewed to take over large portions of society, if necessary by political means, to build the kingdom of God before the final days. A second, small, but forceful group has been the ''replacement theology'' camp, arguing that God has rejected Israel as his chosen people and has given that mission to the renewed Christian church. Reconstructionist leaders, as a third alternative, attract some followers with teachings that call for implementation of Old Testament law as the basis for a new world order. Leaders spend considerable time criticizing one another, a feature that has led the great majority of mainline charismatics to stay close to their own traditions. These people also find attractive the so-called Faith Movement ministry of Kenneth Hagin of Oklahoma, which presents a variety of new alternatives in spiritual renewal, confession, and healing.[50]

For mainliners these new options have shown how volatile any kind of Holy Spirit revival can become. That volatility has made any helpful statistical kind of membership growth analysis extremely hard to carry out. Perhaps the most accurate, given the problems of rapid movements in and out of groups, has been that of David Barrett, a researcher for the Foreign Mission Board of the Southern Baptist Convention. He gauges that in 1988 in North American mainline charismatic movements (including Protestants, Roman Catholics, Orthodox, blacks, and those who identify with radio and television charismatics) totaled some 6,027,330 members. A specialist in church growth, C. Peter Wagner, estimates that in the 1980s the growth rate among charismatics declined about 50 percent in comparison to the growth rate of the previous decade. In round numbers this would mean that on the average within a mainline or Roman Catholic body, the number of charismatics would total between 10 and 15 percent.[51]

That figure, of course, can mean different things to different people. It means considerable growth since the movement started in the early 1960s. It also can mean that the movement has not moved ahead in numbers anywhere near the expectations of its leaders. By and large the mainline bodies have absorbed the charismatic renewal. Those who decided that they could not stay loyal to their faith by keeping membership in the parent church had, for the most part, left by 1990.

As that trend emerged, observers took the opportunity to look back over what had happened during the thirty-some years of charismatic ministry. Those who understood its appearance as the result of supernatural activity found that its strength had emerged from its strong emphasis on inner renewal through prayer and personal reflection; from its inspired leadership, which kept the movement alive and held members within the parent church; from renewed emphasis on Bible study; and from lay leadership. To these observers, the charismatic movement, as it has unfolded, has pointed the way in which seekers can travel in the future.

From those, however, who have studied the movement from a more academic perspective, its growth is attributed to the fear of secularization and the specialization of society. That is, the more specialized into interest groups ("tribes") an industrial society becomes, the more specialized the religious needs of the seekers become. As Christians find themselves increasingly fragmented among business, family, recreation, politics, and the like, which in a pluralistic society have no explicit religious foundations, they find wholeness and resources to combat secularism in a strong renewal movement such as this. To these seekers, the irenic middle-of-the-road course of denominations simply does not meet the increasingly heavy demands for a faith adequate for their particular times. Charismatics believe that God was making this movement available for these times, this post-awakening America. Modernization, with its disdain for traditional authority (as had been reflected in the churches) had left these seekers in need of some source of certainty and absoluteness. The claim that there was a supernatural outpouring of divine power in the spiritual gifts met that need.[52]

Also, charismatic renewal followed traditional socioeconomic class lines, by and large. Those not ready to join the more boisterous, blue-collar, classical Pentecostalists or a totally separated, independent renewed congregation could find social identity among the reference group they had already known, the local congregation. Within that body they developed specific interest groups, finding renewed confidence that they were on the right track by their close spiritual fellowship and sharing with others of the local parish.[53]

Critics of the movement made clear throughout the decade their objections. They pointed out that the charismatics showed little sustained concern for the poor and underfed; they pointed to the lack of formal educational training for many leaders in positions of power; they found instances where such power had led to unchristian bitterness, hostility, and suspicion within congregations. Friends and critics agreed that the movement showed considerable anti-intellectualism, romantic emotionalism, a "desire for thrills and emotional highs," excessive concern for physical health and repose, a "preference for folk-type music with poetically uncouth lyrics," and "cultivated informality."[54]

Yet contrary to the other major crises facing mainline bodies in the 1980s, charismatic renewal offered perhaps more opportunity than liability for restrengthening the faith. It had survived considerable, often unfair criticism earlier in its history. Now it could point to the achievement by some participants of some important theological reflection on how it belonged within its respective denominational affiliations. Further, it had not been directly rejected by the parent churches' leadership, who in turn became more comfortable in working with these newly enthused converts. It offered proof that within the traditional framework of denominations for embracing a variety of emphases, the mission of the charismatics could continue. That same determination to avow that despite all the problems, the work must go on showed up in the mainline shift, not to the sidelines, as its critics claimed, but, as this book will now argue, to a frontline position in the midst of a troubled, often frightening world.

NOTES

1. Martin E. Marty, "The State of the Disunion: A Hard Look at Ecumenism," *Commonweal*, January 29, 1988, p. 43.

2. For evangelicals, see the excellent discussion by George Marsden in the Introduction to his *Evangelicalism and Modern America* (Grand Rapids, Mich.: Wm. B. Eerdmans, 1984), pp. vii–xix; David S. Luecke, *Evangelical Style and Lutheran Substance: Facing America's Mission Challenge* (St. Louis: Concordia Publishing House, 1988), pp. 52–62.

3. Martin E. Marty, "Afterword," in Martin E. Marty, ed., *Where the Spirit Leads: American Denominations Today* (Atlanta, Ga.: John Knox Press, 1980), pp. 232–34.

4. Mark Noll, "Catholics and Protestants since World War II," in Robert N. Bellah and Frederick E. Greenspan, eds., *Uncivil Religion: Interreligious Hostility in America* (New York: Crossroad, 1987), pp. 86–107.

5. See Ellen M. Rosenberg, *The Southern Baptists: A Subculture in Transition* (Knoxville: University of Tennessee Press, 1989).

6. Marty, "State of the Disunion," pp. 44–45; Ronald H. Nash, ed., *Evangelical Renewal in the Mainline Churches* (Westchester, Ill.: Crossway Books, 1987), pp. 22, 23, 34, 36, 70, 92, 95, 130.

7. James Davison Hunter, *Evangelicalism: The Coming Generation* (Chicago: University of Chicago Press, 1987), pp. 191–94; Martin E. Marty, "Religion in America since Mid-Century," in Mary Douglas and Steven M. Tipton, eds., *Religion and America: Spirituality in a Secular Age* (Boston: Beacon Press, 1982), pp. 281–86.

8. News story, *Christian Century*, July 20–27, 1988, pp. 660–62; Nash, *Evangelical Renewal*, pp. 79–85; news story, *Eternity*, July–August 1988, p. 2; *Washington Post*, June 25, 1988, p. B6.

9. Nash, *Evangelical Renewal*, p. 54; news story, *Christianity Today*, February 21, 1986, pp. 36–38; *Touchstone*, Spring 1988, pp. 20–22; John Booty, *The Episcopal Church in Crisis* (Cambridge, Mass.: Crowley Press, 1988); *New York Times*, June 21, 1989, p. 12.

10. Nash, *Evangelical Renewal*, p. 60; Patrick Henry Reardon, "Whither Episcopalians?" *Touchstone*, Spring 1988, pp. 9ff.; *Los Angeles Times*, July 2, 1988, sec. 2, p. 3; *New York Times*, July 12, 1988, p. 9; *Seattle Times*, July 2, 1988, p. C9; *Episcopalians United*, Spring 1988, p. 1.

11. See the publications of Episcopal Renewal Ministries, P.O. Box 1370, Fairfax, VA 22030; *Charisma and Christian Life*, February 1989, p. 31.

12. News story, *Christian Century*, August 2–9, 1989, pp. 710–11; *National Christian Reporter*, February 20, 1989, p. 1; ibid., October 7, 1988, p. 1; *Washington Post*, February 27, 1989, p. D16.

13. *Washington Post*, February 27, 1989, p. D16; *National Christian Reporter*, June 16, 1989, p. 1.

14. *The Yearbook of the Evangelical Lutheran Church in America* (Minneapolis: Augsburg Fortress, 1989), p. 563.

15. *Lutheran*, January 27, 1988, p. 26; news story, *St. Paul Dispatch Pioneer Press*, April 9, 1988, pp. B1, B4; *Lutheran Commentator* 1 and 2 (1987) (P.O. Box 1093, Minnetonka, MN 55345–0093); American Association of Lutheran Churches, *Evangel*, 1988 issues (P.O. Box 17097, Minneapolis, MN 55417; publications of the Living Word Lutheran Church, Eagan, Minn.: Nick Cavnar, "Charismatics and the Lutheran Merger," *Charisma and Christian Life*, March 1988, pp. 46–55.

16. *Minneapolis Star Tribune*, June 24, 1989, p. 6A; *Christian News*, July 10, 1989, p. 6; ibid., July 31, 1989, p. 24.

17. Constant Jacquet, ed., *Yearbook of American and Canadian Churches, 1988* (Nashville, Tenn.: Abingdon Press, 1989), p. 261.

18. *Chicago Tribune*, January 8, 1988, sec. 1, p. 9; *New York Times*, June 20, 1989, p. 14; St. Paul Dispatch Pioneer Press, July 22, 1989, p. 3B.

19. *Los Angeles Times*, August 12, 1989, sec. 2, p. 7; *Washington Post*, May 7, 1988, p. 86; report of the 1988 convention, *This World* 25 (Spring 1989): 109–18; *New York Times*, May 3, 1988, p. 13.

20. Nash, *Evangelical Renewal*, pp. 17–39.

21. *National Christian Reporter*, November 25, 1988, p. 4; *National and International Religion Report*, September 26, 1988, p. 3.

22. Jacquet, *Yearbook, 1988*, p. 261.

23. "Restructuring of the American Presbyterian" (Lecture by Wuthnow, Louisville Presbyterian Theological Seminary, March 7, 1989).

24. *Los Angeles Times*, March 4, 1989, sec. 2, p. 7; *Washington Post*, June 18, 1988, p. B7; *Washington Post*, July 15, 1989, p. C11; *Christian Century*, August 16–23, 1989, pp. 745–46.

25. Jacquet, *Yearbook, 1988*, p. 261.

26. *National Christian Reporter*, July 21, 1989, p. 2; *Christian Century*, July 19–26, 1989, pp. 676–78.

27. *National Christian Reporter*, December 9, 1988, p. 1; ibid., May 19, 1989, p. 1; Nash, *Evangelical Renewal*, pp. 121–39.

28. *National Christian Reporter*, May 19, 1989, p. 1.

29. Wade Clark Roof and William McKinney, *American Mainline Religion: Its Changing Shape and Future* (New Brunswick, N.J.: Rutgers University Press, 1987), pp. 204–9.

30. Roberta Hestenes, "Women in Leadership: Finding Ways to Serve the Church," *Christianity Today*, October 3, 1986, p. 4-I-10-I.

31. Ibid.; Letha Scanzoni and Nancy Hardesty, *All We're Meant to Be: Biblical Feminism for Today*, rev. ed. (Nashville, Tenn.: Abingdon Press, 1986).

32. Marilyn Hickey, "Women in Ministry," *Charisma and Christian Life*, August 1985, p. 83; Jacquet, *Yearbook, 1988*, p. 275; *National Christian Reporter*, March 24, 1989, p. 1; *Newsweek*, February 13, 1989, p. 59.

33. Denise Haines, "Women's Ordination: What Difference Has It Made?" *Christian Century*, October 15, 1986, pp. 888–89; Martha Long Ice, "Clergywomen and the Future," *Word and World* 8, 4 (1988): 357–65.

34. See, for instance, Dan Dervin, "Making Utopia out of Dystopia: The Role of Men as Poison Containers in Radical Feminism," *Journal of Psychohistory* 16, 4 (Spring 1989): 427–43; Mariana Valverde, *Sex, Power, and Pleasure* (Toronto: Women's Press, 1985), pp. 192–203; news story, *Christian Century*, May 17, 1989, pp. 516–17.

35. Rick Wolff, "Clergywomen," *Cresset*, April 1988, pp. 16–20; DeAne Lagerkvist, *From Our Mother's Arms: A History of Women in the American Lutheran Church* (Minneapolis: Augsburg Publishing House, 1987); "Women in the Church" (Symposium), *Sojourners*, July 1987, pp. 14–38; *Newsweek*, February 13, 1989, p. 59; Clark Morphew column, "On Religion," *St. Paul Dispatch Pioneer Press*, January 30, 1988, p. 3B. See the macho ideas in George Gilder, *Men and Marriage* (Gretna, La.: Pelican, 1986); *National Christian Reporter*, January 27, 1989, p. 4.

36. *Touchstone*, Summer/Fall 1988, p. 43; Richard Quebedeaux, "We're on the Way, Lord! The Rise of 'Evangelical Feminism' in Modern American Christianity," in Ursula King, ed., *Women in the World's Religions* (New York: Paragon House, 1987), pp. 129–44.

37. "Women's Theological Center," *Women of Power*, no. 2 (1985): 72; Gregory Baum, "The Church and the Women's Movement," *Ecumenist*, November/December 1988, pp. 12–15; Ronald B. Flowers, *Religion in Strange Times: The 1960s and 1970s* (Macon, Ga.: Mercer University Press, 1984), pp. 199–230. Any recent issue of *Sojourners* has the latest titles in this rapidly growing field of research.

38. Marcia Bunge, "Feminism in Different Voices: Resources for the Church," *Word and World* 8, 4 (1988): 321–26; Mary Hull Mohr, "Feminism Comes of Age," ibid., pp. 327–33. See the work of Carol Gilligan et al., eds., *Mapping the Moral Domain: A Contribution of Women's Thinking to Psychological Theory and Education* (Cambridge: Harvard University Press, 1988).

39. Kenneth Woodward, "Feminism and the Churches," *Newsweek*, February 13, 1989, pp. 58–59; Asoka Bandarage, "Feminist Theory," *Women of Power*, Spring 1986, pp. 81ff.

40. Sandra Schneiders, quoted in *Newsweek*, February 13, 1989, p. 61.

41. Gretchen E. Ziegenhals, "Meeting the Women of Women-Church," *Christian Century*, May 10, 1989, pp. 492–94; Miriam Therese Winter, *Womanpower, Womansong* (Bloomington, Ind.: Meyerstone Books, 1988); Judith Plaskow and Carol P. Christ, *Weaving the New Pattern* (San Francisco: Harper and Row, 1988); Anne E. Carr, *Transforming Grace: Christian Tradition and Women's Experience* (San Francisco: Harper and Row, 1988).

42. Barbara Brown Zikmund, "Women and the Churches," in David Lotz, Donald W. Shriver, Jr., and John F. Wilson, eds., *Altered Landscapes: Christianity in America, 1935–1985* (Grand Rapids, Mich.: Wm. B. Eerdmans, 1989), p. 136.

43. Ibid.; Nancy R. Hardesty, "Whosoever Surely Meaneth Me: Inclusive Language and the Gospel," *Christian Scholar's Review* 17, 3 (1988): 231–40; interview with R. R. Reuther, *Sojourners*, January 1984, pp. 17–19.

44. Roland Mushat Frye, "Language for God and Feminist Language: A Literary and Rhetorical Analysis," *Interpretation*, 1989, p. 48; Donald G. Bloesch, *The Battle for the Trinity* (Ann Arbor: Servant Books, 1985). See also Paul Holmer, "A Fragment of Thought about Feminism, Language, and Church," *Reflections* (Yale Divinity School), January 1985, pp. 44ff.

45. Margaret Poloma, "The Charismatic Movement," in Jeffrey K. Hadden and Anson D. Shupe, eds., *Prophetic Religions and Politics* (New York: Paragon House, 1986), p. 330.

46. Elaine I. Lawless, *God's Peculiar People: Women's Voices and Folk Tradition in a Pentecostal Church* (Lexington: University of Kentucky Press, 1988), pp. 42–43; Mary Jo Neitz, *Charisma and Community* (New Brunswick, N.J.: Transaction Books, 1987), pp. 30–62. See the many articles in Stanley M. Burgess and Gary B. McGee, eds., *Dictionary of Pentecostal and Charismatic Movements* (Grand Rapids, Mich.: Zondervan Publishing House, 1988).

47. P. D. Hocken, "Charismatic Movement," in Burgess and McGee, *Dictionary of Pentecostal and Charismatic Movements*, pp. 138–41; Wagner, "Church Growth," ibid., p. 192; news story, *Religion Watch*, October 1988, p. 6.

48. Ibid., see the same sources.

49. The story on "Signs and Wonders," Burgess and McGee, *Dictionary of Pentecostal and Charismatic Movements*, pp. 184ff., 374.

50. News story, *National and International Religion Report*, December 28, 1988. pp. 7–8; P. D. Hocken, "Church Theology," in Burgess and McGee, *Dictionary of Pentecostal and Charismatic Movements*, pp. 216–17; D. R. McConnell, *A Different Gospel* (Peabody, Mass.: Hendrickson, 1988). On healing see *Charisma and Christian Life*, October 1987, pp. 19–24; David Barrett, "Twentieth Century Pentecostal/Charismatic Renewal," *International Bulletin of Missionary Research*, July 1988, pp. 119–27.

51. Barrett, "Twentieth Century Pentecostal/Charismatic Renewal," pp. 119–27.

52. Good case studies are in Margaret Poloma, *The Charismatic Movement* (Boston: Twayne Publishers, 1982), pp. 197–206. See also Jess Moody, "A Baptist Preacher Looks at the Charismatics," *Christian Retailing*, April 15, 1988, pp. 18ff.

53. J. W. Shepperd, "Sociology of Pentecostalism," in Burgess and McGee, *Dictionary of Pentecostal and Charismatic Movements*, pp. 798–99.

54. J. I. Packer, "Piety on Fire," *Christianity Today*, May 12, 1989, pp. 18–21.

3

The New Social Gospel

Running through the accounts of the several mainline struggles is a current indigenous to all of religious history—the suggestion that this field of study is more fully understood when it is viewed through the eyes of irony and paradox. To give three examples: high ideals often lead pursuers down paths they have never intended to travel; good intentions often lead to regrettable results; and serendipity and fulfillment break out in highly unlikely places.

This condition clearly illuminates the social outreach ministry of the mainline during the 1980s. The internal squabbling, the decline in membership, and the contests over priorities and identity all sapped energy away from the potential for renewal. Yet at the same time many mainliners, awakened in the 1960s, found fulfillment in a heretofore unlikely place—a militant, sometimes personally risky social outreach ministry. This development is entitled "from mainline to frontline," signifying the decision made by many church-related citizens to become directly involved in a variety of peace and justice issues in the name of their convictions.

This was the more ironic because sociologically minded observers had been predicting that the forces of secularization and privatization would predominate; that middle-class, largely white college-educated people would simply phase themselves out of organized religious life. This failed to occur in the movement discussed here. Paradox abounded when this new social gospel directed much of its energy against the prevailing cultural mores of the day, those being the domain of evangelicals. Where once the latter had been more the outsider looking in, now they enjoyed direct access to the White House and other accoutrements of power, while mainliners-turned-frontliners now stood more as the dissenting minority.

Finally, where once critics had accused mainliners of being overly bureaucratic and top-heavily organized, the new activism turned into a multifaceted, very loosely connected movement. It attracted adults of all ages, all regions, Protestants, Catholics, and Jews. It flourished both within and apart from denominational structures. It turned up in both multiple-purpose and single-issue crusades on the local, state, and national levels. It embraced a wide variety of issues: social, economic, sexual, racial, ecological, political, and educational. In the eyes of the participants, this was a pressing-on call to recapture the prophetic voice of Scripture, summoning a people back to righteousness. To the holders fast, the movement was more evidence of continued drifting away from the true faith.[1]

Long under criticism by conservatives for lacking a scriptural foundation for their activism, pressers in postawakening America brought together several themes to meet the needs of the day. Although no one major spokesperson of the stature of a Reinhold Niebuhr came forward, the contributions of Gabriel Fackre and Alan Geyer stand as highly representative of the new foundations. From Andover Newton Theological Seminary, Fackre defined a new concern. Rather than focus on the classical Protestant theme of God's answering word of forgiveness to sin, the direction had turned.

People do not lie awake anymore worrying about Luther's question, "How can I find a gracious God?" People's anguish is not over the alienation between the soul and God but rather over the estrangement between black and white, rich and poor, male and female, East and West. The question is: "How can I find a gracious neighbor?" The many crises in the world lead seekers to concentrate on historical suffering as the focus, and on "hope in action" as the believer's response.[2]

Hence the renewed interest in issues such as racial and gender equality, poverty, hunger, biomedical ethics, and similar issues. This renewed focus, Fackre stated, would not rule out the ongoing search for knowing God's purposes in this world.

But as Alan Geyer, an influential Protestant critic, stated, it does mean recognizing how wide the scope of evangelizing in the world truly is.

God's will is for nations and peoples as well as for individuals. Prophetic faith from Amos to Jesus engages our spirits at their very depth in confrontation with an active God of justice, of peace, of liberation and reconciliation—and commands us to struggle with principalities and powers. Thus conflict and controversy are among the most precious marks of faithfulness. Social action which does not become political action risks becoming cheap grace; it is likely to be escapist, sentimental, and ineffective.[3]

During the 1980s evangelicals would come close to saying much the same thing about becoming involved in the world. Where they and mainliners parted ways became clear when each camp expressed its political loyalties. Mainliners moved strongly into the camp of the liberal Democrats, while evangelicals took their stand with the reigning Republican party.

Several trends helped lead the mainliners to and keep them associated with reform liberalism. Choosing a middle ground between the conservative's preference for a laissez-faire/free-market kind of capitalism and any Marxist-type revolution, they endorsed a mixed economy. There private and public sectors would work together for the common good. Second, the rising concern over protection of the environment and prudent use of energy attracted concerned mainliners toward the Democrats.[4]

Further, throughout the decade several extremely wealthy investors in the stock market came to represent the aspirations and values of growing numbers of citizens. *Newsweek* commented that "the 80s were the decade in which material success became a kind of free-floating standard of excellence." President Ronald Reagan was "openly comfortable with wealth and the wealthy," in contrast to the defeated incumbent, Jimmy Carter. Energetic investors, many under the age of thirty, started making money quickly, emerging in popular parlance as "yuppies," young upwardly mobile professionals, who believed the advertisement telling them that they could have it all.[5] Such identification of conservatism with ostentatious wealth led some mainliners to look for alternatives.

From the world of academe came the charge that the United States was spending too much of public funds on armaments at the expense of shoring up the escalating social crises in unemployment, housing, crime, welfare, damage to the environment, and medical care. The immense prosperity of the age, the indictment stated, was only camouflage for the fact that the huge federal deficit and unfavorable overseas trade balance would soon reduce the United States to a second-rate power.[6]

With their theological outlook being what it was, and with a growing distaste for where the entrepreneurial spirit of acquisition seemed to be taking America, mainliners found reason to move toward liberal reform politics. Studies suggested how far the leaders had made the identification. The Center for the Study of Political and Social Change (of Northampton, Massachusetts) showed that of the 178 religious leaders they polled (89 Catholics, 61 mainline, 23 fundamentalist, and 5 "unclassifiable"), 85 percent of self-described religious liberals were also political liberals, and 89 percent of self-described religious conservatives were politically conservative as well. The two groups differed over how each ranked the performance of large corporations and capitalism, over the government's need to reduce the gap between the rich and poor, over abortion, over requiring job-related work of mothers on welfare, over means to combat communism, over recognizing the rights of homosexuals, and over care for the underclass and the poor, among some twenty-six general issues.[7]

This renewed expression of involvement in peace and justice issues came to the public in enormously varied patterns of organization. Both this diversity of structure and the range of matters within its domain gave the "new social gospel" its distinctive personality. Not strictly the product of the awakening of the 1960s, "special-purpose groups" (as entitled by Robert Wuthnow) started growing rapidly in number during that decade and have continued rapid growth down to the present.[8]

The growth statistics suggest their importance. Defined as those nonprofit, voluntary associations that meet the Internal Revenue Service's qualifications for religious bodies other than denominations or churches, well over 1,000 of these flourished by the late 1980s. By contrast, only 20 such groups existed prior to

1860. Between World War II and 1960 over 460 such bodies appeared. Since 1960, 293 additional organizations, 36 percent of the grand total, have been created.[9]

These groups fully represent the wide variety of mainline and evangelical interests in public ministries. They have focused on an enormous range of human concerns that could be managed only by some social agency. They took their legitimating mandates from their religious sources, all the way from local interest groups within congregations to vast, multilayered national enterprises. At times they appeared to achieve a single goal, such as a referendum on a local issue, and then disappeared. At other times they would branch off, splinter, or join like-minded crusaders in parallel groups. Such was the case with some very unlikely partners joining together to protest the national government's prosecution of the Reverend Sun Myung Moon for income tax evasion charges.

Professor Wuthnow suggests that special-purpose groups grew rapidly during these years for several reasons, the first being the greater degree of professionalization among the leaders. More of them now had earned higher-education degrees, giving them a better understanding of administration and leadership. Second, many groups replicated the existing secular models, such as civil rights, anti-illiteracy, or care-for-the-homeless groups. Third was the growing level of affluence, giving people more money and time for such voluntary causes. Greater public awareness based on extensive mass-media coverage and the availability of direct-mail computer fund-raising and educational programs allowed these bodies to reach millions of otherwise uninvolved citizens.

Perhaps most importantly, these organizations expanded because as private agencies they attempted to stop, assist, or supplement the enormous increase of government activity in the same spheres. Just as the federal, state, and local governments became involved in civil rights, education, health care, equal rights legislation, programs for the elderly, and hundreds of other causes, so the church-related volunteer agencies emerged to advance and protect their special-purpose priorities.[10]

During the 1980s mainliner individuals and special-purpose groups gave public-policy involvement very high priority. Denominations put forward programs for peace and arms control, for environmental protection, for welfare reform, and for protection of those abused by husbands and fathers, in short for much of human wrongdoing. Alongside these organizations came renewed efforts from such interdenominational bodies as Clergy and Laity Concerned (CALC) to supplement and expand such ministries. Added to these efforts were such local-congregation programs as that of the Riverside Church in New York City for disarmament and the Washington, D.C., Church of the Savior program for peacemaking.

The long-standing source of leadership for mainliners, the National Council of Churches, provided a variety of services: educational materials, seminars and workshops on specific issues, lobbying efforts in legislatures and in Congress for specific issues, and public-relations services to keep these issues in the public eye. After careful assessment, one observer concluded, "In fact, the attempt of religious leaders to influence political policies and the relationship between religion and politics in America has been one of the major news stories of the past decade."[11]

The wide-ranging scope and many-sided forms of organizations defy any satisfactory means of summarizing their work. A major expression of this new social gospel has been the many voluntary services positions for participants, lasting from a few months to a few years. Every major body has a "volunteers for . . ." agency working in health care, education, agriculture, evangelism, community development, emergency shelters for the abused, and related problems.[12]

By contrast to the highly publicized financial and television activities of celebrity leaders in the 1980s, these volunteer agencies received little or no attention. Yet, as a commentary on President George Bush's famous call for "a thousand points of light," volunteer work for America's domestic crises, the record shows that there were "millions of points of light already illuminating America—in homeless shelters, foster homes for AIDS babies, soup kitchens, tutoring programs, food delivery services, emergency hotlines, Mothers Against Drunk Driving, church outreach programs and settlement houses."[13]

Certainly the boldest and often the most dramatic and risky form of outreach ministry occurred in the general field of peace issues such as opposition to nuclear weaponry, to arms buildups, and to the location of atomic-powered plants in civilian areas, and in withholding taxes to protest spending for the military. Briefly, the peace movement became in this decade a major element in the mainline political expression of opposition to the course of events of the Reagan administration. Each denomination sponsored in a variety of ways its own Peace Fellowship, agencies providing a variety of educational materials for both general and specific peacemaking programs. The fellowships often led participants in specific localities in commemorating such days as the dropping of the atomic bomb on Hiroshima. They sponsored interdenominational worship services, such as Peace Pentecost in Washington, D.C., to commemorate past peacemakers and encourage members to continue working for that cause.

With so large and varied a record, we can look at only a few stories here to illustrate the depth and degree of personal commitment made by the "peaceniks." In Minneapolis demonstrations were made annually at the Honeywell plant where armaments such as cluster bombs, fuses, mines, jet fighter components, and major systems for such arms as the Trident submarine and others are manufactured. Each year the demonstrators attempted to convince the stockholders to reject the government's contracts for such materials; each year they engaged in civil disobedience and were arrested. The program has been supported by a variety of community volunteer organizations and peace fellowships.[14]

In Seattle, at Puget Sound, a protest against having the nuclear-powered Trident submarine stationed there occurred in 1982. Civilians had long worried over the presence of such potentially hazardous installations. Since the mid-1970s various protests had been made, but without success. After considerable planning, with ecumenical support from a number of church-related and civic organizations, a group of forty-five men and women risked jail sentences of up to ten years by sailing out into the bay to stop the incoming Trident from going in any further than Bangor. One of the protesters was Ruth Youngdahl Nelson, seventy-eight, voted some ten years before the national mother of the year, and the mother of John Nelson, one of the protesters' leaders. As they sailed near the Trident, a Coast Guard sailor aimed a water cannon at Mrs. Nelson and others in their crafts. She looked at him, pointed her finger, and said, "No, no, young man. Not in America, you wouldn't do that."[15] Eventually all participants were fined, and some were jailed.

Another group, the eight members of Plowshares Disarmament Actions, started a movement, picked up by others across the country, to attempt to prevent, largely by symbolic means, the production of nuclear weaponry. From the first such action in 1980, led by Philip and Daniel Berrigan, until September 1986, some seventeen Plowshares actions occurred. In each the participants would attempt to enter a military manufacturing plant, planning to destroy the weaponry found there. They would spill blood ceremoniously, offer prayer, and accept in civil disobedience fashion their arrest and jailing.[16]

The antinuclear crusade spread quickly throughout both mainline and evangelical circles, as well as in the traditional "peace" churches (Brethren, Mennonite, Amish, Quaker, and so on). During the first years of the Reagan administration, church people were moving toward something like a direct confrontation with that government over nuclear weapons and deterrence policy. For example, the Roman Catholic Bishops drafted a pastoral letter in sharp protest over the administration's arms policies. Congregations held special antinuclear services. They found reason to believe that the world and the nuclear superpowers were not doomed by some kind of fate to continue nuclear brinkmanship until one or the other went over the edge. To them God's creation was far too precious to risk such bravado as they perceived to be coming from Washington and Moscow.

In addition, the Reagan administration's leaders took little care to explain their stepped-up production of nuclear arms. In 1984 the bishops published their statement, a major study that raised serious doubts both ethically and militarily over the seemingly imminent nuclear holocaust. Among Protestants, the National Council of Churches joined with denominations and ad hoc committees to support the "freeze" movement, a proposal to halt all further production of nuclear weapons.[17]

The freeze idea caught on quickly, soon developing into a full-blown crusade. Across the country volunteer freeze committees made up of Catholic, Jewish, and Protestant members as well as others organized with the aim of convincing Congress to vote for this special purpose. Most major denominations passed resolutions and sponsored educational programs in their parishes aimed at opposing further nuclear weapon development. Perhaps the best known of these was the United Methodist Bishops' *In Defense of Creation: The Nuclear Crisis and a Just Peace.*[18]

This organizing led to rallies such as the one in New York City in 1982, when nearly one million people rallied for the cause of disarmament. Across the country city councils, congregations, county councils, New England town meetings, and twelve state legislatures by late 1982 endorsed a freeze proposal. In Washington and other metropolitan areas volunteer peace groups organized, providing educational materials and opportunities through forums and workshops for citizens to lobby their members in Congress. The international peace organization, SANE (Committee for a Sane Nuclear Policy), became a clearinghouse for information, keeping ties with synagogues and churches in need of leadership and information.[19] Within a few years the movement would fade into obscurity, but its strength, popularity, and idealism during the early 1980s represented the fact that mainline social ministry could find cause for renewal of its sense of mission.

The continuing hardline anticommunism of the Reagan administration probably contributed as much as anything to increased mainline opposition to its programs during the remainder of the decade. A list of specific campaigns would include mainline opposition to the president's programs in South Africa, for the Contras in Nicaragua, and for a legal crackdown on the sanctuary movement for illegal refugees seeking asylum in U.S. churches from the civil wars in Central America, as well as other opposition. In each situation the mainline churches at various levels of administration would sponsor rallies, workshops, seminars, educational materials, and often direct lobbying in Washington for its alternatives.

Congressional leaders stated that in at least one highly controversial area, funding the Contras, the church lobbies and grass roots letter writing played a major role in contributing to the defeat of the rebels' support at the Capitol.[20] Leading the campaign were the Washington offices of the National Lutheran Council, the United Presbyterians, the United Church of Christ, and the Disciples of Christ, among others. Also influential was the interdenominational service agency, IMPACT, consisting of several mainline denominations pooling their resources for a more united ministry.

The sanctuary movement sprang up at about this same time. A large number of refugees fleeing possible arrest and execution for political activities in their respective Central American nations made their way to the United States during the early and mid-1980s. The U.S. government saw them as being in this country without permission and sought to have them returned. For some refugees this would mean severe punishment. Most American mainline churches and the Roman Catholic church quickly seized on this opportunity to provide protection. Using a medieval tradition that churches had the right to provide sanctuary for the needy without fear of government intervention, they offered living quarters for some of the refugees. Altogether, more than 1,000 were helped in different parts of the country, with the clear understanding that the Immigration and Naturalization Service was ready to make arrests and seek prosecution of those U.S. citizens involved with the program.

The issue reached a nationally focused climax in Tucson, Arizona. There an informally organized coalition of Christians had provided sanctuary for several refugees. The Immigration and Naturalization Service sent undercover agents into their churches, often anonymously and with devices for recording the proceedings, to obtain legal evidence of the sanctuary leaders' violation of immigration laws. That, coupled with the hostility shown toward the Reagan administration's nuclear arms and freeze policies, its failure to support the invoking of economic sanctions against the government of South Africa, its endorsement of President Ferdinand Marcos in the Philippine Islands, and its support for the Contras and hostility toward the governing Sandinistas, all played a part in the scene now being acted out in the Southwest.

In a major trial in which the defendants, Lutherans and Roman Catholics, were supported by their churches, the government prosecuted the coalition for violation of the existing laws. The defendants were found guilty and given suspended sentences. The refugee problem eventually took a different turn as domestic violence in the homelands subsided, if only briefly. The exhilaration of becoming involved in so bold and far-reaching a matter as this movement, however, played a major role in revitalizing the enthusiasm of mainline members for their causes.[21]

Obviously, such programs received sharp, sustained criticism within the mainline bodies, leading to conflicts over national politics such as those described in Chapter 1. Unquestionably, the growing power of evangelicals and fundamentalists in shaping national policies through the leadership of Jerry Falwell, Pat Robertson, and others played a direct role in the controversies of these years. When one of the televangelists would make a withering critique of the peaceniks, the mainline would find cause to continue the battle.[22]

As some of the center-ring battles of the 1980s faded from the spotlight, mainliners through a variety of means started other forms of outreach programs. Many of these were already in place, led by civic groups. Among the more prominent programs receiving mainline support were, first, citizen diplomacy. In 1987 over 120,000 Americans visited the USSR, many working on a one-to-one basis for ending the cold war by making friends there. Second, other mainliners joined programs such as social investment programs. These aimed at directing investors' money away from companies that made harmful products, did business in South Africa, or had repressive worker conditions. Funds rather were steered toward providing investments for companies making ecologically mindful products and using fair labor practices. A third type of program was community organization, where church-related ad hoc groups would join civic neighbors to battle for toxic cleanup, co-op restaurants, and related campaigns. Others included communitywide prayer and meditation groups, conferences for people-to-people diplomacy, and continued education on nuclear and arms control issues.[23]

The peace movement found itself somewhat stalemated, largely because of the less aggressive Bush administration foreign policy and the signals from the Soviet Union that it was undergoing changes in its foreign policy. Mainliners, however, continued throughout the decade their lesser-known but sustained organized lobbying and advocacy programs. All mainline bodies funded such work in Washington, each lobbying agency usually being staffed by three to ten people knowledgeable in the broad fields of foreign policy, disarmament, or other areas of concern to the churches. These officials found friends on Capitol Hill interested in making known to Congress their church's thinking. The lobbies also presented expert testimony before congressional committees considering new legislation. Further, these offices spent considerable time enlisting grass roots support from denominational members on behalf of specific bills or resolutions.[24]

By contrast to legislative efforts before the awakening of the 1960s, mainline lobbying and advocacy in Washington and at the state legislatures has expanded enormously in recent years. This of course reflects the vastly expanded definition of what religion should be involved with in everyday life. The list of issues has grown steadily, the most important during the 1980s being antidrug bills, protection of families from abusive husbands and fathers, welfare for the homeless and poor, loans for college students, tax reform to help citizens in their gift giving to the churches, educational opportunities for the handicapped, biogenetic research, consumer-protection laws, toxic waste disposal, immigration-law reform, military appropriations, welfare measures for Native Americans, environmental protection measures, and the many church/state questions such as prayer in public schools. Of course, not every mainline denomination lobby worked on each of these measures; this listing, however, shows the scope of concern. (As will be seen later, evangelical bodies also maintained vigorous lobby and advocacy programs in the same places.)

Both mainline and evangelical members continued to spend much if not most of their outreach time on local problems. Through the National Council of Churches and related state and local agencies, mainliners offered services and support for teenagers in trouble, for chemical addiction, for improving inner-city housing and law enforcement, and for foodshare sources, usually known as "loaves and fishes" ministries. Parishes continued to offer their buildings for community service programs such as Alcoholics Anonymous, Scouts, day-care centers, men's and women's support groups, senior citizens, weight-control programs, and the like.

All of these reflect the point made earlier that such outreach programs demonstrate clearly that privatization and secularization, however powerful they might be elsewhere, made little headway among those who expressed their faith in such public programs. As the churches moved from the mainline to the frontline, they found themselves in a highly precarious position. Clearly their numbers and support were in decline rather than on the upswing. Clearly morale and high enthusiasm for maintaining denominational life, the identity of each of the major bodies, was often hard to sustain. The bitter battles over who the true Presbyterians or Methodists were continued on into the 1990s. The contests over expanding the leadership role of women and over inclusive language showed no signs of abating. The charismatic movement offered genuine renewal opportunities for some seekers but continued to keep others distracted or divided over its proper place within congregational life.

All these factors were the negatives, and in total they added up to the mainline clearly being in far more trouble concerning its survival than even its critics were projecting. The continuing social gospel ministry was the major positive in the equation of the 1980s. That organized religious life underwent enormous change during the decade was obvious. That change for the mainline is the more clearly understood when the fortunes of the evangelicals during the same time period are examined. Looming beyond all of the change and turmoil was the presence of the third of our three major forces, New Age privatization. The embattled mainline/frontline in the 1980s found these competitors to be formidable indeed.

NOTES

1. Leonard I. Sweet, "The 1960s: The Crises of Liberal Christianity and the Public Emergence of Evangelicalism," in George Marsden, ed., *Evangelicalism and Modern America* (Grand Rapids, Mich.: Wm. B. Eerdmans, 1984), pp. 44–45; Thomas Sieger Derr, "Continuity and Change in Mainline Protestantism," in Richard John Neuhaus, ed., *The Believeable Futures of American Protestantism* (Grand Rapids, Mich.: Wm. B. Eerdmans, 1988), pp. 49–71.

2. Gabriel Fackre, "Sober Hope: Some Themes in Protestant Theology Today," *Christian Century*, September 23, 1987, p. 790; see also Larry Rasmussen, "New Dynamics in Theology," *Christianity and Crisis*, May 6, 1988, pp. 178–83.

3. Alan Geyer, "Religious Roots of Social Action," *E/SA*, February 1979, pp. 10–14; see also Arthur Simon, *Christian Faith and Public Policy: No Grounds for Divorce* (Grand Rapids, Mich.: Wm. B. Eerdmans, 1987), pp. 14–29; J. Philip Wogaman, "The Churches and Political Institutions," *Religious Studies Review* 3 (July 1984): 237–44; a mainline critique of this position is William Willimon, "A Crisis of Identity," *Sojourners*, May 1986, pp. 24–28.

4. J. Philip Wogaman, *Christian Perspectives on Politics* (Philadelphia: Fortress Press, 1988), p. 103.

5. *Newsweek*, January 4, 1988, p. 41.

6. Peter Schmeisser, "Taking Stock: Is America in Decline?" *New York Times Magazine*, April 17, 1988, pp. 25ff.; Laurence Shames, *The Hunger for More: Searching for Values in an Age of Greed* (New York: Times Books, 1989); Louis Menand, "Don't Think Twice: Why We Won't Miss the 80s." *New Republic*, October 9, 1989, pp. 18–23.

7. Robert Lerner et al., "Christian Religious Elites," *Public Opinion*, March/April 1989, pp. 54–58; Gannet News Service release, April 15, 1989, in the *Tucson Citizen*, p. 45; another list by Edd Doerr, *Humanist*, July/August 1989, p. 25; Danny Duncan Collum, "Doing the Lord's Work: Churches Energize the Left," *Progressive*, February 1989, pp. 34–37.

8. Robert Wuthnow, *The Restructuring of American Religion: Society and Faith since World War II* (Princeton: Princeton University Press, 1988), pp. 100–31; idem, "The Growth of Religious Reform Movements," in Wade Clark Roof, ed., *Religion in America Today*, Annals of the American Academy of Political and Social Science, Vol. 480 (Beverly Hills, Calif.: Sage Publications, 1985), pp. 106–16.

9. Wuthnow, *Restructuring*, pp. 113–14; *Washington Post*, November 5, 1988, p. C14.

10. Wuthnow, *Restructuring*, pp. 113–14.

11. Gary Scott Smith, "Reassessing the Relationship between Religion and Social Reform," *Christian Scholar's Review* 14, 4 (1985): 330; James Davison Hunter, "American Protestantism: Sorting Out the Present; Looking toward the Future," *This World*, no. 17 (Spring 1987): 59–61.

12. See Philip Harnden, "Doing Theology with Your Sleeves Rolled Up," *Other Side*, January/February 1986, pp. 16–28. Each year's edition of Constant Jacquet, ed., *Yearbook of American and Canadian Churches* (Nashville, Tenn.: Abingdon Press) contains the lists of such agencies.

13. Morton Kondracke, "Just Say Yes," *New Republic*, April 24, 1989, p. 12.

14. Paul Rogat Loeb, *Hope in Hard Times: America's Peace Movement and the Reagan Era* (Lexington, Mass.: Lexington Books, 1987), pp. 1–18.

15. Ibid., pp. 184; the full story is here, pp. 157–202.

16. Arthur J. Laffin and Anne Montgomery, eds., *Swords into Plowshares: Nonviolent Direct Action for Disarmament* (San Francisco: Harper and Row Perennial Library, 1987), pp. 32–72.

17. L. Bruce van Voorst, "The Churches and Nuclear Deterrence," *Foreign Affairs*, Spring 1983, pp. 827–52.

18. United Methodist Bishops, *In Defense of Creation: The Nuclear Crisis and a Just Peace* (Nashville, Tenn.: Graded Press, 1986); *Washington Spectator*, October 15, 1985, p. 2; the history is in Pam Solo, *From Protest to Policy: Beyond The Freeze to Common Security* (Cambridge, Mass.: Ballinger Publishing Company, 1988); news story, *Sojourners*, December 1982, p. 6. For all these issues, see Randall Forsberg and Carl Conetta, eds., *Peace Resource Book, 1988–1989: A Comprehensive Guide* (Cambridge, Mass.: Ballinger Publishing Company, 1988).

19. See again all sources in note 18.

20. Allen D. Hertzke, *Representing God in Washington: The Role of Religious Lobbies in the American Polity* (Knoxville: University of Tennessee Press, 1988); Wilbur Edel, *Defenders of the Faith: Religion and Politics from the Founding Fathers to Ronald Reagan* (New York: Praeger, 1987), pp. 124–39.

21. Gary MacEoin, ed., *Sanctuary: A Resource Guide* (San Francisco: Harper and Row, 1985); *U.S. News and World Report*, April 21, 1986, pp. 16–17.

22. Wuthnow, *Restructuring*, pp. 125–31; a critique of the "religious left" by Michael Novak, "Commentary," *Minneapolis Star Tribune*, July 8, 1985, p. 13A.

23. Helen Cordes, "A Field Guide to the New Activism," *Utne Reader*, March/April 1988, pp. 74ff.

24. Hertzke, *Representing God*, chap. 6.

PART II

THE TRANSFORMATION OF EVANGELICALISM

INTRODUCTION

During the 1980s the evangelicals passed through a period of enormous growth and frequent crisis. Like the mainliners, they seemed to be caught up in a pattern where large-scale change continued to accelerate at a growing rate. Needing to hold fast to that which was good, they would encounter heavy pressures for major overhauls in three general areas of their religious expression: in politics and making public policy; in the expansion of evangelism through the mass media; and in coming to terms with the attractions of popular culture as an appropriate model of expression of their faith. These three topics constitute the subjects of Part II.

In each case the social forces of modernization, secularization, and privatization came sharply into play, carrying the believers by 1990 toward areas of religious life they could only dimly have foreseen ten years earlier. By contrast to the record of the mainline, theirs was one of continued numerical growth. But like their counterparts, evangelicals also faced something similar to the Kelley thesis problem. Clear signs emerged throughout the decade that their earlier fidelity to orthodox doctrine, conservative politics, and moralistic life-styles was beginning to weaken. This issue we will call the "Hunter thesis," named for James Davison Hunter, a prominent sociologist who became in the 1980s the Kelley of the evangelicals.[1]

The history of the evangelicals during this decade paralleled that of the mainline in another important respect; not all their activities were expressed through politics, the media, or popular religion, or through their respective denominations. Much of the holding/pressing battle would break out in the world of personal life-style, family involvement, and individual values, issues that will be discussed in Part III.

Further, the tidy, logical categories used here to differentiate among the several groups often fall short of accounting for the decidedly nonpatterned behavior of evangelicals during the decade. Like mainliners, they move in and out of elective

53

politics, they support and then drop certain media ministries, and their tastes in popular religion often fall into several different, at times conflicting, categories. But that only reminds us that religious life is best understood through the lenses of irony and paradox.

Although estimates vary as to the total numbers of Christians in America who call themselves evangelical, experts agree that it is somewhere around 25 percent of churchgoers, at least by the late 1980s. As to their demographic profile, they tend by contrast to mainliners to be more numerous in the South and Midwest, to have somewhat lower incomes and less formal education after high school, and to have higher attendance at religious meetings.[2]

Considerable agreement, in and out of evangelical circles, does exist, however, over the major boundaries for family membership inside the clan. Acknowledging their enthusiasm for defining who is who (one typology consists of fourteen different groups within the fold), the specialists agree that there exist four major camps, those that will be used in this study: mainline evangelicals, left-wing evangelicals (such as Sojourners), classical Pentecostalists, and fundamentalists.

The last-named group differs from the others not so much in doctrine as in its long-standing policy of separating itself from any association with Christians who associate with mainliners. Fundamentalists also take pride in a more acrimonious, sharply honed style of verbal attacks on those outside their camp. During this decade, however, the historical unity of fundamentalism started to come apart. Led by the Reverend Jerry Falwell, many moved toward a more "progressive" or "neofundamentalist" position. Holding fast to their doctrine, they would show much greater cooperation with evangelicals and others in the conservative political camps.[3]

Classical Pentecostalists, meanwhile, espouse most evangelical doctrine, adding a stronger emphasis on the spiritual gifts of glossolalia, discernment of spirits, exorcism, and related ministries. All, however, are decidedly antimainline, antiliberal, and adamant in their determination to contend earnestly for the faith once delivered unto the saints. Left-wing evangelicals hold to a conservative orthodoxy in doctrine while working for many left-wing liberal sociopolitical causes.[4]

Within these broad categories flourishes a wide variety of emphases on doctrines concerning the end times, the inerrancy of the Bible, and the blessings on earth that the believer should expect. In this study the key to understanding evangelical separateness from the mainline is in the members' extremely strong loyalty to parachurch organizations rather than to one specific denomination. Over the course of American history evangelicals have worked freely with parachurch organizations in missions, education, charity, and morality crusades, among others. If thwarted or deflected from carrying out a program with a specific denomination, evangelicals have been able to move on to another body. One observer made a telling insight: "It is not uncommon for good Evangelical Christians to pass through three, four, or five denominations, let alone congregations, in the course of their spiritual journey. When Fuller Seminary's student body is analyzed by denomination, the largest grouping is 'no denomination.' "[5]

Hunter finds the same pattern. Evangelicals have developed parachurch organizations in almost every area of social life: colleges, universities, think tanks, publishing houses, magazines, bookstores, law firms, businesses, and even dating services and "Cowboys for Christ."[6] By contrast to mainliners' warring over identity, evangelicals focused on what they believed that the Bible taught for their lives. That practice has produced considerable controversy within the family, but it has allowed evangelicals to bypass much of the agonizing, energy-sapping internecine wars of mainline life.

From the early 1940s evangelicals have come together under some national direction for ministries of common interest. Best known of these has been the National Association of Evangelicals. It has coordinated many programs of its 45,000 churches representing some seventy-eight denominations. It claims a constituency of 10 to 15 million members. It avoids by design the kinds of doctrinal and public-policy controversies that led the National Council of Churches to near self-annihilation by 1989.[7]

In brief, evangelicals and mainliners faced some but not all of the same excruciating problems throughout the 1980s. At times some cooperation and overlap did exist. Certainly, as Harry S. Stout suggests, evangelicals produced the same kinds of programs already under way in the mainline by stepping up their political activity, by producing more translations of the Bible, by greater use of the arts in church worship, and by participating more in Christian forms of personal counseling.[8]

Important as these were, they would be overshadowed by the need to resist the ever-present allurements of the secular world. Modernity seemed to threaten the very foundations of morality with its permissiveness for individual behavior. Privatization could lead believers into the trendy but self-indulgent realms of occult and New Age practice. Secularization might well take time-honored priorities of piety and service and reshape them into forms beyond restoration.[9] The 1980s came to be a pivotal decade for all these contests.

NOTES

1. James Davison Hunter, *Evangelicalism: The Coming Generation* (Chicago: University of Chicago Press, 1987). See the controversy this book has created in an account of an evangelical symposium on it, *World*, March 11, 1989, pp. 5–6; news story, *Christianity Today*, April 21, 1989, p. 42.

2. Robert Webber, *Common Roots* (Grand Rapids, Mich.: Zondervan, 1978); Robert Wuthnow, *The Restructuring of American Religion: Society and Faith since World War II* (Princeton: Princeton University Press, 1988), pp. 135–42, 177–81; George Marsden, "Fundamentalism" in Charles H. Lippy and Peter W. Williams, eds., *Encyclopedia of the American Religious Experience*, Vol. 1 (New York: Scribner, 1988), pp. 947–62; R. Stephen Warner, *New Wine in Old Wineskins: Evangelicals in a Small-Town Church* (Berkeley: University of California Press, 1988), pp. 51–59; Samuel S. Hill, "Fundamentalism and the South," *Perspectives in Religious Studies* 13, 4 (Fall 1986): 47–53; Edward Dobson, *In Search of Unity: An Appeal to Fundamentalists and Evangelicals*

(Nashville, Tenn.: Thomas Nelson Publishers, 1985). Richard John Neuhaus states that there are 50 million evangelicals in the United States; *Religion and Society Report* 4, 3 (March 1987); 2.

3. Dobson, *In Search of Unity*; editorial, *Fundamentalist Journal*, January 1987, p. 12; Dinesh D'Souza, "Jerry Falwell's Renaissance," *Policy Review*, no. 27 (1984): 41–42.

4. Grant Wicker, "Pentecostalism," in Lippy and Williams, *Encyclopedia*, Vol. 1, pp. 933–46; Robert Booth Fowler, *Unconventional Partners: Religion and Liberal Culture in the United States* (Grand Rapids, Mich.: Wm. B. Eerdmans, 1989), pp. 130–35.

5. David S. Luecke, "Mission Insights from our Evangelical Colleagues," (Paper delivered at a Lutheran Church–Missouri Synod conference, March 26, 1986; available from the LC–MS, St. Louis, Missouri), p. 7.

6. James Davison Hunter, "American Protestantism: Sorting Out the Present; Looking toward the Future," *This World*, no. 17 (Spring 1987): 59, 67.

7. Neuhaus, *Religion and Society Report* 4, 3 (March 1987); 2.

8. Harry S. Stout, "Soundings from New England: Mainline Protestants Today," *Reformed Journal*, August 1987, pp. 7–12.

9. David A. Roozen, *Varieties of Religious Presence* (New York: Pilgrim Press, 1984), pp. 7–8; Eric Woodrum, "Moral Conservatism and the 1984 Presidential Election," *Journal for the Scientific Study of Religion* 27, 2 (1988): 206–7; George Marsden, "Secularism and the Public Square," *This World*, no. 11 (Spring/Summer 1985): 48–62; Kenneth S. Kantzer, "The Priorities of Love," *Christianity Today*, January 17, 1986, pp. 29–31.

4

Politics for Holders: The New Christian Right

Among the many upheavals that restructured American evangelicalism during the 1980s, none attracted more attention, criticism, and soul searching than the entrance of fundamentalists and evangelicals directly into elective politics on a heretofore unprecedented scale. Having since their foundation years stood apart from what they had perceived as the corruptive forces of compromise and secularity, these religionists made a total reversal of course, in the process creating what is known as the "New Christian Right."

Its main contours are so well known as to require no fresh definition here. For our purposes its story illustrates clearly the complexity and unpredictability of the pressers/holders conflict. If the Bible taught believers that they must refrain from politics in the name of holding fast, then could that inerrant source be made to say that in the 1980s they must now press on? That transformation did occur; the reasons it occurred serve also as the reasons for the rise of the "New Christian" or, more accurately, "religious" Right.[1]

Throughout the unfolding of the awakening of the 1960s, a substantial number of Americans viewed many of its results with considerable dismay. The rapidly changing status of women meant that the traditional nuclear family was being threatened. The Supreme Court decision in 1973 to make legal abortions available seemed a direct threat to life itself. Calls for an Equal Rights Amendment sounded more like calls for social revolution. Greater freedom in obtaining divorce would threaten the sanctity of marriage. The ease with which pornography was now available, the increasingly open expression of homosexuality in public, and the inclusion of sex education in the public schools all were threatening the moral foundations of society.

The schools could no longer include Bible reading or mandatory prayer, thanks to the Supreme Court decisions. The level of literacy and respect for traditional learning seemed to be sinking fast in the name of reform of public education. Those parents who sent their children to private religious day schools learned that the Internal Revenue Service was investigating to see whether these were fronts for racially segregated institutions.[2]

Throughout the 1970s various conservative think-tank officials started probing ways in which the growing anger of certain church-related people could be channeled into direct political action. Activists such as Richard Viguerie, an expert in computerized direct-mail fund-raising, Howard Phillips of the Conservative Caucus, and Paul Weyrich of the Committee for the Survival of a Free Congress explored various forms of organization and leadership to mobilize those conservatives who heretofore had stayed clear of elective politics. They were encouraged by the 1976 campaign, in which, for the first time in sixteen years, the religious faith of the presidential candidates became an issue. This suggested that people could be enlisted by appeals to their faith as well as to their pocketbooks. By that time certain televangelists such as Pat Robertson and Jerry Falwell were building strong support through effective preaching about the moral tailspin in which America was caught.[3]

Also standing before the viewing public was the one-time Hollywood star and now two-term governor of California, Ronald Reagan. He started talking about born-again faith in terms familiar to the evangelical audiences. He vowed in the primaries to uphold their demands to restore morality in public life, end elective abortions, and reduce the scope of government's power over the lives of the citizenry.

In addition, Reagan exuded a quality of confidence, congeniality, and everyday homespun exuberance for the future of the American republic that had enormous appeal. Although the incumbent president, Gerald Ford, eventually received the Republican nomination, Reagan served notice that he would return.

A final ingredient helping to bring evangelicals into politics came with the appearance of a catch-all explanation for why America was headed toward destruction. In a 1961 Supreme Court decision, *Torcaso* v. *Watkins*, Justice Hugo Black had coined a phrase, "secular humanism," which he entitled to be a religion. Over the next several years conservatives picked up on that term, finding it the rationale needed to explain why America stood close to destruction: the liberals and atheists, those in control of higher education, the news media, and much of government and mainline religion had chosen to eliminate religious faith from its traditional center of American life. In the name of separating church and state, the humanists had instead established an alternative religion, one glorifying the achievements of humankind, seeing to it that God and religion would stay out of any influential position in the nation's public life.[4]

Thus by the end of the 1970s the ingredients for a transformation were available. The think-tank leaders explored the list of celebrity conservative preachers who might head up an antiabortion, antipornography, antihomosexual political coalition. In a meeting with Falwell, Weyrich stated, "Jerry, there is in America a moral majority that agrees about the basic issues. But they aren't organized. They don't have a platform. The media ignores them. Somebody's got to get that moral majority together."[5] That phrase became the energizing force for the newly created Moral Majority, with Falwell as president. To him and his supporters, the traditional resistance to organized politics had to be reversed because America could be saved now only by direct intervention by that moral majority acting in organized politics. It all fit together: the crises, the organizational structure, the vision, the cause, and the funds. In various forms Moral Majority was to lobby for causes, raise funds for candidates, and educate the general public; its time had arrived.[6]

The first direct mail under Falwell's leadership, *Moral Majority Report*, was sent out in January 1980 to 77,000 recipients. By October, in the heat of the presidential campaign, Moral Majority was mailing out 482,000 *Reports*. The think tankers and Falwell had broken new political organizing ground by enlisting the support of an informal network of conservative, largely fundamentalist Baptist ministers to find voters receptive to their messages. Advertised as an action organization to appeal to all groups, including supportive Catholics, Jews, and Mormons, the Moral Majority in reality revolved around the ministerial world of fundamentalists.[7]

Already in place, but not quite as well funded, was a similar political action group, Christian Voice. Organized in 1976 under the title Citizens United, it took its new title two years later. Its leaders included Rev. Robert Grant (president), Gary Jarmin (chief lobbyist), and Colonel Donor (chief fund raiser; "Colonel" is his first name). Its first mailings centered around enlisting votes to stop gay rights measures in California.

By 1980 Christian Voice found its identity when it published its first series of what it entitled "Moral Report Cards." Candidates for office were rated either for or against a short but strongly felt series of public-policy issues. The criteria for what was moral or immoral were those of the Christian Voice leaders. The cards, at first five by seven inches in size, were mailed out in large quantities and distributed at parking lots. Candidates came out as either "Christian" or "un-Christian." Although the leaders disavowed the charge by critics that they were calling those in disagreement somehow "immoral," that impression could hardly be overlooked.[8] Also, by 1980 Christian Voice organized a tax-exempt political action committee and an educational foundation. It had on its letterhead the endorsement of well-known U.S. senators such as Orrin Hatch (R.-Utah) and Gordon Humphrey (R.-N.H.).

In sum, the hopes by think-tank leaders that somehow the conservative Protestants could be organized politically now became a reality. All that remained was the approval of the national Republican ticket. That event came just after the nominating convention when Reagan addressed a group of evangelical and fundamentalist ministers meeting in Dallas: "I know you can't endorse me, but I want you to know that I endorse you and what you are doing."[9] As events later would demonstrate, that endorsement linked the very loosely organized religious Right to the fortunes of one of the two major political parties. It created the momentum (what sociologists call the "legitimation") for their cause. For the next eight and one-half years their fortunes would rise and fall on the basis of that president's position toward them.

The religion issue during the fall campaign attracted considerable attention because both the incumbent president, Jimmy Carter, and the independent candidate,

Representative John Anderson (R.-Ill.), were avowed born-again Christians, as was Reagan. Nothing like that had happened before in American history. From the outset Carter found himself unable to overcome the criticisms about runaway inflation and his inability to rescue the hostages in Iran or generally to deflate the perception that he was incompetent. Reagan, meanwhile, knew the benefits of photo opportunities, of focusing on pocketbook issues, and of invoking patriotic symbols.

During the campaign the news media gave extensive coverage to the religious Right, especially the Moral Majority. They featured a poll showing that one-third of all American adults claimed having a born-again experience, that half believed that the Bible was inerrant, and that over 80 percent thought that Jesus was divine. Pat Robertson responded, "We have enough votes to run the country."[10]

Reagan's resounding victory attracted considerable attention to and from the evangelicals. One of their own, Carter, had been defeated, and a second, Anderson, had conducted a credible campaign. More important was the claim (repeated nine years later by Falwell as he closed down Moral Majority) that the evangelical Right voting bloc was the force that defeated five of six targeted liberal Democratic senators running for re-election: Birch Bayh, Indiana; Frank Church, Idaho; John Culver, Iowa; George McGovern, South Dakota; and Gaylord Nelson, Wisconsin. (Alan Cranston of California was re-elected.) That claim, made throughout the decade, continued to bolster the credibility of the religious Right among the faithful. But analyses made over the next several years showed that in each case local issues far outweighed any evangelical cohesion as a motivation for voting. Experts found no evangelical voting bloc as such in existence.[11]

During the first Reagan term in office, Moral Majority demonstrated considerable expertise in using the media for promoting its agenda against abortion, civil rights measures for homosexuals, and ERA and for tax breaks for parents of children in parochial schools, voluntary prayer in public schools, and heavy spending for armaments and support of all anti-Communist regimes globally.

What is the more remarkable is that the Moral Majority itself was little more than a special-purpose interest group. News services talked of it as a monolithic, vote-producing powerhouse of evangelicals determined to support the administration all the way. In reality Moral Majority, Christian Voice, and a 20,000-member friend-of-Israel group named the Religious Roundtable, plus Robertson's political arm, Freedom Council, were competing for the same supporter dollars and media attention. This they were doing with great adroitness. Falwell convinced reporters that his televised Sunday service from Lynchburg, Virginia, "The Old Time Gospel Hour," was being watched by 25 million viewers. In fact it attracted 1.4 million. Moral Majority claimed 2 million members, although it had around 400,000 on the mailing lists. Robertson, Falwell, and the Moral Majority vice president Cal Thomas became experts at sound bites, "punchy, outrageous quotes" well suited for lead paragraphs and twenty-second clips on the evening news, such as Thomas's statement about abortion, "We're becoming a society with a chicken in every pot and a baby in every trash can."[12]

Unquestionably, the national media—press, news magazines, and television— were dominated by political liberals who were trying to show how antiquated and out of touch with the public the religious Right really was. Thus they gave heavy coverage to the movement's support for creationism as science, the patri- archal quality of its anti-ERA statements, and its unrestricted red-white-and-blue patriotism. They unwittingly were giving credence to what the religious Right would later claim as a major victory for their cause—the introduction of absolutist morality into the legislative-political arena as a legitimate source for discussion.[13]

Once the Reagan administration set its conservative tone, both Christian Voice and Moral Majority expanded their programs. The former continued to circulate its best-known product, the moral report cards well suited for quick reads in the media. It and Moral Majority aimed their fund-raising not at every potential sup- porter but at uncommitted or hostile evangelicals and fundamentalists.

By the end of fiscal 1981 Moral Majority had raised some $6 million, published full-page ads in leading daily newspapers, sent out 840,000 copies of its monthly newsletter, and counted some 300 radio stations broadcasting its daily commen- tary. Market analysis had shown both groups that their best donors were from the small-sized category, not large corporations. The latter sent its funds for political education largely to the increasing number of conservative think tanks in the early 1980s.[14]

Once in the political arena, the Moral Majority joined battle with the liberals at many points; it opposed the nuclear freeze proposal, supported the anti- Communist administrations in South Africa and the Philippine Islands, and opposed the ERA, among other issues. Asserting that it spoke for the Biblical position on the contests in Congress and the statehouses, the leadership pressed hard for more recognition. This was given when Falwell and a close ally, the Reverend Tim LaHaye, stated that "the countdown to Armageddon," the final struggle between Christ and the forces of Satan on earth, had begun. Christians, however, need not fear a nuclear holocaust because God would never allow so devastating an event to occur.[15]

The White House, with its political intelligence network alert to the changing character of evangelicalism, responded with both formal and informal approval of the religious Right. Several of its favorites received appointments to high posi- tions: Morton Blackwell (an aide to Richard Viguerie) became the president's religion advisor, with Carolyn Sundseth, a highly regarded evangelical, on his staff; Moral Majority officer Robert Billings received a high post in the Depart- ment of Education; Pentecostal leader James Watt was appointed secretary of the interior; and antiabortion Dr. C. Everett Koop became surgeon general. However, in the off-year elections of 1982 the religious Right could not deliver enough votes in the senatorial campaigns to unseat any of the targeted liberal incumbents.[16]

President Reagan kept open his communications with this bloc, most notably in a memorable speech to the National Religious Broadcasters in January 1983. There he endorsed tuition tax credits for parents of children in parochial schools, called for a return of voluntary prayer to the public schools, condemned the *Roe v. Wade* abortion decision, and made what became a memorable quotation about the Soviet Union being "an evil empire." That theme especially was strongly cherished by many evangelicals.[17]

The administration moved slowly on many issues on the social agenda but decided after the 1982 elections to make a full effort on school prayer. With Christian Voice, Robertson's 700 Club, the support of televangelists Jimmy Swaggart and Jim Bakker, and a large offensive by Moral Majority, supportive congressional officials prepared the measure. It read,

Nothing in this Constitution shall be construed to prohibit individual or group prayer in public schools or other institutions. Neither shall the United States nor any State compose the words of prayers to be said in public schools.

The full weight of media pressure came onto Capitol Hill from the religious Right and from many church- and synagogue-related bodies opposed to the measure. For a moment it seemed that the Senate would support the amendment, but when the final soundings of public opinion were made, it went down to defeat. It would be the last time the White House would give its full support to that measure.[18]

What surprised most members of Congress apparently was the highly organized and substantial opposition by the religious community. Despite televangelist and Moral Majority claims to speak for the Judeo-Christian tradition, the postvote analyses showed that community sharply divided not only between conservatives and liberals, but between evangelicals and fundamentalists.

Partly in response to that experience, in 1983 a new kind of political action group with support from religious conservatives appeared, named American Coalition for Traditional Values (ACTV, pronounced "active"). Headed by Tim LaHaye and funded largely by television ministries, it was created to revitalize the evangelical vote for the re-election of the Reagan-Bush ticket in 1984. Its endorsers read like a Who's Who among conservative televangelists: James Robison, Jimmy Swaggart, Kenneth Copeland, Rex Humbard, Jim Bakker, and Jack Van Impe. Others on the board were Bill Bright of Campus Crusade, Ben Armstrong of the National Religious Broadcasters, Robert Dugan, chief of public affairs for the National Association of Evangelicals (NAE), and media celebrity on family matters James Dobson.[19] The linkage between the Republican party and the leadership of the religious Right was now made public.

LaHaye added the resources of Christian Voice and Falwell to the ACTV program, supported by a million-dollar grant from a White House program, Leadership '84. Some 350 field directors were enlisted and given instructions on how to identify and register sympathetic voters through the churches. LaHaye summed up the reasons for intense religious Right campaigning: "If the liberals regain control of the Senate and White House in the coming election (they still control the House of Representatives) it will be all over for free elections by 1988. Oh, we may vote in 1988, but it will be no contest, for by then the liberals will have curtailed our access to the minds of the American people."[20]

Much of the same intensity from the religious Right appeared in other sources. The presence of Representative Geraldine Ferraro, a Roman Catholic who supported the *Roe* v. *Wade* decision as public policy, produced considerable discussion in those circles. So too did Falwell's ongoing criticisms of what he perceived to be expanding homosexual influence throughout American society. Much of the rhetoric was sharply worded, such as his calling homosexuality "a perverted lifestyle . . . performed only by humans . . . . most people look on this sin in a different way than all other sins. Most Americans look with great contempt on the homosexual. That is why we cannot help homosexuals."[21]

Christian Voice developed its moral report cards further by adding an attractively printed "Candidates' Biblical Scorecard," published in association with the Biblical News Service led by David Balsinger, a veteran conservative campaign director. The document drew very sharp differences between the respective national candidates and circulated in millions of copies across the country.

For some evangelicals, however, the LaHayes, Falwells, and Christian Voice campaigning were unacceptable. A respected scholar and columnist, Richard Lovelace of Gordon-Conwell Theological Seminary, wrote that "Christian Voice's scorecard on Reagan and Mondale is so ridiculously partisan that it dresses up the President as King Arthur, while the affable Mondale is made to look like the antichrist." On Falwell, he stated, "Dr. Falwell's fund-raising materials are so filled with fear and hatred of homosexuals that they turn off those concerned for biblical ministry to gays."[22] Such conclusions represented the intensity and breadth of difference over the participation of evangelicals in partisan politics, now in effect for four years.

As the campaign unfolded, it became clear that the economic record of the incumbents and the strong military buildup against the Soviet Union had great appeal for the voters. So too did the incumbents' media campaign. Professor Ralph Whitehead summarized this well:

In 1984 the Reagan campaign captured this spirit of the New Middle Americans. Reagan was photographed out of doors with cultural leaders, his hair stirred by the wind. Walter Mondale was indoors in Washington, D.C., pointing to charts with numbers and columns. Reagan pitted sunlight against dreariness, bunting against red tape, insurgency against settled arrangements, the heartland against the Capitol. Reagan evoked balmy weather, a three-day weekend, the smell of charcoal fires, and the easy rhythm of a doubleheader. Mondale conjured up sweaty palms and deadlines and a nick in the wallet. Reagan was life and liberty. Mondale was death and taxes.[23]

Other analyses pointed to the same general conclusion. The religion-in-politics issue and the role of the religious Right leadership for Reagan-Bush dimmed in comparison to the economic and foreign-policy appeals of the incumbents. An important study completed for the conservative think tank, the Institute for Government and Politics, headed by Paul Weyrich, made a convincing argument. No matter whether voters were evangelical, interpreted the Bible literally, and had a strong personal commitment to the faith, they voted according to "the social background and current social standing of the individual (in a sociological sense)."[24] Thus even with the exit polls of the *New York Times* and CBS showing the Reagan-Bush ticket winning 81 percent of the white born-again vote, the decisive factor was social identity.[25]

The actual outcome of the race was not in doubt after early September. Mondale carried only his own state, Minnesota, while Reagan won some 59 percent of the popular vote, a landslide by anyone's definition. However, the total number who voted moved downward from 53.9 percent in 1980 to 53.1 percent in 1984. Apparently the alarmist tones of religious Right leadership calls failed to stir a significant portion of the public. In the Senate the Democrats gained two seats; in the House some fifteen new Republicans were elected, not enough to gain a majority. Evangelical leaders claimed credit for the re-election of Pat Swindall in Georgia, Jesse Helms in North Carolina, and Phil Gramm in Texas, as well as four new House candidates. But religious Right support for Senator Roger Jepsen in Iowa and Representatives Dan Crane of Illinois and George Hansen of Idaho failed to stop their defeats. Christian Voice acknowledged that "the Christian community still remains largely unorganized" politically and pledged to start working on that task immediately.[26]

What stood above the many postmortem evaluations was the fact that the religious Right had a friend in the Oval Office for four more years. Not always as responsive to their immediate needs as they wanted, President Reagan remained their best hope. The times and the issues were stirring; the opportunities were great. In four years the religious Right had made known its presence; now it would learn if it had also accumulated power.

NOTES

1. Good general works are Gillian Peele, *Revival and Reaction: The Right in Contemporary America* (New York: Oxford University Press, 1984); Steve Bruce, *The Rise and Fall of the New Christian Right: Conservative Protestant Politics in America, 1979–1988* (New York: Oxford University Press, 1988); Sara Diamond, *Spiritual Warfare: The Politics of the Christian Right* (Boston: South End Press, 1989); Matthew Moen, *The Christian Right and Congress* (Birmingham: University of Alabama Press, 1989).

2. Bruce, *Rise and Fall*, pp. 35–44; Susan D. Rose, *Keeping Them out of the Hands of Satan* (New York: Routledge, 1988); Richard John Neuhaus, "What the Fundamentalists Want," *Commentary*, May 1985, p. 45.

3. Robert Wuthnow, *The Restructuring of American Religion: Society and Faith since World War II* (Princeton: Princeton University Press, 1988), pp. 114–31; James Dunn, "Wise as Serpents at Least: The Political and Social Perspectives of the Electronic Church," *Review and Expositor* 71 (Winter 1984): 79–80.

4. Erling Jorstad, *The New Christian Right, 1981-1988* (New York: Edwin Mellen Press, 1987), pp. 27-36; Rebecca E. Klatch, *Women of the New Right* (Philadelphia: Temple University Press, 1987), pp. 68-71.

5. Jerry Falwell, *Strength for the Journey: An Autobiography* (New York: Simon and Schuster, 1987), p. 359.

6. Ibid., pp. 357-81; Diamond, *Spiritual Warfare*, pp. 45-63.

7. James L. Guth, "The New Christian Right," in Robert C. Liebman and Robert Wuthnow, eds., *The New Christian Right: Mobilization and Legitimation* (New York: Aldine Publishing Company, 1983), pp. 31-45; Robert C. Liebman, "Mobilizing the Moral Majority," ibid., pp. 49-73.

8. News story, *Christian Century*, August 15-22, 1979, p. 781; Ronald B. Flowers, *Religion in Strange Times: The 1960s and 1970s* (Macon, Ga.: Mercer University Press, 1984), p. 170; Diamond, *Spiritual Warfare*, chap. 2, passim (see her documentation).

9. *Christianity Today*, September 19, 1980, p. 1070; *Christian Century*, September 24, 1980, p. 872.

10. Michael Leinesch, "The Paradoxical Politics of the Religious Right," *Soundings* 66, 1 (Spring 1983): 91-99; idem, "Right-Wing Religion: Christian Conservatism as a Political Movement," *Political Science Quarterly* 97, 2 (Fall 1982): 403-25; Clyde Wilcox, "The Christian Right in America," *Review of Politics* 50, 4 (Fall 1988): 669-71.

11. S. M. Lipset, "Evangelicals and the Elections," *Commentary* 71, 3 (1981): 25-31; Guth, "New Christian Right," p. 38; Robert Zweir, "The New Christian Right and the 1980 Elections," in D. G. Bromley and Anson Shupe, eds., *New Christian Politics* (Macon, Ga.: Mercer University Press, 1984), pp. 173-95; news item, *Christianity Today*, December 12, 1980, pp. 52-53; Jim Castelli, "The Religious Vote," *Commonweal*, November 21, 1980, pp. 650-51; Arthur H. Miller and M. P. Wattenberg, "From the Pulpit: Religiosity and the 1980 Elections," *Public Opinion Quarterly* 48 (1985): 301-17; Leo Ribuffo, "Fundamentalism Revisited," *Nation*, 231 (November 29, 1980): 570-71.

12. Tina Rosenberg, "Have the Media Made the Moral Majority?" *Washington Monthly*, May 1982, pp. 26-34.

13. Ibid.; Michael Parenti, *Inventing Reality: The Politics of the Mass Media* (New York: St. Martin's Press, 1986), pp. 89-99.

14. Liebman, "Mobilizing the Moral Majority," p. 55.

15. Andrew J. Weigert, "Christian Eschatological Identities and the Nuclear Context," *Journal for the Scientific Study of Religion* 27, 2 (1988): 175-91; news item, *Charisma*, October 1984, p. 32; Jerry Falwell, *Nuclear War and the Second Coming of Jesus Christ* (Lynchburg, Va.: Old Time Gospel Hour, 1983); S. R. Shearer, "The Evangelical/Jewish Coalition," *Catalyst* 1, 1 (1987): 59-67. Nancy T. Ammerman, "Fundamentalists Proselytizing Jews," in Martin E. Marty and F. E. Greenspan, eds., *Pushing the Faith: Proselytization and Civility in a Pluralistic World* (New York: Crossroad, 1988), pp. 109-22.

16. Jorstad, *New Christian Right*, pp. 115-26; Richard V. Pierard, "Religion and the 1984 Election Campaign," *Review of Religious Research* 27, 2 (December 1985): 98-104.

17. Pierard, "Religion," pp. 102-3.

18. See the cogent defense against school prayer by John W. Baker in *Report from the Capital*, May 1984, pp. 10, 14, published by the Baptist Joint Committee on Public Affairs.

19. Diamond, *Spiritual Warfare*, pp. 66-68; Jorstad, *New Christian Right*, pp. 132-34.

20. Tim LaHaye, quoted in Diamond, *Spiritual Warfare*, p. 67.

21. Jerry Falwell in a symposium of conservatives on sexual issues in *Policy Review*, no. 29 (Summer 1984): 12-31, especially p. 25; "Issues," *Charisma*, November 1984, p. 9.

22. Diamond, *Spiritual Warfare*, pp. 68–69; "Issues," *Charisma*, November 1984, p. 9.

23. Ralph Whitehead, "The New Middle American," *New Perspectives Quarterly* 5, 3 (Fall 1988): 17–18.

24. Stuart Rothenberg and Frank Newport, *The Evangelical Voter: Religion and Politics in America* (Washington, D.C.: Institute for Government and Politics, 1984), p. 112; see all of their Chapter 7, "The Importance of Religion."

25. See documentation in Diamond, *Spiritual Warfare*, pp. 67–68; *New York Times*, November 7, 1984, pp. 1, 21.

26. S. M. Lipset, "Beyond 1984—the Anomalies of American Politics," *PS* 19, 2 (1986): 222–36; Eric Woodrum, "Moral Conservatism and the 1984 Presidential Election," *Journal for the Scientific Study of Religion* 27, 2 (1988): 192–210; Paul R. Abramson et al., *Change and Continuity in the 1984 Elections* (Washington, D.C.: Congressional Quarterly Press, 1987), pp. 141–42; memorandum from Christian Voice, "Save America," Vol. 2 (1985): 1–8.

5

A Lifetime in Four Years: The Evangelicals in Power, 1984-1988

At the inauguration ceremonies for President Ronald Reagan in January 1985, the religious Right could justly claim that it was well on the way to achieving its original goals. It had direct access to the highest political office in the land, it had televangelist spokesmen commanding huge annual revenues and loyal supporters, it had found ways to penetrate organized political agencies, and it knew that its liberal adversaries in politics and religion were dispirited and leaderless. Yet within five years much of this promise would be drastically altered and, in some cases, evaporated. While the faith of the evangelical rank and file held fast, much of its best-known leadership would find that it had misunderstood that faith or greatly overrated its own durability to remain at the top.

This is best illustrated by looking at the careers of four of the most influential televangelists allied with the religious Right. In 1985 Jim Bakker, Jerry Falwell, Pat Robertson, and Jimmy Swaggart were each bringing in more than $50 million annually to their treasuries (see p. 68). All were vigorously expanding their technology and their educational and charitable programs; all had become household words. Yet by late 1989 Bakker had been convicted on twenty-four counts of fraud and conspiracy for financial mismanagement. Falwell had disbanded the Moral Majority leadership and returned home. Robertson had made an all-out effort to win the Republican nomination for the presidency and had been forced to withdraw early in the primaries. Jimmy Swaggart faced a greatly diminished ministry as his publicly confessed sexual behavior left that program weak and in steady decline. All of this occurred in four years; perhaps the speed could be traced to the fact that the medium that they used—television—was so great a creator of accelerating speed, burnout, and overexposure that it somehow quickly devoured or overpowered these four, all of whom flourished and failed through the power of electronic ministry.

This chapter explores the course of that transformation, seeing it as a major symptom of deeper troubles within evangelicalism. Just as mainliners were close to collapse by decade's end, so too evangelicals were by that moment anything but harmoniously prepared to assume the role of leading the center of energy in American religious life. The story unfolds largely on the national scene, where the power to restore the values cherished by evangelicals was located.

Yet evangelicals continued through the 1980s to be active in the ministries they had been conducting on the local levels for decades. Many were either embarrassed or highly critical of the superstars who in their judgment failed to express the norms of righteousness demanded by evangelicalism.[1] This chapter looks also at some of the more influential of the evangelicals' activities, especially as they affected the shaping of the public policy. The picture that emerges is something like a quilt, something like a kaleidoscope, and something like a mosaic. Yet a pattern in the carpet does exist, suggesting that growing secularization, documented by James Davison Hunter, had by decade's end made its influence evident.

The four televangelist leaders oriented toward the political agenda of the religious Right commanded their contributions in 1985 as follows:

Show	Income	Viewers
"PTL," Jim and Tammy Faye Bakker	$52.9 million	13.0 million homes
Jimmy Swaggart	$140.0 million	197 markets
"700 Club," Pat Robertson	$233.0 million	250 markets
"Old Time Gospel Hour," Jerry Falwell	$100.0 million	1.5 million homes[2]

In the eyes of the general public these figures represented the major voices within evangelicalism, even though Billy Graham was still considered the most respected of all such spokespersons, and Oral Roberts held the loyalty of his supporters.[3]

Yet for all their public presence, they cooperated with at least one organization, the American Coalition for Traditional Values, to implement the religious Right political agenda. In 1985 ACTV moved its headquarters to Washington, D.C. Its program, made credible by its letterhead endorsements by all of the leading evangelists except Graham and Robertson, worked to enlist ministers to spread ACTV educational materials and sponsor local voter registration and get-out-the-vote drives. In 1985 some 300 members attended a conference aimed at spreading the message of the religious Right social agenda. Its funding came from vigorous solicitation of known and potential donors already in Right organizations. Even under the energetic leadership of the Reverend Tim LaHaye, however, ACTV never attracted the momentum its founders had envisioned. When the disappointing results of the 1986 congressional races became known, it faded into obscurity.[4]

The one religious Right group that expanded during these years was, coincidentally, the one headed by Bev LaHaye, spouse of Tim. Her group, Concerned Women for America (CWA), founded in 1979 as an antiabortion crusade, became the most influential of all such crusades. Within conservative evangelical circles Beverly had noted growing anxiety and anger over the attention the national media were giving to the women's movement, especially the National Organization for Women, and to the ERA movement. To her, these did not speak for all American women. "The average Christian women didn't know what was happening. We were concentrating on raising our families and working in our churches. We didn't know what ERA stood for; we didn't know what NOW was doing. I saw a great need to educate Christian women."[5]

With volunteer help the CWA started off in the LaHayes' house, then in San Diego. It quickly attracted considerable interest, enough to give it the means to open an office in Washington, D.C., in 1985 with experienced legal and lobbyist help. By that time it claimed a membership of some 235,000.

LaHaye found CWA support coming largely from local congregations. Working with their ministers, the CWA would organize local chapters. Shortly it had an attractive monthly newsletter and addresses and telephone numbers of members within cities and states, all creating supportive networks.

Its agenda contained the standard items of the religious Right: resistance to elective abortion, resistance to perceived humanistic trends in public education, resistance to Communist expansion, and opposition to pornography. Considerable emphasis was placed on prayer to support the members' study and discussion of the agenda. Each local chapter would have a specific list of items on which to read, pray, and lobby, especially by individual letters to legislators. State and regional conventions brought delegates together for further exchange and support. The annual convention in Washington, D.C., was considered the highlight of the year; there delegates would hear well-known conservative speakers. In 1984, during the campaign, LaHaye read a letter from President Reagan to the convened audience, "America is on the way back in no small part due to your efforts."[6]

By late 1988 Concerned Women had become arguably the most influential of all religious Right organizations. It claimed over 500,000 members, although, as critics said, this total included anyone who had sent no more than a general inquiry to its Washington office.[7] It faced some competition from a somewhat comparable activist group working out of Alton, Illinois, the Eagle Forum, headed by Phyllis Schlafly. Both leaders pointed out that they were not working against each other for membership. But despite Schlafly's long-standing record of achievement in the religious Right, the CWA came to a position of larger influence. For instance, during the intensive campaign in the fall of 1987 over the nomination of Judge Robert Bork to the Supreme Court, President Reagan, needing a public forum for an advocacy speech, chose to make it at the annual CWA convention.

Beyond that, CWA became extremely influential in providing legal counsel for cases going as high as the Supreme Court over public-education curriculum and textbooks. In the decisive cases, those in Tennessee and Alabama, CWA along with Robertson's staff furnished the legal counsel. It also provided a refugee camp in Costa Rica for escapees from the Sandinista regime in Nicaragua. All in all, its lobbyists have been considered among the most effective in Washington.[8]

Other active groups outside the televangelist orbits included Christian Voice. It also found its fortunes changing drastically after the 1984 election. Being largely a small-staffed advocacy lobby specializing in the report cards, it was best known for its belligerent, often polemical political rhetoric. For example, one fund-raising letter opened this way: "I have a shocking thing to tell you: The main source of funding the homosexual movement is the American taxpayer—you!"[9] It promoted the standard religious Right agenda, legitimating its claims to leadership by having on its executive board such luminaries as Tim LaHaye and Hal Lindsey, author of *The Late Great Planet Earth*. "Congressional advisors" included politically conservative House members such as Jack Kemp (R-N.Y.), Trent Lott (R.-Miss.), Mark Siljander (R.-Mich.), and Guy Vander Jagt (R-Mich.), among others.

The changes started when Donor decided to leave. Moving to California, where, apparently, he became involved in charismatic groups, he brought out a sharply worded criticism of much religious Right activity, charging in 1988 that the Republican party had opened itself to their work only to win their votes, not to follow their teachings.[10] With his absence, President Robert Grant moved the Christian Voice more toward absorption into another attempt at a coalition of rightist groups, the American Freedom Council. With strong financial support from the Unification church, and with the mailing lists of Richard Viguerie and others, Christian Voice maintained its presence. But it had other problems. Its ownership of the "Presidential Biblical Scorecard" was taken over late in 1986 by David W. Balsinger and moved to California. During the 1988 campaign Christian Voice was bringing out "Voters 88 Guide," a close imitation of the original report card. Like ACTV, however, it had failed to produce much cooperation among the several religious Right groups for concerted lobbying. Thus it had lost Donor, its pioneering crusader, and its identity with its original product, the "Scorecard." Finally, by accepting support from the Unificationists, it had opened itself to very sharp criticism from Balsinger and other leaders on the Right. In brief, it had not by 1990 been able to serve as any umbrella or unitive agency to focus religious Right energies.[11]

Within the larger evangelical community, a significant number of laity and ministers chose to make their own witness, standing apart from the religious Right. None came anywhere close to commanding the financial resources of the groups just discussed; several were connected with the larger academic community. All strove to make their sociopolitical activism harmonious with scriptural teaching, recognizing that they might well remain numerically small but faithful to what they believed.[12]

Among the first to appear was Evangelicals for Social Action (ESA), which was founded in the 1970s as an attempt to demonstrate evangelical concern for peace and justice issues. Its call to arms, the 1973 "Chicago Declaration of Evangelicals to Social Action," showed its sense of mission to be educational. As articulated by its driving force, Professor Ron Sider of Eastern Baptist Theological Seminary, it offered for the next several years carefully studied position papers on a wide range of issues: nuclear weaponry, disarmament, feminism, liberation theology, hunger and homeless concerns, and church/state relations.

Sider became something of a lightning rod, often sharply criticized from the Right for what seemed to be his full support for leftist issues. However, when the abortion issue came to the foreground, ESA and Sider took a full antiabortion position.

To join hands with other Christians in that movement, some ESA members and others created Just Life, a coalition of evangelicals and Roman Catholics. Just Life also focused on an educational ministry, presenting a variety of documents and conferences on life-related issues: war and peace, abortion, and hunger. It claimed some 3,200 members by 1988.[13] Evangelicals also worked closely with WorldVision, a global relief and educational agency aimed at providing food and related necessities to the starving. It has been in many respects parallel to the Bread for the World organization associated more with the mainline.

Perhaps the largest parachurch outreach ministry has been that directed by the National Association of Evangelicals. Staying clear of public elective politics and of televangelist connections, it started bringing out an increasingly large and carefully researched series of educational items for a variety of congregational audiences. It created a considerable stir in the mid-1980s when it produced a study of nuclear war and peace issues, closely paralleling in timing the document on the same subject by the National Council of Catholic Bishops. This work was something of a first for the NAE, which became increasingly willing to explore Biblical foundations and specific activist programs for issues discussed by ESA, Just Life, and other groups.

The NAE also increased its coverage of social justice issues in its monthly newsletter and in books such as that edited by Richard Cizik, *The High Cost of Indifference: Can Christians Afford Not to Act?* From a decidedly conservative framework, its authors examined the social issues related to the media, pornography, crime, religious liberty, abortion, peace issues, and the turmoil in public schools.[14]

Obviously, on the local scene evangelicals provided much the same kind of social ministry to the needy as did the mainliners. These included ministries to the hungry and homeless, to troubled youth, to the aged and handicapped, and to those in jail or hospitals—the full range of outreach.[15] As was true with the mainline, activist evangelicals in the 1980s found little evidence that their faith was being permeated by either privatization or secularization.

However, the greatest public and media interest in evangelicalism continued in these years to focus on the national political arena. Much of this emerged from the increasing criticism made of the religious Right by a growing number of religious and politically oriented agencies. Best known was People for the American Way, created by television producer Norman Lear. With a membership of some 200,000 and expert media technicians, it provided to newspapers and radio and television stations a steady flow of liberal criticism and alternative solutions to each major religious Right maneuver. Much the same counterattack against the religious Right was made by the Clergy and Laity Concerned (CALC), the American Civil Liberties Union, and the National Education Association.[16]

Through such exposure, as well as from the generally liberal bent of the mass-media press and news television, the leaders of the religious Right came under careful public scrutiny. Much of this pleased them because the critics were seen as the secular humanists destroying the nation. Shortly after the inauguration of President Reagan in 1985, the political Right, the religious Right, and everyone else concerned with elective politics started to ponder the incumbent's successor four years hence. Knowing that that prize would be the supreme victory for their cause, leaders of the religious Right started in 1985 and 1986 to make sustained efforts to take control of or at least to deeply penetrate Republican party ranks. Across the country in most states those citizens calling themselves the "Christian Right" worked diligently to place their delegates and candidates in key electoral positions. To them the traditional political tactics of compromise and pragmatic solutions fell short of their commitment to enact their religious ideals into everyday legislation, but they also knew that they had no other alternative in a democratic society but to work through the existing machinery. It would become a matter of holding and pressing at the same time. [17]

That condition turned into a major headache for the GOP leadership. Knowing that evangelicals, estimated by them to total 22 million, had voted 80 percent to 20 percent for Reagan-Bush in 1984 (whereas in 1976 they had voted 56 percent to 43 percent for Carter-Mondale), they also were aware that the general public held highly negative ratings for both Jerry Falwell and Pat Robertson. [18] On learning this, Falwell responded with two moves. He endorsed the candidacy of Vice President Bush for the White House in 1988, thus saying to the religious Right early in the campaign that he would not support the pending candidacy of fellow televangelist Pat Robertson. Early in 1986 he restructured Moral Majority into a new organization, named Liberty Federation. The Moral Majority would stay in existence, working strictly on "moral issues," while the federation would center on a wide variety of matters such as federal budgets, the Strategic Defense Initiative ("star wars"), and foreign-policy issues.

Observers noted that Moral Majority had fallen short of its original goals and was creating negative reactions among voters. The Democratic National Committee chair, Paul G. Kirk, suggested that "Liberty Federation won't stand for true liberty any more than Moral Majority represents the moral values of most Americans." The rival Christian Voice leader, Gary Jarmin, pointed to other Falwell problems: a large drop in revenues had led to a reduction of some 10 percent of the latter's total staff. Jarmin suggested that Falwell had got in way over his head and was now praying that God would provide. "Well, it looks like he might not be ready to." [19]

On a deeper level the polarization produced by the maneuvers of religious rightists within Republican ranks developed out of their desire to follow a single-issue strategy. Some pursued the single issue of elective abortions; others pursued increased expenditures for the military. The net result came to be that they were not bringing more than their own already-committed fellow believers into their crusades. [20]

Republican rightists also were dividing and battling over the candidacies of Jack Kemp, a staunch conservative, and the imminent announcement by Robertson that he would run. Falwell had taken his stand for Bush. The problem came down to which candidate would best be able to translate the social agenda of the religious Right into legislation.[21]

One answer came from the vice president's campaign managers. George Bush started early in 1985 to win more support of the religious Right without losing his existing hold on the party's center. His aide, Doug Weed, an Assemblies of God minister, began circulating actively in religious Right circles, showing leaders where Bush stood on the social agenda. Bush also met with some fifty prominent evangelical leaders and communicators at his home in Washington, D.C., listening to their concerns and explaining his own faith. In attendance were Bev LaHaye, Jim and Tammy Faye Bakker, and Jimmy Swaggart.[22]

In September 1986 Robertson announced that he had reached his goal, some 3 million signatures by registered voters endorsing his candidacy. Now he could announce his formal candidacy for the Oval Office.

For the 1986 congressional races ACTV made only a modest effort to bring back its 1984 voter registration programs. Christian Voice News produced a forty-page "Candidates' Biblical Scorecard." It listed some twenty-three issues as crucial for the promorality, profamily movement. Twelve of these were established as the norm by which voters could evaluate the records of the office seekers. Friendly ministers were asked to circulate the magazine within their congregations so members would know how the "candidates stand on the biblical-family-moral-freedom issues."[23]

In sum, by election day 1986 the religious Right leadership had shown that it was still sharply divided into self-contained organizations competing with one another for the dollars and endorsements of the voters. Swaggart and Bakker avoided any direct involvement but kept up their criticism of the secular humanist takeover threat, stating that it could be stopped at the polls.

Such an outcome, however, failed to occur. Despite the active campaigning of President Reagan and energetic pleas by the conservatives, every candidate running for the Senate who had been supported by the religious Right was defeated. This included the prorightist candidacies of incumbent Senators Jeremiah Denton (R.-Ala.) and James Abnor (R.-S.D.) (with a 100 percent rating approval by the Liberty Federation) and the defeat in Georgia of Mack Mattingly, a strong conservative. In California the incumbent liberal Alan Cranston turned back the Falwell-endorsed Ed Zschau, and incumbent Dale Bumpers won in Arkansas against the challenge of fundamentalist Asa Hutchinson. In Nevada the endorsement of prorightist Paul Laxalt (retiring from the Senate) could not bring his candidate, James Santini, to office. In Florida a favorite religious Right candidate, incumbent Paul Hawkins, was defeated by Governor Bob Graham.[24]

On the state level the story was much the same. Here local issues prevailed over those of the Right's social agenda, so that victory there reflected different support than for national-office candidates. What did seem surprising to observers was the extensive activity, and sometimes takeover, of power by religious Right leaders on the local, county, and state levels of electioneering. Already the

Robertson forces had started to organize and were able to make some headway in several states. Usually this was accompanied by extremely bitter feelings between the regulars and the newcomers.[25]

Two conclusions seemed inevitable. Falwell had said, "Conservatives owe everything we are and have achieved in the 1980s to one man—Ronald Reagan." His coattails failed to cover any incumbent acceptable to the religious Right. In addition, many evangelicals concluded that the religious Right had not spoken for them; their interests extended beyond single-issue militancy.[26]

Still, elective politics being the highly competitive, often nasty combat it is, the religious Right had made some progress in its six years on the national scene. What would happen in 1987, however, was almost exactly what the religious Right least needed to happen, the saga of Jim and Tammy Faye Bakker and the PTL ministry.

The main outlines of the story are well known enough to not require repeating here. The final history of it has yet to be written, since Bakker and his associates were in 1990 still in litigation with the government over the convictions handed down by a jury in October 1989 on twenty-four fraud and conspiracy felonies.[27] Here we look at Bakker's role in the political religious Right, the manner in which the general public looked upon the scandal, and its impact on the larger evangelical scene.

Jim and Tammy Faye Bakker by the early 1980s were among the four most prosperous televangelist enterprises in the country. In 1983 Bakker made a direct commitment to ending elective abortion.

Until now, no one has ever gone on national television and said the things that I am saying. No one has dared to speak as I have about the hideous crimes going on in our country. . . . I have exposed the mass murders of unborn babies and cried out against rulers in government who are trying to play God! I believe God has raised up the PTL as a voice in these last days.[28]

In 1984 he became a member of the board of ACTV. In that year also PTL published what became a staple religious Right primer on citizen involvement, *The Great American Arena: Positive Strategies for 20th Century Patriots.*[29]

That involvement became very important for two reasons. First, it placed the Bakkers directly in the sphere of the celebrity religious Right political televangelists. The general public repeatedly in the next years would not differentiate the PTL from the overt politicking of the others. Second, the Bakkers after 1984 chose to move their format away from the controversial world of public policy and fully toward their unique style of popular religion: easy listening to upbeat songs, positive messages about God's blessings, including economic rewards for the righteous, and ample camera time for Tammy Faye to sing, witness, interview, and comment.

By this time the Bakkers had established their own identity, offering "health and wealth" to those who believed as they did. Martin E. Marty suggested that their program had become much like a lottery: people were being encouraged to send in money for which they would receive benefits of improved material and spiritual living. Tammy Faye reversed the older tradition of Assemblies of God women not wearing makeup or fancy clothes. Now she was marketing her own cosmetics line.[30] The Bakkers, in other words, wanted to be seen as separate from the politically minded televangelists. But as events unfolded, they could not achieve this.

Their major financial problems began late in the 1970s when the Internal Revenue Service and Federal Communications Commission started investigating allegations that proper accounting procedures were not being followed and the promises of goods and services to donors by the Bakkers were not being honored. Charges were leveled claiming fraudulent fund-raising and misappropriation of funds sent in for a specific cause, such as foreign missions, by donors. PTL was charged with using such designated funds for other programs. Rumors turned up also about the expensive tastes in consumer goods used by the Bakkers. Much of the latter charge was overlooked by supporters who endorsed the Bakkers' enjoyment of the earned material benefits of this life.[31] But the financial mismanagement and fraud that led to the Bakkers' downfall was already being carefully investigated by the government in the early 1980s.

What was not known until 1984 was the specific catalyst that started the downward slide for Jim and Tammy Faye. In 1980 Bakker had a sexual encounter with Jessica Hahn at a Florida resort hotel. This was kept quiet until 1984. The *Charlotte Observer*, tracking the financial story, learned from Hahn about the tryst. Late in 1984 additional church officials and reporters came to know of the event. Hahn had been paid some $265,000 hush money to keep her quiet. Various attempts at negotiating a permanent settlement continued through 1985. The IRS also continued its probes into PTL finances.

In 1986 the net broadened to involve another of the four major televangelists. Jimmy Swaggart, having heard of the Hahn-Bakker event, demanded that the parent church organization, the Assemblies of God, in which both were ordained ministers, discipline Bakker. Swaggart's motives may well have been inspired by his desire to keep clean the reputation of fellow Assemblies of God ministers. His charges, as later research showed, may well also have resulted from his realization that potential viewer support for him was being sent to the PTL, whose Pentecostal theology paralleled his own.

Evidence shows also that Bakker and his closest associate, the Reverend Richard Dortch, started to pay themselves and other high-ranking staff members huge bonuses as well as continuing to live extravagant life-styles. Swaggart and fellow televangelist John Ankerberg pressed church officials for disciplinary action, Swaggart referring to PTL as "a cesspool of sin and filth."[32]

For reasons that may never be fully understood, the whole PTL empire began to unravel quickly at this point. The general public learned of the Hahn story, with *USA Today*, for instance, carrying photographs of her dressed in apparel somewhat more sexually suggestive than that of the church secretary she had been.

Then the national news media discovered the story, aided by Swaggart's blasts about PTL being "a cancer" and the hints of fraud and deception in the entire financial structuring.[33]

Now the third of the four major televangelists, Jerry Falwell, stepped into the spotlight. Aware that continued public suspicion of the Bakkers might well discredit his and similar ministries, and apparently not adverse to flexing his own muscle on the national scene, he boldly moved in to reduce further damage. As a fundamentalist, he had over the years frequently criticized in polemical terms the kind of spiritual gifts ministry of the Pentecostalists; they likewise had little affection for his kind of what they believed to be wooden, literalist views of religious life. But Bakker agreed to temporarily give PTL control over to Falwell and a board of directors to be chosen by the latter.

Well aware of the long-standing tensions, Bakker told the public that he gave control to Falwell because he feared a hostile takeover from, as it turned out in his thinking, Jimmy Swaggart. That kind of conspiracy accusation was played out daily in the news media. The charges and rebuttals soon led to satire and ridicule in television talk shows and radio call-ins, bringing the sordid details directly to the general public. An enormously messy, nasty series of accusations, plots, and counterplots followed.

When Falwell and his associates saw the financial mismanagement at PTL, they realized that the situation was far more threatening not only to those Bakker had allegedly cheated but to the entire television ministry. Bakker and Dortch were defrocked by the Assemblies of God; Swaggart temporarily kept silence, but the exposés continued. The fourth major televangelist, Pat Robertson, commented publicly, "I think the Lord is housecleaning a little bit. I'm glad to see it happen."[34]

Then Bakker accused Falwell of wanting to take over PTL, despite the theological chasms that divided the fundamentalists from the Pentecostalists. Falwell answered in kind, stating publicly that Bakker was not fit to be a minister and accusing him of homosexual behavior and creating a "blood covenant" as a cult kind of religious expression of loyalty by followers to Bakker. The latter's bodyguard denied that charge, but all the while more reporters and more government officials continued to find how extensive the fraud and chicanery had become.

Across the country the whole story became a standing, and soon stale, national joke. Newspaper cartoonists freely lampooned with biting caricature the Bakkers, Swaggart, and Falwell. The weekly tabloids such as *National Enquirer* and *Star* carried lurid headlines of even more scandal to be revealed. Local radio disc jockeys wrote parodies such as "Would Jesus Wear a Rolex Watch?" (as did Jim Bakker). The comedian Chevy Chase started making a satirical movie, *Fletch Lives*, drawing on the script being created in the daily news media.

Falwell continued to make sharply worded criticisms of the Bakkers, who claimed that they had never intended to give him control of the PTL. Hahn became something of a national celebrity, moving into the *Playboy* magazine mansion of Hugh Hefner in Los Angeles and soon coming out in seminude photographs with an accompanying two-part story of the 1980 adventure with Bakker. No one seemed to know where to stop "the story without an end," as it became known.

Finally, in October 1987 Falwell and his associates resigned from the PTL board. A bankruptcy judge had ruled on the case in such a way that Bakker might have been able to regain control. That was too much for Falwell, who left the matter in the hands of the courts.[35]

As with the many interpretations of Swaggart's original motivations, so too observers pondered Falwell's motives. He clearly had no intention of taking control of PTL properties, but by jumping into so ludicrous a scandal he could not keep some of it from running off on himself. He apparently believed that he was strong enough to be the prime leader in changing the moral fabric of American society, but he failed. Professor Marty suggested that Falwell had simply changed his theatre.

The whole matter was brought before a grand jury in the area. After some fourteen months of investigation they called for an indictment of Bakker and Dortch for diverting more than $4 million from the ministry, a major felony. On October 5, 1989, Bakker was found guilty on the twenty-four counts of fraud and conspiracy leveled against him.[36]

The pollsters moved out quickly to test public reaction to the battles among the televangelists. They found in the spring of 1987 what evangelicals had feared. Confidence in these leaders had declined drastically. A few statistics showed this. In the Gallup poll of April 1987, television evangelists dropped as "trustworthy" from 63 to 23 percent. These ministers were characterized as "honest" by 34 percent, "dishonest" by 53 percent. Seven years earlier these figures had been 53 percent honest, 26 percent dishonest. Among specific individuals, Billy Graham's ratings remained very high, only 24 percent being "unfavorable." Bakker went from 48 percent being favorable in 1988 to 87 percent being unfavorable seven years later. Falwell, not rated in 1980, now had a 38 percent favorable and 62 percent unfavorable rating. Swaggart went from 76 percent favorable in 1980 to 70 percent unfavorable in 1987.[37]

In essence, all four televangelists turned up losers: Bakker, of course, because he has to face criminal charges; Swaggart because he was charging fellow ministers with sexual obsessions that turned out to match his own behavior; Falwell for having grandiose dreams beyond his grasp; and Robertson, who when seeking votes later attempted to retract the "housecleaning statement." His staff also rewrote his presidential campaign biography, with the revised edition showing that Bakker was not very important to the Christian Broadcasting Network (CBN) ministry.[38]

But evangelicals in 1987 knew little of this. Throughout the scandal evangelical press and radio leaders disassociated their ministries from these televangelists and called for a general accounting of all financial donations and expenditures for such programming. They criticized much of the popular media for their excesses but acknowledged that without careful reporting, such as that by the *Charlotte Observer*, the scandals might have gone unexposed. Further, in the

Bakker case (as with Swaggart later) the Assemblies of God leadership provided the general public with evidence that righteousness and accountability were required of even the most popular, revenue-producing ministers.[39]

Explosive as the Bakker case was for evangelicals, they found themselves caught up with other Americans in the summer of 1987 with new controversies involving the religious Right. The two issues attracting great attention and suggesting the increasing difficulties of that Right were the nominations of Judge Robert Bork to the U.S. Supreme Court and the so-called Iran-Contra story involving Colonel Oliver North. In these cases the leadership came from Falwell, Robertson, and Concerned Women for America. By the summer of 1987 the country was so polarized over the highly conservative ideology espoused by the White House and the Right that it came by informal consensus to allow these two cases to serve as examples of the battles over who was in control of the government. Few citizens were willing to compromise on either of the major issues concerned; with Bork it was abortion rights, and with North it was anticommunism and constitutional separation of powers. Both issues were central to religious Right loyalties.

The Supreme Court by 1987 was divided ideologically between four more liberal and four more conservative justices. The sudden resignation of Justice Lewis Powell gave President Reagan the opportunity to appoint a justice favorable to the antiabortion cause he and the full Right had championed. He nominated Judge Robert Bork, formerly of the Yale Law School faculty. The nomination set off an uproar of protest and support on both sides by a variety of activist, special-purpose groups everywhere. Bork was portrayed as a great intellectual, a proven jurist, and one who honored the principle of "original intent," that is, that judges in constitutional decisions must honor and follow the intentions of the Founding Fathers as they wrote the Constitution in 1787.[40]

That position attracted strong support among conservatives and many evangelicals. A huge array of petition drives, rallies, fund-raising programs, and related opinion-shaping activities took center stage for Christian Voice, Concerned Women for America, Liberty Federation, Moral Majority, and the campaigning of Pat Robertson for the presidency. Bork represented the vote that would repeal elective abortions; he would furnish the vote that would turn back the liberal agenda on civil rights, equal opportunity and affirmative action, criminal justice, and a host of other legal and moral issues.

Beyond his endorsement by the leadership of the religious Right, several major church denominations took the unprecedented step of making their official positions known on Bork. The National Association of Evangelicals endorsed him, as did the largest Protestant denomination, the Southern Baptist Convention. Concerned Women for America in national convention heard President Reagan make a personal plea to them and the nation for Bork. As they cheered, Reagan quipped, "It makes me feel as if reinforcements have just arrived."[41]

CWA also collected 76,000 signatures to present to the Senate as a petition for Bork. It paid for hundreds of newspaper and radio ads, public service announcements, and op-ed pieces. Some 350 CWA members came from several states to lobby those same senators. Bev LaHaye testified before the Senate Judiciary Committee on behalf of the 500,000 members claimed by the organization.[42]

On the other hand, a variety of church-related, labor, feminist, civil rights, and similar activist groups demanded that the Senate turn down the nomination. Among these were the Americans United for Separation of Church and State (largely a Baptist group), the National Council of Churches, and the United Church of Christ. Bork was seen by them as hostile to their interests and as a judge whose mind was already made up on the momentous issues facing the nation's highest tribunal.[43]

Clearly everyone involved understood that this was a battle to the end, with no compromise possible. It made logical sense to the liberals (including the American Civil Liberties Union and People for the American Way) on the one side and Moral Majority, CWA, and Pat Robertson on the other. When the Senate voted the nomination down, the religious Right leadership claimed that this was one more step toward the takeover by secular humanism. That argument was short-lived, however, because the administration, after putting forward a candidate who confessed to once having smoked marijuana, now named an experienced justice from California, Anthony Kennedy. His nomination went through with little conflict.

The other major battle of the summer of 1987 came during the hearings in Congress over the discovery that the administration had devised a plan to bring about the release of American hostages held in Lebanon. Briefly, Iran would pay America for arms, the profits of which would go toward financing the Contras, the anti-Sandinista army largely in military control of Nicaragua and seen by the Right as being agents against Russian communism in the Western Hemisphere. When the secrecy of this plan and its extensive network of finances and communications under the leadership of Colonel Oliver North and Admiral John Poindexter became known, a huge outcry of protest went up around the country. Most conservatives, including religious Right leaders, praised the courage and patriotism of North, who risked his career to carry out what he believed were constitutional and anti-Communist activities. Critics, mostly liberals, pointed to the several instances of secrecy, destruction of evidence, violation of congressional rules to keep it informed of foreign-policy matters, and related issues as evidence that the administration had gone amok in its foreign policy.

The story is well known enough to need no repetition here. Religious Right leadership almost unanimously claimed North to be a long-overdue but entirely praiseworthy hero for his activities. He was fighting the Communists, he was carrying out orders, and he freely displayed his love of country in the congressional hearings and frequent fund-raising speeches around the country.

Several religious Right groups moved in for support. Using the occasion both to praise North and to raise funds, Falwell's Liberty University gave him an honorary doctorate. CWA sponsored his speeches around the country and gave him extensive publicity. When it became clear that at least some evidence discovered could lead to his conviction, these groups and Pat Robertson called on President Reagan to issue a pardon before North came to trial.

Like the Bork debate, the Iran-Contra battle continued to polarize the nation. Critics of Falwell saw it as a chance for him and the religious Right to regain respectability after the PTL scandal. (This occurred after the Swaggart story also.) Moral Majority, Christian Voice, and CWA mounted their most extensive campaigns to date to get petitions asking for a pardon. When President Reagan did not act before leaving office, the conservative community sharply criticized him for the omission. In 1989, when North was convicted of three counts by a jury, with President Bush refusing to intervene, they found reason to wonder if America was going soft.[44]

By early 1988, with control of the White House and the Senate at stake, supporters of the political televangelists found their potential clout with voters in serious trouble. Robertson was running hard but making little headway. Bakker was in disgrace, casting about for a villain on whom to blame his problems. Falwell was suspect to both fundamentalists and Pentecostalists for his forays into PTL management. But at least there still stood Jimmy Swaggart, the man who was preaching to more viewers around the world than any other evangelist in history. In 1986 the Swaggart ministries' income was over $146 million; at the Baton Rouge, Louisiana, headquarters some 700 students were attending the two-year-old Jimmy Swaggart Bible College; his television program was carried on 3,000 stations, not including cable outlets, and was seen in 195 nations. In front of his headquarters was World Ministry Avenue, framed by flags of those 195 nations. Within the offices were ministries providing food, medicine, hospitals, and schools in underdeveloped nations around the world. The Swaggarts' private residence was valued at some $2 million.[45] In brief, he stood as the most influential televangelist in the United States and overseas.

Yet by May he stood defrocked and disgraced, confessing to a pattern of sexual practices with at least one prostitute in nearby New Orleans. By 1990 his ministry had been reduced to far below half of what it had once commanded.[46] His fall helped strengthen the general public's perception that all wealthy televangelists were alike: greedy, power hungry, and bent on advancing their own interests through the guise of religious faith.

Swaggart had risen to such power largely by his skillful use of television and his carefully prepared self-image. Endorsing the full religious Right social agenda, he gave special attention to attacking Roman Catholicism, rock music, pastoral counseling, and politicoreligious liberalism. He identified himself with the tradition of "anointed" preaching within Pentecostalism, emphasizing the necessity for righteous living.

His success came from his remarkable skills to mock academics, liberals, mainline elites, and critics of his ministry. Portraying himself as a country boy, he catered to the resentments of those who found themselves scorned and outside the inner circles of educated Americans. One observer noted, "His warm style

and honky-tonk sound attracted crowds who regarded him as the most able expo-
nent of the true Pentecostal message. Many Pentecostals enjoyed seeing one of
their own become a star. Having gone unnoticed for many years, they took pride
in and lavished funds on those who gave them visibility."[47]

The actual collapse unfolded in a sordid story of involvement for some years
with at least one prostitute in New Orleans. His activities had been followed by
another Assemblies of God minister, Marvin Gorman, deposed from the clergy
roster for alcoholism but now building a nearby ministry competitive to that of
Swaggart. When church officials were notified by Gorman of Swaggart's visits
to the prostitute, a chain of events developed that led by late spring to Swaggart's
being defrocked. Swaggart, in turn, created his own independent ministry.[48]

The news media gave Swaggart's story the full treatment of sarcasm, ridicule,
linkage with Bakker, and greed. The cancellations of his media productions started
coming in quickly; CBN, with a viewership of 37 million homes, was among
the first to cancel his telecasts. Other broadcast and cable systems followed the
CBN lead. Within a year Swaggart had dropped from 2.298 million to 836,000
households. His book and other merchandise sales dropped as rapidly. More
reliable financial data could not be collected because the Swaggart financial records
have remained very closely guarded.[49]

None of this helped the campaign of the fourth major televangelist, Pat Robertson, for the Oval Office. Even though few expert political observers gave his
candidacy any chance of success, his followers hoped that he might at least solidify
the religious Right into a solid voting bloc within the Republican party.

Robertson fell from front-page and prime-time coverage early in the 1988 campaign because his campaigning could not convince the voters that he had been
given a divine mission to be elected. Nor could his operatives match the expert
know-how of the George Bush team. He was basing his credibility on his expertise in a wide variety of public-policy issues as demonstrated on his highly popular
talk show, "The 700 Club." There he had endorsed the full agenda of the religious
Right, emphasizing "the things that made this country great and the good old-
fashioned values that most Americans believe."[50]

His candidacy rested on the premise that he would be supported by the
evangelicals as well as Pentecostalists and many conservatives from both major
parties. He and his staff, however, had not counted on both the sharp-edged attacks of other Republicans and the criticisms of his statements made before his
candidacy, as well as his several serious misstatements during the primaries. He
had in 1981 claimed that only Christians and Jews would be qualified to run the
government. He suggested that when he was in the White House, he would deal
with the terrorist Colonel Qaddafi of Libya by having him killed. He asked supporters to pray that the old liberals on the Supreme Court "either retire or be
graduated to that great courtroom in the sky."[51]

Having endorsed the cooperation he received from Jim and Tammy Faye Bakker in their earlier joint television programs, he now in an updated campaign
biography gave them very short attention. Such statements led fellow rightists

such as Bev LaHaye to state, "When he starts giving answers like we're hearing, you begin to wonder whether he can really handle the highest position in the land." She was referring to Robertson's charge that George Bush had started the Swaggart scandal to discredit him as a televangelist. Robertson resigned his Baptist ministry credentials to demonstrate to voters that he was not the captive of any controversial group, only to be criticized for that by Billy Graham, Jesse Jackson, and other Baptist clergy.

For the moment, when Robertson came in second in the Iowa primary after Senator Robert Dole, his candidacy seemed to have credibility. Then, in a total effort, his team campaigned throughout the South, claiming it as a natural constituency for this "Super Tuesday," the day fifteen presidential primaries in that region were held. Robertson failed in each one, losing badly in his own state. At that point the campaign died.[52]

One final battle contributed to the failure of the religious Right to win acceptance as a viable special-interest bloc within the GOP. This was *Grove City College* case, named for a private Pennsylvania college charged by the government with racial discrimination in applying federal funds to some of its internal programs. Congress wanted all federal funds withheld from Grove City College or any institution involved in such discrimination; it passed a bill to achieve that. President Reagan announced that he would veto the measure.

The religious Right, especially Falwell and Dr. James Dobson of the "Focus on the Family" program, started a massive effort to prevent any override of the promised veto. Acting apparently with White House information, they claimed that the congressional bill would force the government to entitle practicing homosexuals, AIDS patients, and drug addicts, among others, to receive protected federal funds. They convinced their followers to send what was called a "tidal wave" of letters and telegrams and to make personal lobbying visits to Capitol Hill.

Within a few days the lawmakers found that the situation had gotten out of hand. The protesters were making erroneous judgments; they were tying up telephones and other media sources. Friends of the religious Right such as Jamie Buckingham, editor of *Charisma*, stated that the Falwells and Dobsons were "just plain wrong." Sympathetic senators such as Orrin Hatch and Alan Simpson sharply criticized the Dobson/Falwell offensive, as did the National Association of Evangelicals. Congress overrode the veto, 73–24 in the Senate and 292–133 in the House.[53]

At stake for the religious Right was the viability of its power to influence Congress and its reputation as a responsible special-purpose group within the Republican party. Its leaders had chosen, as it turned out, the wrong measure at the wrong time, using wrong information, and they were badly defeated. It was a lesson they would not forget.

NOTES

1. Randall Balmer, *Mine Eyes Have Seen the Glory: A Journey into the Evangelical Subculture in America* (New York: Oxford University Press, 1989), pp. 8-9.

2. *Time*, February 17, 1989, pp. 63-65; Stewart M. Hoover, *Mass Media Religion: The Social Sources of the Electronic Church* (Los Angeles: Sage Publications, 1988), p. 64; *Christianity Today*, February 3, 1989, pp. 34-35; George Gallup, Jr., and Jim Castelli, *The People's Religion: American Faith in the 90s* (New York: Macmillan, 1989), pp. 158-64.

3. Marshall W. Fishwick and Ray B. Browne, eds., *The God Pumpers: Religion in the Electronic Age* (Bowling Green, Ohio: Bowling Green State University Popular Press, 1987), pp. 60-74.

4. See the Southern Baptist Convention publication, *Light*, January 1986, p. 12; news story, *Church and State*, October 1985, pp. 203-4; ibid., February 1986, p. 130; Sara Diamond, *Spiritual Warfare: The Politics of the Christian Right* (Boston: South End Press, 1989), pp. 66-67: "Memo," *Christian Century*, January 26, 1983, p. 79; transcript of the "Donahue Show," Multi Media Entertainment, Cincinnati, Ohio, in a debate between Tim LaHaye and Representative Patricia Schroeder (D.-Colo.); news item, *Inside the American Religious Scene*, June 20, 1986, p. 2.

5. Interview with Beverly LaHaye, *Fundamentalist Journal*, April 1984, p. 4; Diamond, *Spiritual Warfare*, pp. 83, 106-8.

6. Diamond, *Spiritual Warfare; Charisma*, December 1984, p. 88; Richard G. Peterson, "Electric Sisters," in Fishwick and Browne, *God Pumpers*, pp. 132-36; *Moral Majority Report*, April 1984, p. 10; *Concerned Women*, November 1987, p. 18.

7. News story, *Ms.*, February 1987, p. 26; Diamond, *Spiritual Warfare*, pp. 107-10.

8. Allen D. Hertzke, *Representing God in Washington: The Role of Religious Lobbies in the American Polity* (Knoxville: University of Tennessee Press, 1988), index, "Concerned Women from America"; profile, *Washington Post*, September 26, 1987, pp. C 1ff.; profile, *New York Times*, June 15, 1987, pp. 34-36; Rebecca E. Klatch, *Women of the New Right* (Philadelphia: Temple University Press, 1987), passim; Jerome L. Himmelstein, "The Social Basis of Antifeminism: Religious Networks and Culture," *Journal for the Scientific Study of Religion* 25, 1 (1986): 1-15.

9. Christian Voice, Newsletter, October 25, 1985, p. 1.

10. Letter to supporters from David W. Balsinger, September 1988; Diamond, *Spiritual Warfare*, pp. 69-72; David W. Balsinger, *The Samaritan Society* (Brentwood, Tenn.: Wolgemuth and Hyatt, 1989); *Christianity Today*, February 7, 1989, pp. 38-39; Sara Diamond, "Shepherding," *Covert Action Information Bulletin*, no. 27 (Spring 1987): 18-31.

11. Linda Blood, "Shepherding/Discipleship Theology and Practice of Absolute Obedience," *Cultic Studies Journal* 2, 2 (1986): 235-45; Diamond, *Spiritual Warfare*, pp. 78-79; this writer attended the American Freedom Coalition conference in Washington, D.C., Spring 1987; Balsinger, *Samaritan Society*; Dave Racer, *Not for Sale: The Rev. Sun Myung Moon and One American's Freedom* (St. Paul: Tiny Press, 1989), passim.

12. Other small religious Right groups included the Rutherford Institute and the Christian Legal Society, established to advance their causes through the legal system, and *The Other Side* magazine and community; see Dean C. Curry, "Evangelicals, the Bible, and Public Policy," *This World*, no. 16 (Winter 1987): 34-49; Myron S. Augsburger, "Pluralism Gone to Seed," *Christianity Today*, January 17, 1986, p. 20-I.

13. See the publications of Just Life; Joyce Hollyday, *Turning toward Home: A Sojourner of Hope* (San Francisco: Harper and Row, 1989).

14. Richard Cizik, ed., *The High Cost of Indifference: Can Christians Afford Not to Act?* (Ventura, Calif.: Regal Books, 1984).

15. See, for instance, the stories in the biweekly newspaper, *Twin Cities Christian*; "Action Guide," *Christian Herald*, January 1989, p. 1; news story, *Washington Post*, November 5, 1988, p. C14.

16. See Erling Jorstad, *The New Christian Right, 1981–1988* (New York: Edwin Mellen Press, 1987), index, for references; People for the American Way, *Forum*, March 31, 1986, pp. 1–8.

17. See the analysis in Rob Burwitt, "The 1986 Election Generates GOP Power Struggle," *Congressional Quarterly*, April 12, 1986, pp. 802–7; news story, *St. Paul Pioneer Press Dispatch*, July 7, 1985, p. 6H.

18. *New York Times*, March 17, 1986, p. 12.

19. See the documentation in Jorstad, *New Christian Right*, pp. 162–63, 172–73; John Judis, "The Charge of the Light Brigade," *New Republic*, September 29, 1986, pp. 16–18.

20. Jill Kiecott and Hart M. Nelson, "The Structuring of Political Attitudes among Liberal and Conservative Protestants," *Journal for the Scientific Study of Religion* 27, 1 (1988): 48–57.

21. See the in-depth case study by Kenneth D. Wald et al., "Churches as Political Communities." *American Political Science Review* 82, 2 (June 1988): 531–48.

22. News story, *Charisma*, November 1986, p. 63; "George Bush: Where Does He Stand?" *Christian Herald*, June 1986, pp. 14ff.; news item, *National Christian Reporter*, August 22, 1986, p. 1. See the news story about the Bush-Bakker political meeting, *Washington Post National Weekly Edition*, December 26, 1988–January 1, 1989, pp. 23–26; a 1987 "Frontline" television investigative program suggested that the White House called off the 1985 investigation by the IRS of PTL so as not to alienate pro-PTL voters.

23. "Candidates' Biblical Scorecard," 1986 edition (Washington, D.C., 1986); Jorstad, *New Christian Right*, p. 247.

24. Jorstad, *New Christian Right*, pp. 257–58; Jim Castelli, *A Plea for Common Sense: Resolving the Clash between Religion and Politics* (San Francisco: Harper and Row, 1988), pp. 109–39.

25. See the account in *Minneapolis Star Tribune*, December 7, 1986, p. 39A, and the many references to Robertson's campaigning in Jeffrey K. Hadden and Anson Shupe, *Televangelism: Power and Politics on God's Frontier* (New York: Henry Holt, 1988); People for the American Way, *Election, 1986;* People for the American Way, *Religion and Politics* (Washington, D.C.: 1987); David R. Runkel, ed., *Campaign for President: The Managers Look at 1988* (Dover, Mass.: Auburn House, 1989), pp. 26–31, 186–88, 237.

26. *National Christian Reporter*, January 9, 1987, p. 1; *Christianity Today*, December 12, 1984, p. 43; the detailed explanation of Reagan and the religious Right in K.O.U. Kejon, "One Nation Under God: President Ronald Reagan and the Religio-Political Neo-Conservative Movement in Contemporary America" (Ph. D. diss., Department of Religious Studies, University of California at Santa Barbara, 1987); Judis, "Charge of the Light Brigade," p. 19; Roger J. Nemeth and Donald A. Luidens, "The New Christian Right and Mainline Protestantism: The Case of the Reformed Church in America," *Sociological Analysis* 49 (1989): 342–52.

27. See the splendid biography by Charles E. Shepard, *Forgiven: The Rise and Fall of Jim Bakker and the PTL Ministry* (New York: Atlantic Monthly Press, 1989).

28. Newsletter, PTL, August 10, 1983, p. 1; ibid., September 21, 1983, p. 1.

29. Vernon K. McLellen, *The Great American Arena: Positive Strategies for 20th Century Patriots* (Charlotte, N.C.: Associates Press, 1984).

30. Shepard, *Forgiven,* passim; *New York Times,* March 28, 1987, pp. 1, 7; *Los Angeles Times,* March 25, 1987, pp. 1, 20; Joe E. Barnhart, *Jim and Tammy: Charismatic Intrigue inside PTL* (Buffalo: Prometheus Books, 1988), pp. 121–30.

31. See again the *Los Angeles Times,* March 25, 1987; Barnhart, *Jim and Tammy.*

32. John Stewart, *Holy War: An Inside Account of the Battle for PTL* (Enid, Okla.: Fireside Publishing, 1987), p. 108; Larry Martz, *Ministry of Greed: The Inside Story of the Televangelists and Their Holy Wars* (New York: Weidenfeld and Nicolson, 1988), pp. 99–101 and Index references to Ankerberg; Barnhart, *Jim and Tammy,* pp. 3–17.

33. See the account in Martz, *Ministry of Greed,* pp. 99–101, Stewart, *Holy War,* p. 108.

34. *New York Times,* March 24, 1987, p. 30; ibid., March 29, p. 24; that was the last public statement on this issue made by Robertson. Billy Graham withheld any comment; see the account in *Los Angeles Times,* April 11, 1987, sec. 2, pp. 3–5.

35. *New York Times,* October 9, 1987, p. 9; *Washington Post,* November 21, 1987, pp. D1ff.; Timothy D. Whelan, "Falwell and Fundamentalism," *Christianity and Crisis,* October 12, 1987, pp. 328–31.

36. *New York Times,* October 6, 1989, pp. 1ff. The brilliant interpretation of the Bakkers' saga by Frances Fitzgerald appeared too late to be used in this study; see Fitzgerald, "Reflections: Jim and Tammy," *The New Yorker,* April 23, 1990, pp. 45–87.

37. Gallup Poll, *Gallup Report,* no. 259, April 1987, passim, especially pp. 57–71; Gallup and Castelli, *People's Religion,* p. 160.

38. Martz, *Ministry of Greed,* p. 240.

39. See Margaret Poloma, *The Assemblies of God at the Crossroads* (Knoxville: University of Tennessee Press, 1989).

40. See the discussion in Jorstad, *New Christian Right,* pp. 217–29, and the refutation of "original intent" by Leonard W. Levy, *Original Intent and the Framers' Constitution* (New York: Macmillan, 1988).

41. *National and International Religion Report,* October 5, 1987, p. 8; *National Christian Reporter,* October 9, 1987, p. 1.

42. *Concerned Women,* January 1988, p. 2; Ethan Broner, *Battle for Justice: How the Bork Nomination Shook America* (New York: W. W. Norton and Company, 1989); see the case for Bork in Gordon Jackson, "Robert Bork's America," *Policy Review* 42 (Fall 1987): 32–39.

43. *National Christian Reporter,* August 5, 1987, p. 1; ibid., September 18, 1987, p. 4; ibid., October 2, 1987, p. 2.

44. Ben Bradlee, *Guts and Glory: The Rise and Fall of Oliver North* (New York: D. I. Fine, 1988); William S. Cohen and George Mitchell, *Men of Zeal: A Candid Inside Story of the Iran-Contra Hearing* (New York: Penguin USA, 1989). North was convicted of obstructing Congress, destroying documents, and receiving an illegal gratuity; *New York Times,* May 5, 1989, pp. 1ff.

45. Lawrence Wright, "False Messiah," *Rolling Stone,* July 14–28, 1988, pp. 97ff.; "Jimmy Swaggart," *Current Biography Yearbook, 1987* (New York: H. W. Wilson Company, 1987), pp. 537–40; Steve Chapple, "Whole Lotta Savin' Goin' On," *Mother Jones,* July/August 1988, pp. 36ff.

46. *Christianity Today,* February 3, 1989, pp. 32–34; *Time,* September 11, 1989, p. 76.

47. Edith Blumhofer, "Swaggart and the Pentecostal Ethos," *Christian Century,* April 6, 1988, p. 334; Swaggart's strong support for right-wing Latin American leaders is

documented in Diamond, *Spiritual Warfare*, pp. 32–35; on Catholics see Karl Keating, *Catholicism and Fundamentalism: The Attack on "Romanism" by "Bible Christians"* (San Francisco: Ignatius Press, 1988), pp. 86–98; *Washington Post*, April 8, 1987, pp. A1ff.

48. *U.S. News and World Report*, March 7, 1988, pp. 62–64; *National and International Religion Report*, February 13, 1988, p. 4; *St. Paul Pioneer Press Dispatch*, April 1, 1988, p. 5A; Art Harris, "Swaggart Agonistes," *Washington Post National Weekly Edition*, March 7, 1988, pp. 12ff.; *Washington Post*, April 4, 1988, pp. C1ff.; *New York Times*, April 9, 1988, p. 1.

49. *New York Times*, May 3, 1988, p. 2; "Swaggart's Fall: What Pastors Are Saying," *Charisma and Christian Life*, May 1988, pp. 72–78; news item, *Christian Retailing*, April 15, 1988, p. 3; *Newsweek*, July 11, 1988, pp. 26–28; *Christianity Today*, February 3, 1989, p. 33; *Minneapolis Star Tribune*, November 9, 1988, p. 16A; ibid., February 13, 1989, p. 5A; *Twin City Christian*, September 22, 1988, p. 3A; *Time*, September 11, 1989, p. 76.

50. See the sympathethic study in Hadden and Shupe, *Televangelism*; also see the extensive detailed analysis in Hoover, *Mass Media Religion; Time*, February 17, 1987, pp. 62–65; Jim Wallis, "A Wolf in Sheep's Clothing," *Sojourners*, May 1986, pp. 22–23.

51. Malcolm Gladwell, "Chuck Colson vs the Fundamentalists," *American Spectator*, February 1986, pp. 21–23; *Congressional Quarterly*, October 3, 1987, p. 2387; *Christian Herald*, March 1988, p. 20; David Bennett, *The Party of Fear: From Nativist Movements to the New Right in American History* (Chapel Hill: University of North Carolina Press, 1988), pp. 387–403; Pat Robertson on "The 700 Club," January 11, 1981; *U.S. News and World Report*, February 22, 1988, pp. 21–22; *National Christian Reporter*, October 16, 1987, p. 2.

52. *Detroit Free Press*, December 28, 1986, p. 1; Steve Bruce, *The Rise and Fall of the New Christian Right: Conservative Protestant Politics in America, 1979–1988* (New York: Oxford University Press, 1988), pp. 129–31; Balmer, *Mine Eyes Have Seen the Glory*, pp. 107–37; Mark Noll, "Pat Robertson and the Iowa Caucuses," *Reformed Journal*, March 1988, pp. 9–12; *Washington Post National Weekly Edition*, February 15–21, 1988, p. 6; *Washington Post*, March 8, 1988, p. 1A; *Congressional Quarterly*, May 14, 1988, p. 1268; *Christianity Today*, February 3, 1989, pp. 33–34; *Los Angeles Times*, May 21, 1988, sec. 2, p. 6; Cal Thomas in *Eternity*, May 1988, p. 18; "Media," *Washington Post National Weekly Edition*, May 23–29, 1988, p. 20.

53. *Twin City Christian*, June 2, 1988, p. 7A; *Report from the Capital*, May 1988, p. 9; *National Christian Reporter*, April 1, 1988, p. 4; People for the American Way, *Forum*, Fall 1988, p. 2; *Time*, March 28, 1988, p. 26; *Christianity Today*, April 22, 1988, pp. 38–39; *New York Times*, March 22, 1988, p. 12; *Liberty Report*, April 1988, p. 3; *Concerned Women*, May 1988, p. 23.

6

End and Beginnings: The First Bush Years

By contrast to the crusades for Bork, North, Grove City College, and Robertson, the religious Right involved itself only quietly in the 1988 campaign. There was no doubt that George Bush would be their candidate, he who had cultivated the leaders' friendship and talked openly about his faith. By contrast, evangelicals hardly knew Governor Michael Dukakis, the Democratic presidential nominee, or very much about his Greek Orthodox faith. As the much-analyzed and highly controversial campaign unfolded, evangelicals were far more sympathetic toward the Republican stand on abortion, tuition tax credits, anticommunism, and voluntary school prayer than they were with the Democratic alternative.[1]

They also could support the strong Bush-Quayle show of patriotism and pledging allegiance to the flag, as well as a perceived stronger stand on punishment for criminals. Bush freely associated with such religious Right leaders as Falwell and welcomed Robertson's support for the November election. Even though Bush belonged to a mainline body, the Episcopal Church, his regular attendance seemed to impress some evangelicals who had wondered about the lack of attendance by the incumbent president.[2]

While the campaign played itself out showing Bush commanding an ever-increasing lead and the Democrats unable to mount any effective appeal, the public watched another major battle erupt. It focused on the issue of abortion, the most divisive domestic social issue in the United States since the time of slavery. From the outset the religious Right and most of the evangelical community had opposed elective abortion, with various positions being taken on whether to allow it in case of rape or incest, to save the life of the mother, or under no conditions. Most important, however, was the growing conviction that elective abortion, the *Roe* v. *Wade* decision of 1973, must be overturned. The Republican ticket was pledged to that end.

However, even though antiabortion demonstrations and educational and lobbying programs had been conducted by the religious Right since its first days, it had not been able to bring together either a mass movement or effective leadership to win over those who were neutral or even prochoice. Throughout the evangelical community in the 1980s leaders and laity gave the most serious attention to the moral issues. The major charge was that elective abortion was simply murder: that the fetus at conception was alive, and that abortion was taking that life. By contrast, of course, the prochoice people argued for the freedom of females to make the decision for themselves, not to leave it in the hands of politicians or judges; a woman had a constitutional right to privacy, and that right included the decision to elect an abortion.[3]

The political importance of the abortion issue became vividly clear by early 1986. On the grass roots level, several antiabortion groups had started working to win support of political office seekers. With some support of prominent Republican leaders, these activists chose the GOP as the better suited of the two major parties to achieve their goal. They found friends such as Representative Jack Kemp, Senator Robert Dole, Vice President Bush, and aspirant Pat Robertson willing to endorse their cause. In brief, antiabortion and mainstream Republicanism became something of a partnership in the spring of 1986.[4]

At the same time, some evangelical groups started expanding older, smaller programs to meet the problem of a woman not wanting or able to keep her baby. In Lynchburg, Virginia, at the Thomas Road Baptist Church, a maternity home for such persons was opened, with the option of adoption being provided. That became a prototype for later programs, with agencies opening in several states. The experience offered the women the time to make their own plans under medical supervision without pressures from family, boyfriends, or husbands.[5]

Within mainline denominations the majority of policy makers generally endorsed the *Roe* v. *Wade* options. In the later 1980s, however, an increasing number of antiabortion groups appeared, such as Lutherans for Life or the National Association of Episcopalians for Life. But beyond the fact than many mainline members held strongly feminist views about freedom of choice, liberal Protestantism could not, as one analyst stated, attract strong public support for "its own highly nuanced reflections on abortion and, with some unfairness, has become identified in the public mind simply with undifferentiated support for legal abortion."[6]

Still the antiabortion movement seemed fragmented and listless until the appearance of a powerful new organization, Operation Rescue. Its leader was Randall Terry, a graduate of Elim Bible Institute of Elim, New York. From its founding in 1987 it grew to be a powerful catalyst in organizing antiabortion forces.[7]

Basically, Terry, a highly skilled organizer, motivator, and articulate fundamentalist, convinced supporters to practice civil disobedience in trying to stop (their term is "rescue") an abortion at a medical facility. This was done by massive numbers of nonresistant bodies blocking entrances to such facilities, or locking themselves inside abortion clinics and thus shutting down operations. The rationale was both to win public attention by these nonviolent means and to stop women about to have an abortion from carrying out their plans.[8]

What helped make Operation Rescue so effective was its blunt language and strategy; abortion was simply called "murder" or "killing." Potential demonstrators were encouraged to stand their ground when on a mission and accept the punishment of the law and the court. As it unfolded, the movement mushroomed dramatically overnight. By 1988, usually on weekends at large city medical facilities, hundreds of demonstrators, ready to be arrested and fined for breaking the law, would stop the flow of persons going in. The movement continued to spread in 1989, with the media carrying stories of sometimes thousands of demonstrators being arrested, fined, and released. Despite the shrill and confrontational nature of the protest, the movement under Terry's direction continued to pick up strength.[9]

In some instances, where ties to Operation Rescue were not clear, major damage resulted. Demonstrators in Corpus Christi, Texas, were fined $800,000 for picketing a doctor's home to protest abortions; they were convicted of gross negligence and causing mental anguish to the physician and his family. In Philadelphia protesters were fined $110,000 for attempting to stop abortions at a women's center. The judges ruled that the demonstrators were breaking federal racketeering laws aimed at those who would use force, threats, and trespassing to intimidate employees and related personnel. Other such incidents broke out in every section of the country, with no definitive amount of evidence being available to ascertain how far the civil disobedience movement met with resistance from the law. What occurred in Los Angeles was perhaps typical. Demonstrators were arrested, given suspended sentences, and released.[10]

Within the evangelical community a huge controversy developed over the planned civil disobedience. Despite the fact that Falwell and Robertson endorsed Operation Rescue, large numbers of evangelicals stated that they could not accept deliberate lawlessness no matter how noble the motives. Debates within congregations, seminaries, weekend rallies, and denominational meetings focused on the increasingly bold and disruptive nature of Operation Rescue. When it was learned that Terry himself was a fundamentalist, some hailed that as a great advance for the movement. Others claimed that once the laws were violated by personal choice, a citizen could pick and choose which to obey and which to violate.[11]

As the abortion showdown moved into the streets in the fall of 1988, it helped polarize an electorate already sharply divided over the nasty presidential campaign's verbal brawls about patriotism, the rights of criminals, capital punishment, and the loyalty of the American Civil Liberties Union—all matters carrying with them deep emotions not easily resolved by traditional political discourse and debate. Adding to the campaigning were two other religious Right crusades, Christian Voice and Biblical Scorecard. Apparently, when Christian Voice became identified more closely with the Unification Church, the head of Biblical Scorecard, David Balsinger, decided that he could not participate in the move. As the campaign heated up, Balsinger presented the "Presidential Biblical Scorecard," with the familiar standards of judgment used in earlier campaigns.[12] Christian Voice, led by Dr. Robert Grant, brought out "Voters '88 Guide," with much the same kinds of material. In their postmortems after the elections, neither organization could present convincing evidence that their publications had been more than preaching to the choir. However, it seems clear that the direct mailings from Moral Majority, Robertson, and Tim LaHaye did capture some national headlines and television programs, giving the religious Right another window to influence the voters.[13]

Perhaps if the abortion issue had never arisen, the Republicans would have won anyway. That conclusion must await the verdict of historians years away from the present. What can be concluded is that the religious Right made no visible difference, despite its showing of 80 percent exit-poll support for Bush-Quayle. Again the election showed what had happened in 1980 and 1984: the voters made their choices on the basis of issues other than the special-purpose crusades of the Right. In some six instances where candidates for house seats chose to identify with the religious Right, all were defeated.[14]

The lack of appeal of the ideology espoused by the religious Right showed up in such anomalies as Bush winning in Ohio, as did the very liberal incumbent Senator Howard Metzenbaum, or Bush winning in New Jersey along with liberal incumbent Senator Frank Lautenberg against a very attractive candidate, Peter Dawkins.

As the postmortems set in, evangelicals made an assessment of how much President Reagan had actually helped their cause. They knew that his successor, George Bush, would select a conservative for the next Supreme Court appointment, thus tipping the balance five to four in their direction. But they also heard the president's closest advisor, Edwin Meese, comment that their social agenda issues "were not the primary objectives of the President." Apparently the latter believed that such matters belonged in state legislatures and the courts.[15] Another conservative commentator, Wilfred M. McClay, made the point that "although he [Reagan] liked to speak to conservative Christian social and moral concerns, he had no intention of doing much about them. Rarely has a political pressure group been more effectively coopted, for the evangelicals' political clout was almost entirely tied to Reagan, and Reagan would never risk his popularity by departing too far from the curve of mainstream public opinion."[16]

Sensing such a mood, other evangelicals moved quickly to create the feeling that progress would continue under the new president. Representative William Dannemeyer (R.-Calif.) introduced into the House a measure to allow voluntary prayer in public schools, a move blasted by other conservatives. Bev LaHaye and CWA announced a full slate of issues for the next round of battles, including no federal funds for prochoice organizations, "no special rights for gays and lesbians," support for the "freedom fighters" (the Contras), and an end to elective abortions and pornography. Some twenty evangelical leaders met with the president-elect during December to make clear their priorities. Among them were Falwell, Bev LaHaye, Robert Dugan of NAE, James Dobson, Stephen Strang of *Charisma* magazine, and Rev. James Robison. Earlier that day Pat Robertson and the president had exchanged viewpoints.[17]

Much to the surprise of most evangelicals was the news announced in the spring of 1989 that the president would delay action on enacting tuition tax vouchers for parents of children in private and religious schools. This issue had ranked at the top of the evangelical list. After consultations with Bush, some evangelicals stated that he was only delaying, not canceling his campaign promises there. Others remained more than a little dubious that this mainliner would actually fulfill his pledge.[18]

Some evangelicals wondered also why the president gave total support for the candidacy of Senator John Tower to be secretary of defense. They held a very low opinion of his personal life, replete with stories of womanizing and drinking. Others felt a sense of bewilderment that one of their own, the staunchly evangelical surgeon general, Dr. C. Everett Koop, disagreed so sharply with many of their strongest convictions. These included his recommendation that people use condoms to help reduce the spread of AIDS. Such a recommendation was considered tantamount to endorsing homosexual acts. Koop also stated that research had not conclusively proved that the experience of abortion was necessarily damaging to the mental health of the woman. That too had already been rejected by evangelicals. Koop went so far as to make a very strong criticism of two evangelical leaders, James Dobson and televangelist Rev. James Kennedy, who, he claimed, had written about AIDS with at best faulty and at worst "reprehensible" data.[19]

Well into 1989 the Bush program regained considerable credibility with the July 3 decision of the Supreme Court to greatly restrict the availability of legal abortions. The Court also left open the agenda to hear additional cases, perhaps to overturn *Roe* v. *Wade* entirely.[20] The credibility of Randall Terry, head of Operation Rescue, rose accordingly. He let it be known that abortion was the first of several planned crusades: against pornography, against judicial activism, and to restore "moral sanity" to the arts, universities, and mass media. He included homosexuality on his list of targets. He stated that mothers, if financially possible, should stay at home with their children. He also intended to deny teenagers access to birth-control information without parents' consent.[21] Terry's organization started producing audiotapes, recordings, and videotapes about him; a four-color magazine featuring Operation Rescue was on the planning boards. In brief, here might well be a new leader to unite the social agenda of the religious Right.[22]

Such a leader might well be needed, because in May 1989 Falwell announced that he was closing down Moral Majority and Liberty Federation and himself retiring from national elective politics. Such a move was not altogether surprising. Observers had noted that he had continued to move toward the evangelical center and away from his separationist origins. The financial picture for his political operations remained bleak after the televangelist scandals. The heavy public appearance schedule of the last eight years had left him little time for his interest in Liberty University. (He had, for instance, become the most interviewed Protestant preacher on the television "Nightline" show in recent years.)

Critics pointed to the timing of the withdrawal, stating that the religious Right had made no appreciable difference in the 1988 elections. It continued to struggle for funds, and new leaders such as Dr. James Dobson, Randall Terry, and Bev LaHaye were attracting more support. Moral Majority's strength had depended upon its being against issues; now, as a part of the power establishment in Washington, it could less easily be on the anti side.[23]

Admitting that he was more of a centrist than in 1980 when "we sat in our citadels and fired out cannonballs," he could laugh as the Religious News Writers Association gave him a farewell roast. In commenting on his aggressive fundraising strategies, they found an appropriate text, Luke 16:22, "And it came to pass, that the beggar died."[24]

So within one decade the four major leaders of the evangelical resurgence in public politics had passed into quietude. Robertson could regain his leadership at CBN, but his future in the Republican party depended entirely on the success of President Bush's first term, a matter out of Robertson's control. Swaggart and Bakker were in disgrace. Falwell, claiming that he had achieved his goals, was back in Lynchburg. Unquestionably these and comparable leaders had put the social agenda of the religious Right squarely in the thick of the national political debate; they had moved into the vacuum created by the national political demise of the mainline churches.

Perhaps they had achieved something else. As George Marsden suggests, the religious Right had restructured the entire set of loyalties within evangelicalism. The old charismatic-Pentecostal-fundamentalist-evangelical division had been remade into the conservative-nationalistic political group (the religious Right), the progressive evangelical group (Sojourners, ESA, and allies), and the charismatics. In the early 1990s the distinctive qualities and identifying traits of these embryonic new alignments will become clearer.[25]

In any event, these ten years suggest that whatever inroads modernization and privatization had made in evangelical circles, a substantial number of evangelicals saw themselves and their organizations as the last fortresses of faithful resistance to the encroachments of the world and the forces of secularization. Those who agree with the Hunter thesis regarding the greater worldliness of the evangelicals in the 1980s will have considerable opportunity and evidence at their disposal to explore these implications.

NOTES

1. E. C. Ladd, "The 1988 Elections: Continuation of the Post New-Deal System," *Political Science Quarterly* 104, 1 (1989): 1–18; "Education," *USA Today, The Magazine of the American Scene*, August/September 1988, pp. 77–81; "Reviving Vouchers," *Church and State*, May 1988; pp. 100–103. The Party platforms are in the *New York Times*, August 17, 1988, pp. A20–A21.

2. Doug Weed, *George Bush: Man of Integrity* (Eugene, Oreg.: Harvest House, 1988); *National and International Religion Report*, August 15, 1988, p. 3; *Los Angeles Times*, October 1, 1988, sec. 2, p. 6; news story, *Insight*, May 2, 1988, pp. 18–20, on the friendship between Bush and Falwell.

3. Brenda Hofman, "Political Theology: The Role of Organized Religion in the Anti-Abortion Movement," *Journal of Church and State* 28, 2 (1986); 225–47; "Abortion," theme issue, *Eternity*, January 1986, pp. 1–59, 70–72; Ted Jelen, "Changes in the Attitudinal Correlations of Opposition to Abortion," *Journal for the Scientific Study of Religion* 27, 2 (1988): 211–28.

4. Analysis by Phil Gailey, *New York Times*, June 29, 1986, p. 8.

5. News story, *Eternity*, July/August 1985, p. 6; *Twin City Christian*, June 15, 1989, pp. 1B, 15B; *Newsweek*, April 28, 1986, p. 39.

6. *Christian Century*, August 3, 1988, p. 710; *Time*, July 4, 1988, p. 44; "Special Report: Abortion," *Ms.*, April 1989, pp. 89ff.

7. Garry Wills, "Evangels of Abortion," *New York Review of Books*, June 15, 1989, pp. 15–19; Susan Faludi, "Where Did Randy Go Wrong?" *Mother Jones*, November 1989, pp. 22–28ff.

8. Robert Nolte, "Siege on Abortion," *Charisma and Christian Life*, January 1989, pp. 42–51.

9. Wills, "Evangels of Abortion," pp. 15–19; *New York Times*, May 3, 1989, p. 10; *National and International Religion Report*, March 13, 1989, p. 1.

10. "The Gathering Storm," *Ms.*, April 1989, pp. 92–95; an excellent survey is in the *Los Angeles Times*, March 17, 1989, Part 1, p. 1 and ff.

11. Wills, "Evangels of Abortion," pp. 15–19; *Newsweek*, May 1, 1989, p. 26; *Time*, May 1, 1989, pp. 26–28; *Sojourners*, November 1988, pp. 5–6; *Liberty Report*, September 1988, pp. 11–12; *Christianity Today*, November 4, 1988, pp. 34–35; ibid., December 9, 1988, pp. 52ff.; ibid., April 7, 1989; pp. 42–43; *Minneapolis Star Tribune*, December 12, 1988, pp. 1A, 10A; *New York Times*, April 10, 1989, pp. 1ff. See the attitudinal studies in George Gallup, Jr., and Jim Castelli, *The People's Religion: American Faith in the 90s* (New York: Macmillan, 1989), pp. 167–69.

12. Balsinger letter, Summer 1988, "Presidential Scorecard" (Costa Mesa, Calif.).

13. *Congressional Quarterly*, August 13, 1988, pp. 2249–50, and October 15, 1988, pp. 2941–44; *National and International Religion Report*, November 21, 1988, p. 8; *National Christian Reporter*, November 25, 1988, p. 1.

14. The exit polls are in the *New York Times*, November 10, 1988, p. B6; see also Gerald M. Pomper, ed., *The Election of 1988* (Chatham, N.J.: Chatham House Publishers, 1989), pp. 34ff. See the profiles listed in note 13 from the *Congressional Quarterly*, and the results in the *New York Times*, November 10, 1988, pp. 20–21.

15. News item, *Church and State*, September 1988, p. 185.

16. Wilfred M. McClay, "Religion in Politics: Politics in Religion," *Commentary*, October 1988, p. 43; similiar assessments by evangelicals are in *National Christian Reporter*, February 12, 1988, p. 1, and "Washington Scorecard," *Christianity Today*, October 21, 1988, pp. 32–33; "Sizing Up the Reagan Revolution," ibid., pp. 17–23; John B. Judis, *William F. Buckley, Jr., Patron Saint of the Conservatives* (New York: Simon and Schuster, 1988), pp. 469–70.

17. *Church and State*, June 1989, p. 7; *St. Louis Post-Dispatch*, June 1, 1989, p. 1; *Concerned Women*, January 1989, p. 2; news item, *Charisma and Christian Life*, January 1989, p. 32.

18. Editorial, *Charisma and Christian Life*, May 1989, p. 9; news item, *Journal of Church and State*, Winter 1989, pp. 178–79; *World*, April 15, 1989, pp. 4–5; *Christianity Today*, May 12, 1989, p. 55; *National Christian Reporter*, May 2, 1989, p. 2; *National Review*, May 19, 1989, p. 7; *Church and State*, January 1989, p. 12.

19. *Newsweek*, March 6, 1989, p. 22; *Los Angeles Times*, June 10, 1987, sec. 2. p. 7; *National and International Religion Report*, June 19, 1989, p. 2; *U.S. News and World Report*, May 25, 1989, p. 27.

20. *New York Times*, July 4, 1989, p. 1.

21. *Los Angeles Times*, March 17, 1989, sec. 2, p. 3–4.

22. *Christian Century*, January 4–11, 1989, p. 9; *National Christian Reporter*, February 17, 1989, p. 2.

23. *Washington Post*, June 12, 1989, p. A11; Cal Thomas made much the same conclusion in a debate with this author on KUOM radio, Minneapolis, February 7, 1989. See Stanley Presser et al., "Measuring Public Support for the New Christian Right," *Public Opinion Quarterly* 52 (1988): 325–37; *Minneapolis Star Tribune*, June 12, 1989, pp. 1A, 6A.

24. *New York Times*, June 12, 1989, p. A14; *Los Angeles Times*, June 12, 1989, sec. 1, p. 3.

25. George Marsden, "Unity and Diversity in the Evangelical Resurgence," in David Lotz, Donald W. Shriver, Jr., and John F. Wilson, eds., *Altered Landscapes: Christianity in America, 1935–1985* (Grand Rapids, Mich.: Wm. B. Eerdmans, 1989), p. 75; another carefully nuanced scenario is Kenneth D. Wald et al., "Evangelical Politics and Status Issues," *Journal for the Scientific Study of Religion* 28, 1 (1989): 1–16.

7

The Mass Media: Networks to Power

During the 1980s not only the televangelists but evangelicals of every category found opportunities in the mass media to continue their rise to ascendency. They developed an understanding of both the technology and the needs of the audiences to give them influence unknown before in Christendom to evangelize. Their freedom in being able to work through media-centered parachurch organizations rather than denominational structures opened opportunities for ministry unavailable to (and often unsought by) mainline bodies. A few statistics show the trend. The conservative National Religious Broadcasters administered 85 percent of all Protestant religious broadcasting; periodicals working with the Evangelical Press Association had increased by over 300 since 1950, with a net growth of 20 to 25 periodicals a year. Evangelical publishing houses for books and other print media had grown to over seventy, and evangelical bookstores had increased since 1950 by over 6,000.[1]

What stands out with remarkable clarity during this decade is the manner in which evangelicals constructed and used social (as well as technological) networks for their purposes. "Network" here is defined broadly as a social system created to organize experience and impart meaning and to establish identity and furnish information for participants for both their personal and social lives.[2] Networks connect people and opportunities, and nowhere was this more promising than in adding to the older networks and creating newer ones in the media for believers. Here the tension between pressers and holders reflected great ambiguity and tension. Media proponents were looking for improvement, for the new and different. (They reminded viewers that Jesus preached to at best 20,000 people in his ministry; one television program could reach hundreds of millions at one time.)

But they would have to face an extremely difficult question: did that novelty in some direct manner alter the permanence and the meaning of the gospel, the holding fast? Since so much of popular secular culture reached the general public through the media, especially on television, could the uniqueness and eternal foundations of faith be faithfully transmitted there? That question would be at the heart of understanding how evangelicals and the mass media came together in this decade.

Within that overarching question several other problems faced the evangelicals in media. Were media a substitute for the real thing for the hands-on, eye-to-eye contact of a prayer meeting, a worship service, an educational session, or a counseling opportunity? Was something vital lost by placing a mediating instrument between believers? Was the message, the kernel of faith, somehow subsumed or fundamentally altered to meet the time, schedule, economics, and audience needs of the media giants, both electronic and print?[3] One observer put it this way:

A host of video recorders and playback units, wall-sized screens, video games, home computers, walking stereos, film and slide systems came up from man's hands to spread the light. And Atari, IBM, Apple, Kodak, Digital, Aiwa, GE and Canon said, "That is good." And the people led by the light, sat and stared in silence. And God saw what man had done with His light and said, "That is not good! Not good at all!"[4]

In more formal terms, the evangelical absorption of mass media indicated that much of its growth since the 1970s could be understood at least in part for reasons beyond those given by Dean Kelley. Now, in a manner previously unknown within Christendom, the great truths and the magisterial and formal dignity so long associated with Christian worship and learning were becoming intelligible in terms very close to the secular or popular (meaning widespread) culture. Evangelicals, by contrast to most mainliners, had long known a more personal, experiential kind of spirituality. As Samuel Hill explains: "It is unmediated . . . occurring person to person, without significant reliance on worship forms, clergy certification, sacramental participation, doctrinal propriety or ecclesiastical legitimation."[5] This led to a greater spontaneity for seekers to find the religious direction in their life being expressed in the everyday, ordinary course of events as well as in the more formal, church-related activities. This popular religion had broken free from formal institutions and came to flourish through a rapidly expanding network of communications systems.[6]

They key to understanding here is furnished by the concept of "popular religion." This in essence is one part of the larger entity of "popular culture," well defined by Russell B. Nye. Popular culture is "those productions, both artistic and commercial, designed for mass consumption, which appeal to and express the tastes and understandings of the majority of the public, free from control by minority standards. They reflect the values, convictions, and patterns of thought and feeling generally dispersed through and approved by American society." Popular culture is "neither complicated nor profound," remaining predictable and close to majority standards, dealing "with the known, the fulfillment of expectation, the pleasant shock of recognition, the validation of an experience already familiar."[7]

Scholars such as Robert C. Ellwood and Peter Williams have shown in general terms how popular culture shapes popular religion, the domain of evangelicals, especially through the mass media. Evangelicals, along with others, have both utilized and rejected the fruits of secularization and modernization. They have found especially through the mass media the confirmation of their belief that their faith "is essentially miraculous, experiential and charismatic," the last word meaning "inspirational."[8] The media put them in touch with the millions of other believers around the nation and the world who share at least some of the important essentials of their religious conviction.

These expressions as interpreted by Ellwood are clear, predictable, and familiar, authenticating everyday life experiences. The new technology produces a sense of God's providence and care in a world otherwise dominated by secularists and modernists who either ignore or scorn the popular religion found in the media. It becomes clear at this social level that religious faith among evangelicals emerges strongly "from the bottom up," the everyday lives of ordinary people, rather than being shaped by the "knowledge elite," those leaders from the universities, cathedrals, seminaries, and similar traditional sources of religious leadership. Mass media, which are duplicatable, inexpensively transmittable, mass produced, and results of the modernization process through technology, became the new way, the pressing on, to express one's faith in this new decade.[9]

TELEVISION

Seen as the "great wasteland," the "boob tube," and similar sarcasms, television nonetheless by the 1980s dominated all of American life. In 1988 the Nielsen pollsters reported that average hours of television per day for Americans had increased from five hours and eleven minutes in 1957–1958 to six hours and fifty-nine minutes in 1987–1988.[10]

Robert Wuthnow concludes that television has grown to be of major, virtually immeasurable influence in American life, including its religious life. It had great influence on evangelicals because its broadcasters found successful formulas for keeping their expression of popular religion attractive to their well-analyzed audiences. With its informal, nonauthoritarian structure, evangelicalism has long been receptive to attractive personalities; and television had the capacity for creating such celebrities.

Within the framework of offering diversified themes, the major message of evangelicalism from its early days through the 1980s has been, according to Wuthnow, one of "moral reconstruction." American society was seen as moving toward self-destruction from the collapse of morality; religious television (free, always available, passive) supplied not only religious gratifications in a wicked world, but a sense that when these evangelical leaders and programs started to take charge in American society, then it could be rescued. Religious television provided "an umbrella under which the remnant of God's people could come together."[11] That process could also be understood as the expression of social networking.

Such an outcome had hardly been high on the list of priorities of the pioneer televangelists when they started broadcasting in the 1950s. The ministries of

Billy Graham, Oral Roberts, and Fulton Sheen captured the public's attention but were supplanted in the 1960s and 1970s by the more professional programming of Pat Robertson, Jim and Tammy Faye Bakker, Jimmy Swaggart, Kenneth Copeland, Rex Humbard, Robert Schuller, and others.

The astounding success of these programs, as measured by their huge and annually increasing incomes, told the broadcasters that they were giving the public what it wanted. Religious television, be it in the form of a church service (Falwell, Swaggart, or Schuller), a special crusade (Roberts or Graham), or a talk/entertainment show (Robertson or the Bakkers), turned these communicators into national celebrities, with status equal in the mind of the viewer to that of celebrities on national broadcast television or other forms of entertainment.

Second, the evangelicals saw the possibilities for mass proselytizing and invested huge sums of money in improving the technology of broadcasting. They simply stayed far ahead of the smaller mainline attempts at similar programming, a feature that gave their shows not only wider coverage but greater professional polish and appeal.[12]

Third, the evangelicals succeeded because they drew on previous experience in fund-raising, building their support base among millions of viewers sending in small sums on a regular basis. The advent of computerized direct mailings gave them the financial edge they needed to stay ahead of their expenses.[13]

By contrast, mainline programs generally could not generate the revenue the television stations could obtain from evangelical broadcasters. As a result, by the early 1980s only a handful of mainline programs were being broadcast, none with the clout of the televangelists. By the late 1980s some mainline bodies joined with Jewish, Catholic, and Orthodox television programs to create the Vision Interfaith Satellite Network (VISN). Sponsored by twenty-two churches, it offered a modest schedule of fifteen half-hours of weekday programming and eighteen hours of weekend shows. Its spokespersons described it as "a rich mix of entertainment, music, drama, worship and public affairs" for persons "interested in mainstream religious and values-oriented telecasting." By late 1989 it was being fed to cable companies largely in Southern California, reaching close to 6 million households. *Time* magazine, however, called its programming "dull and dated." But it continued its slow growth.[14]

VISN offered little or no competition for those who had come to understand the evangelical approach to be what "religion" on television stood for. For them the union of popular culture and popular religion had taken place. The question remained, however: Was this real religion or what a public already accustomed to the blandishments of commercial television wanted to view? Was religious television a kind of distortion of reality, a subliminal way to bring viewers around to sending in their donations?[15]

Critics of televangelism waged vigorous polemical battles among themselves over such questions, while the revenues kept increasing. By 1988 some 336 religious television stations were broadcasting, up from 92 in 1985. This growth was helped by the rapid utilization of cable broadcasting and the miles-high communications satellites and satellite dishes that made instant broadcasting to local receivers even simpler than before.[16]

All of this involved huge amounts of money for production, for advertising, for updating donor lists, for keeping up with the latest technology, and, as the scandals revealed, for staying ahead of the competition. The *Wall Street Journal* discovered what the auditors at most television stations already knew: they were being swallowed up by their own success. Demand by the public was far outstripping the supply of programs. The giants on cable such as WTBS started to raise their rates, up as much as four times in two years. This forced the religious broadcasters to give even more attention to fund-raising. The major programs employed marketers and the latest direct-mail technology to expand their revenues. An official from CBN, Paul Virts, explained that computer data banks tabulated multiples—how much donations exceed expenses in a television market. Focus groups of viewers were used to fine-tune shows for their appeal. "We test programs the same way major advertisers test commercials."[17]

Marketing became a highly competitive battle among the leaders, who continued to expand their programs of motivation for winning viewers. Free gifts such as a tape of the viewed program, a booklet, or a lapel pin would be offered. Once the programmer had the inquirer's name and address, the heavy appeals for funds started. When criticized for being so aggressive, John M. Cummuta, a religious broadcaster, replied:

The program must be relevant to the target viewer/listener. When I say "relevant" I mean that, while we are not of this world, we are sure in it; and the programs that are most successful in building responsive audiences are those that help—in a practical, usable way— their target audience members to live the Christian life, right where they are today.[18]

Aware of the decline of public trust in televangelists, a specialist in the field, Bruce H. Joffe, warned broadcasters to avoid overusing the word "personal" in a computer-printed letter and to avoid "emergencies" with "Mail Grams . . . Tel-a-Grams, ALERT-Grams, Action Grams."[19]

At the time the controversy about the Bakkers was boiling over, one of the most familiar of all televangelists, Oral Roberts of Tulsa, made the nation's front pages and prime-time television news during the spring of 1987 with a unique fund-raising appeal. Telling his viewers that God would "call me home" if the total amount requested were not raised, he inadvertently helped to stereotype all such evangelists.[20] Outside the religious community such requests brought on a wave of satire, sarcasm, and disbelief from the general public. HBO put on a spoof, "Glory! Glory!"; *Harper's* magazine ran a story on "Packaging Christ's Second Coming" as that event would be prepared at a televangelist's business office; documentary studies such as "Thy Kingdom Come: Thy Will Be Done" drew large audiences; and a new business, Tongue-in-Cheek, brought out a board game called "Fleece the Flock."[21]

The head of the National Religious Broadcasters (NRB) trade association, Ben Armstrong, replied that such charges were just not true. Studies showed that only one program, PTL, exceeded the average commercial time of secular television. Falwell's fund-raising time was the same as the commercial broadcast average, and the others were all below that norm.[22]

But as the Swaggart and Bakker stories continued to unfold, the NRB moved to re-establish credibility by strengthening its existing watchdog organization for monitoring fiscal accountability. Back in 1979 the NRB had created the Evangelical Council for Financial Responsibility (EFCA), which produced a code of ethics for members. Since few of the controversial ministries joined, in 1987 the NRB created the Ethics and Financial Integrity Commission (EFICOM). To receive accreditation (and thus hopefully win suspicious viewers' support), members had to submit an annual audit prepared by independent public accounting firms. All income sources were to be disclosed; members had to pledge to spend all revenue for the purpose for which it was solicited.[23]

Early in 1988 an ad hoc conference of most of the major evangelical leaders was held to explore the full range of fund-raising issues. Further plans for tightening fund-raising procedures were made. But as EFICOM became known among all NRB members, only a few chose to carry out its strict requirements. Further, the federal government gave indications that it might want to see if the tax-exempt status of religious organizations was being abused. At the decade's end the situation was far from resolved.[24]

The NRB, founded in 1944, had become a professional association of high repute. Its programs during the controversies now came into general view far more than ever before. It had become the chief networking agency for all forms of religious broadcasting: television and radio, commercial and noncommercial. It offered a wide variety of services to its members, including local, regional, and annual national conferences on problems and opportunities. The 1988 national meeting, for instance, featured displays and information by some 1,150 related organizations: technology, print, computers, and various Christian ministries and publishers. Delegates attended workshops on marketing, advertising, promotions, program production, and translations into other languages. In brief, the members met, learned, and exchanged views with others.[25]

Various awards were given over the years for the best programs and contributions in a variety of categories. The political tone of the NRB remained clear at its conventions. The most prominent televangelists, as well as President Reagan and Vice President Bush, had been featured speakers. Some hints turned up in the 1989 convention that some of the more controversial free-lance preachers of the health/wealth school had been deliberately kept off the program. The new headline celebrity that year was Randall Terry of Operation Rescue, who signed autographs among the many display booths of film, jewelry, new equipment, and Bibles on cassettes and computer discs. The industry was thriving.[26]

RADIO

The other major form of electronic evangelism, of course, has been radio. Its flexibility, its low cost for both producer and listener, and its infinite adaptability all made it ideally suited for the parachurch outreach of evangelicalism. By contrast to television, which until very recently required extensive equipment and receivers in fixed places, radio goes everywhere. In fact, its first great successes in the early 1920s emerged out of the radio ministries of two evangelical giants, Walter Maier of "The Lutheran Hour" and C. E. Fuller of "The Old Fashioned Gospel Hour." They set broadcasting precedents and built listener loyalty that has continued to grow to the present. By 1985 there were some 1,043 religious-format radio stations; that increased by 1987 to 1,370 and by 1989 to 1,518. That constituted a gain of more than 22 percent during the 1980s. Some 1,500 organizations were producing religious radio and television materials by 1989, an increase of 33 percent in that decade.[27]

As was true with television, mainline religious broadcasting in radio diminished drastically through the mid-twentieth century. Mainline broadcasters followed a policy of broadcasting only in donated (public-service) time. Evangelicals of all varieties have been able to attract listener support to the extent that by 1990 they produced over 90 percent of all religious radio programming. Some of this comes from the radio stations actually owned by evangelicals, but hundreds of secular stations also have sold them time, such as on Sunday morning or in the late evening. Whatever the outlet, radio has furnished listeners with networking opportunities of almost unlimited variety.

That fact helps explain why religious radio grew so quickly in the 1980s. After remaining mostly programs consisting of preaching, sacred music, and moral exhortation during the mid-century years, religious radio in the 1970s moved ahead rapidly by learning how to attract advertisers and how to present the most attractive "format," the key word in radio programming.

Market research, as it became more sophisticated in understanding listener preference, joined hands with formatting. That is, specific age and music-taste groups were identified, and radio programs were created to please specific groups instead of general audiences. The major categories have been inspirational/MOR (middle-of-the-road), southern gospel, CHR (Contemporary Hit Radio) contemporary hits, CHR/rock, traditional/sacred/beautiful Christian music, teaching/information, and adult/contemporary.[28] These categories are closely parallel to the formats in secular radio such as nostalgia, New Age, R&B (Rhythm and Blues), suburban, contemporary, and lite. Thus audiences that have become familiar with the various formats from that source find the same differentiation to suit their taste preferences in religious radio.[29]

The key has been to match advertisers interested in reaching specific interest groups to these formats. This has been done by marketing analysis and careful watch on competitors. A leader, Gary Crossland, comments, "Since Christian radio has become so many different things, so has the audience. In almost every case, the audience has become more upscale, and they tend to buy many products in far greater quantities than other media groups. Christian radio is replete with what we call 'Guppies' ('God Fearing Urban Professionals')." Crossland found what advertisers wanted to hear: over 90 percent of the listeners, including the large teenage market of eighteen and under, were not yet fifty-five years old. The various formats suited the needs of these people; format radio had found a new form of evangelizing.[30]

Beyond the music format, however, religious radio has grown also because it has established its own form of talk-show programs. These have the advantage of being able, when necessary, to deal with local religious or moral issues in a given community; or they might be connected with several national networks where celebrity broadcasters such as Pat Boone, Hal Lindsey, Charles Swindoll, or James Dobson are heard.

Since radio is so immediate, it can have engaging shows ready almost instantly; much controversy was heard on religious radio over civil disobedience and the antiabortionists, Christian rock music, the idolization of athletes, issues such as respect for the national flag, and—always the staple of all talk shows—personal identity and social relationship issues. Call-in listeners can have their individual questions or dilemmas addressed directly by a specialist or highly respected role model, such as Pat Boone. The controversies, however, center around social issues; rarely do religious talk-show hosts debate doctrine. Celebrity televangelists such as Falwell and Robertson also have short radio programs, with special emphasis on call-ins.[31]

Print media, such as magazines and newspapers, help create a sense of community among listeners by carrying complete daily radio schedules. Desktop publishers furnish stations with up-to-the-moment lists of the top ten or twenty recorded songs in each category and often indicate what is the most popular recording or show in a given city. Some stations, such as KVOI in Tucson, bring out a newspaper of religious interests on a regular basis.[32]

Evangelical radio broadcasters, in their success, have taken a large risk. They have modeled their productions to simulate much of the larger popular culture's taste standards. They enthusiastically present their formats as popular religion, with market sales being largely determinative of what formats will continue to thrive. They are sensitive to religious radio competitors looking for the same advertising dollars. All of this has made their success, as outsiders see it, tied to market values.

However, leaders such as Crossland make another case. Conceding that radio is mostly a background medium, he finds only two formats that are at the forefront of listeners' attention: news talk and Christian radio. People listen carefully to these for the messages conveyed there. "Christian audiences will listen to a Christian station not just because it represents a sound which they prefer but rather it represents what they are. Christian radio listeners do listen because they are Christian."[33] By 1989 *Broadcasting* magazine rated religious/gospel as the third most popular radio format in the United States. Only country and adult contemporary stations attracted more listeners.[34]

The top ten daily syndicated religious radio programs in 1988 were the following:

1. "Focus on the Family"/James Dobson   744 stations
2. "Through the Bible"/J. Vernon McGee   496

3. "Insight for Living"/Chuck Swindoll   481

4. "Back to the Bible"/Warren Wiersbe   421

5. "In Touch"/Charles Stanley   398

6. "Point of View"/Marlin Maddoux   345

7. "Haven of Rest"/Paul Evans   275

8. "Radio Bible Class"/Darrow Parker   232

9. "Minirth-Meier Clinic"/Don Hawkins   216

10. "Faith Seminar of the Air"/Kenneth Hagin   207

The top ten weekly syndicated radio programs in 1988 were the following:

1. "Lutheran Hour"   645 stations

2. "Hour of Decision"   620

3. "Children's Bible Hour"   592

4. "Revival Time"   550

5. "Baptist Hour"   530

6. "Focus Weekend"   510

7. "Unshackled!"   450

8. "Radio Bible Class"   439

9. "Moody Presents"   410

10. "Questions and Answers"   380 [35]

PRINT

Within the world of print media, evangelical expansion unfolded from much the same dynamics as those in electronics; specialization and marketing expertise in popular religion turned the 1980s into a bonanza time for producers and buyers. Mastery of market needs, widespread use of advertising in a variety of other media, the careful development of celebrity authors (who were also popular on the lecture circuit and in television and radio), and improved means of retailing all contributed to the upbeat character of this field.

Nowhere did evangelicals have farther to go in their evangelizing than in strengthening the character of their book ministries. As the movement responded to the awakening of the 1960s, its outreach in books was characterized as having outdated publishing technology, writers more willing to keep alive old theological battles than explore new ground, a reluctance to face the more personal needs of readers such as self-image, sexual morality, and aging, and, finally, doctrinal studies intelligible only to experts, the knowledge elite.[36]

All this was rather quickly turned around. By the mid-1980s the Christian Booksellers Association estimated that its member stores were doing approximately $2 billion a year in retail sales, a figure that had doubled since 1980. In 1989 the figure was estimated to be $2.7 billion. That total was expected by the experts to reach $3.6 billion by 1990.[37]

There were many specific reasons explaining this growth. One specialist, David Hazard, offered the following. As religious faith embraced a more experiential dimension in the 1970s and beyond, readers purchased testimony books in greater quantities. They increased personal identification with special models or heroes such as Nicky Cruz (inner-city ministry), Joni Eareckson Tada (handicapped artist-author), B. J. Thomas (musician), or Catherine Marshall (well-known inspirationalist). This genre became a staple for publishers when Charles Colson, of Watergate scandal fame, brought out his story, *Born Again*.[38] The discovery that the secular market was purchasing such titles led independents such as Harper and Row and Doubleday to set up full-scale religious book departments also.

Then, as television, radio, and improved advertising played their parts, special topics such as "end times" found millions of buyers. The landmark book was Hal Lindsey's *The Late Great Planet Earth*, which sold nearly twenty million copies in one decade. Its end-times interpretation well matched the fears of readers about nuclear disaster. From this success came several similar "look-alike" titles.

Third, as religious faith became more privatized, and believers recoiled from the moral permissiveness of the awakening, a strong market developed for specific advice books on marriage and child rearing. Here were topics ideally suited for popular religion, nondenominational, and in harmony with the increasing number of electronic media programs on relationships. In this category several writers became national celebrities: James Dobson, Charles Swindoll, Beverly and Tim LaHaye, and Charlie Sheed. Close by were popular titles in self-help books on depression, overweight, and retirement, as well as beauty manuals, cookbooks, tips on money management, advice on improving self-esteem, and related topics.[39]

Further, the all-time best-seller, the Bible, held its place at the head of the lists, largely because of the publication of new translations aimed at evangelicals: the Good News Bible, the Jerusalem Bible, the New International Version, several new Scofield Bibles, and Good News for Modern Man. One careful observer, Randall Balmer, suggests that Bible sales by decade's end were running between $60 and $200 million annually in the United States.[40] Retail outlets such as Southwestern sent out thousands of college students during summer vacations to sell oversize family Bibles.

At times the merchandising went to extreme lengths. Bibles were brought out in a wide variety of colors, with exteriors "grained and gilded and marbled and stained and lacquered and civilized in every way conceivable." Extra-large Bibles were offered as incentives for joining the crusades of television personalities such as Rex Humbard and Jerry Falwell.[41] In a supreme example of technology coming to terms with the ageless truths of Scripture, the Bible by 1989 was available in totally computerized fashion, pocket sized, with a complete concordance and indexed counseling guides.[42]

In the late 1980s several of the leading publishing houses were caught up in the international trend of buyouts and takeovers. That had occurred in some instances because of overproduction of certain genres, such as the self-help books and books that carried a more general (some said bland) upbeat inspirational quality rather than an explicit evangelical message.[43]

Whatever the problems facing the leaders, rank-and-file evangelicals bought books in rapidly increasing numbers and at a variety of outlets. In 1984, for instance, 37 million people bought at least one Christian book; 48 percent of these purchases were made in religious bookstores. Many of the others were distributed through religious book clubs such as Guideposts, Family, Christian Herald, Christian Bookshelf, and Word Book Club, with incentives much the same as those of the Book-of-the-Month Club.

Religious magazines, usually owned by publishers, carried monthly best-seller lists, much like those of the *New York Times*. Almost every evangelical magazine also presented a variety of book reviews, some quite critical of other evangelicals. The evangelical groups more oriented to social justice such as Sojourners and the Other Side also carried full book services. In short, networking through parachurch firms in the print media was fully developed by the late 1980s; readers could easily purchase a vast assortment of books knowing largely what these contained. Specific denominations also operated book outlets. Several smaller, independent outlets, selling usually at discount prices, came into the market. The better-known ones were Christian Book Distributors of Massachusetts, Christian Book Bargains of New Jersey, and Christian Light Publications of Virginia.[44]

Much of the leadership and networking for book sales, as in the case of television, has come from the national trade group, the Christian Booksellers Association. It includes mainline firms as well, but it clearly reflects the preponderance of evangelical interests in the field. It brings out a monthly trade magazine, *Bookstore Journal*. It furnishes outlets for an enormous variety of products; it offers specific advice and workshops on the problems facing the retailer; and it has its awards of the year for the best contribution in a variety of mass-media categories.

The national convention during the 1980s has become something of an exaggerated version of popular religion moving into highly controversial exhibits. One critic at the national meeting found more things a person could eat, drink, wear, hang on the wall, or stick on one's car than one could read. Another, Mike Yaconelli, editor of *Wittenburg Door*, an evangelical magazine, called it "nothing more than a money-making flea market of Jesus Junk." There the producers and wholesalers have offered the full gamut of items identified with popular religion.[45]

In a closely related field of newspapers and magazines, the trends for evangelical growth during the 1980s were not quite as successful. Even though such giants as *Christianity Today* were able to build a dynasty in print media, other long-standing journals such as *Christian Life* and *Eternity* closed down; still others, such as *Christian Herald*, greatly cut back on size. In newspapers, although several outstanding models for relevant evangelical journalism were flourishing, such as *Twin City Christian* (Minnesota), no discernible trend developed in other regions for such sources of news and inspiration.

At least two factors contributed to this situation. Television was able to attract far larger advertising revenues than in earlier years. By the late 1980s it stood as the prime media source for most evangelicals, and advertisers knew that. Second, in journalism, as contrasted to books or electronics, the secular press offered a kind of competition evangelicals could not match, The major news magazines, such as *Time* and *Newsweek*, had well-established religion departments with respected writers such as Richard Ostling (himself an evangelical) and Kenneth Woodward. Readers could find recent developments conveniently presented there rather than look through any evangelical press for such information.[46]

Observers also noted that for the daily or weekly print media, readers were habituated to their city or regional newspaper, which at times carried news of the religious world. Along with that, of course, came general news and all the special features only a newsprint vehicle could produce: sports, crosswords, recipes, and the like. However, evangelicals often complained, with justification, that the secular press, with a few exceptions, did not understand religion in modern society and spent too much time talking about the aberrant and sensational rather than the solid news unfolding within the churches.[47]

Some of the problems emerged also from the existence of two nationwide press services, the Associated Church Press (mostly mainline) and the Evangelical Press Association. Until 1988 they had duplicate services, covering much the same developments but using their respective outlets for coverage. Few if any Evangelical Press Service items would appear in, say, the *New York Times*; nor would Associated Church Press items turn up in evangelical journals. The result was a lack of information about the two respective major divisions within American Protestantism. In 1988 the two organizations held their annual conferences jointly, taking steps to eliminate duplication and improve the quality of reporting.[48]

At the root of religious print journalism problems has been the public's penchant for considering the "news" of newspapers and magazines as being "secular" while looking for "religious" news largely from church- or parachurch-related publishers. Evangelical editors made serious attempts in the 1970s and 1980s to make religion relevant to everyday life. At the national level evangelicals watched the rapidly changing dynamics of newsprint media in the 1980s as these affected such established journals as *Eternity, Christian Life* (which merged with *Charisma*), and *Christian Herald*.

From the early 1950s the leader, with clear appeal to mainstream evangelicalism, has been *Christianity Today* of Wheaton, Illinois. Long associated with the ministry of Billy Graham, its expansion well mirrors many of the major trends within evangelicalism as a whole. Its early issues were largely scholarly in scope and language, limited to traditional "religious subjects." As various major battles within the family unfolded, such as inerrancy, *Christianity Today* took careful steps to present the news in a clear, accurate manner, while commenting vigorously for or against a cause in the editorials.

Gradually it expanded, adding regular reviews on movies, the fine arts, books, and international and national events. Its circulation increased to 173,000 for its bimonthly issues. Following the consolidation trend of the decade, its leaders brought out specialty magazines for special readerships: *Ministries Today, Christian Retailing, Today's Christian Woman, Christian History, Campus Life*, and *Leadership* (for ministers). As did several smaller, independent firms, *Christianity Today* provided inserts on topics of general interest to congregations for placement in their weekly bulletins. It established a Christianity Today Institute, made up of well-known experts in various fields who discussed and published "today's critical issues and what they mean in the context of our living faith."[49] More than any other single organization, *Christianity Today* by decade's end came to symbolize the center of mainstream evangelical ministry and outreach. Its several departments demonstrated how influential the informal networking carried out through parachurch organizations could be in evangelical ministry.

In addition, a wide range of special-interest magazines continued to appear throughout the 1980s. Some were denominational; some were associated with such parachurch groups as Campus Crusade for Christ, Inter-Varsity Fellowship, Fellowship of Christian Athletes, several independent charismatic and Pentecostal groups, Sojourners, and the Other Side. Almost every similar organization had its own print organ.

Print journals obviously served another major function, that of bringing information about various products for sale to the readers by advertising. By contrast to mainline journals, those with evangelical connections carried extensive classified sections with notices of a wide variety of goods, most of them within the domain of popular religion. Catalogs for almost every major evangelical body also came into great prominence in the 1980s. From the vast sampling of tapes, books, tracts, videos, and cassettes in the Jimmy Swaggart catalogs to the variety of devotional items and home furnishings in other catalogs, readers had the opportunity to add material items with the ease of credit cards and toll-free numbers. In several metropolitan areas evangelicals brought out Christian business directories. Modeled after the yellow pages, these listed by category of service, anything from accountants to office cleaning to youth organizations, those firms wanting to reach evangelical readers.

Another widely used device for networking and advertising was the direct-mail separate postcard-size advertisements. Those readers on evangelical mailing lists would periodically receive packets with anywhere from twenty to fifty individual cards informing them how to purchase the same kinds of items found advertised in magazine classified ads. These cards also clearly reflected the preference of their users for items expressing a popular religion preference.

In sum, through the rapid development of print media potential, evangelicals had at their disposal a huge assortment of items for the home, the spirit, and the mind for their religious outreach. Most of these avoided the sharp edges and sources of conflict among competing groups, such as Pentecostalists against fundamentalists. Partisans of those armies had available for them their own print media. Thus evangelicalism spread in print both by concentrating on mainstream participation and by acknowledging the need for specialized media for special-purpose groups.

FILM

The technological innovations of the age provided one final major media category, that of film, video, and audio. Some initial resistance by evangelicals to any form of the "movies" had to be overcome; today some participants still avoid any viewing of what they consider a morally damaging industry. By 1988, however, a major evangelical publisher, Thomas Nelson, could bring out *The Movie and Video Guide for Christian Families* in annual editions.

For most evangelicals these three media have been taken up quickly and put to use in a variety of ways. Mostly video has been used for educational purposes both in the homes and within congregations. Usually a company would engage a well-known celebrity, such as Dr. James Dobson or Dr. James Boice, to produce a series of videos on their specialties. These would be made easily accessible and provide to the congregation the services of experts not otherwise available. Dobson's series on the family, for instance, has been shown in over 50,000 churches.[50]

Conferences within a city or a geographical region on topics such as marriage enrichment would have available appropriate video lectures and discussion starters for those in attendance. Training manuals for the local leaders have been made available. Equally popular have been Bible studies, devotional guides, and the full range of religious education subjects for children. These have been made available for rent or purchase and cover such topics as financial management, fund-raising, sexual issues, and Old and New Testament personalities, among others. They are obtained usually through religious bookstores or national distributors. A good example is American Video for Church and Home from Jackson, Mississippi, which stocked a wide variety of videos on almost every conceivably relevant subject for its customers. With its toll-free number it was "Your One Stop Video Source."

The immediate advantage, besides having specialists available, was in using these videos in parish educational programs where a shortage of teachers was a chronic problem. The drawback, as with every medium, has been the distance between the medium itself and the viewer. Often videocassettes and audiocassettes were structured to allow participant interaction within the specified group.

Film ministry followed much of the same course. The major advantage of the large screen was its better adaptability for full-length stories such as films of the lives of church history giants: John Hus, John Calvin, C. S. Lewis, or John Wycliffe.

Audio had the obvious advantages of lower price, greater portability, and ease of reproduction. Audiocassettes were playable in automobiles, while jogging with a Walkman receiver, and in other places inaccessible to video or film. Evangelical firms had been among the first when audio came on the market to promote its educational potential. As was true with all other forms of mass media, audios became accepted because of their adaptability, the wide variety of subjects available, their reliance on celebrity specialists, and ease with which they could be replayed. Easily shared either by hand or through the mails, audio became in the 1980s an accepted form of networking using parachurch producers and suppliers.

CONFERENCES

Although not strictly "media" by definition, the vast array of evangelical conferences, retreats, rallies, camp meetings, and conventions came to serve a crucial need for networking within the parachurch structure. These social events can rightly be described at the conclusion of media because they have shown that they can bring together every dimension of that ministry. Conferences depend upon celebrity preachers and leaders; they make available the latest technological materials for those living out in the grass roots; they usually attempt to transcend denominational lines, bringing together people pursuing charismatic gifts or endtimes prophecy or in need of spiritual regeneration and encouraging seekers to make a decision for conversion at an altar call or to receive physical or mental healing.

Clearly the leadership of Billy Graham, starting in the 1950s, has inspired much of the confidence evangelicals share over large-scale rallies. For over thirty years he has conducted revivals in dozens of countries, as well as continuing his radio preaching. He is so widely known that once when a skeptic asked, "What is an evangelical?" the answer came back, "Someone like Billy Graham."

Rallies have succeeded largely when there has been a sufficiently clear focus on what will occur, but not too much specialization to make it seem exclusivist. Hence the great popularity ever since the 1960s of Christian rock music festivals for youth or conferences on biblical inerrancy or congregational financial management. By contrast, mainliners loyally attend meetings of their respective denomination or specific World Day of Prayer interdenominational meetings. But they have nothing like the multipurpose networks of communication available to evangelicals of all varieties.

The record we call history unfortunately can never do full justice to so complex a topic as evangelical ministry. The most measurable way to analyze it is to see who made the most money, who had the most viewers or listeners, or some other such quantitative measurement. These unquestionably are highly important, but they come up short, as all scholarship does, when the question is raised: What really occurred when the evangelicals moved into the center of American religious life during this decade? Perhaps by the time the final section of Part II is completed, we can better answer that central question.

NOTES

1. James Davison Hunter, "American Protestantism: Sorting Out the Present; Looking toward the Future," *This World*, no. 17 (Spring 1987): 67, 76.

2. See Nicholas Abercrombie et al., eds., *The Penguin Dictionary of Sociology* (New York: Penguin Books, 1984), p. 143.

3. See the discussion in Carol Flake, *Redemptorama: Culture, Politics, and the New Evangelicalism* (Garden City, N.Y.: Anchor Press, Doubleday and Co., 1984); Virginia Stem Owens, *The Total Image: or, Selling Jesus in the Modern Age* (Grand Rapids, Mich.: Wm. B. Eerdmans, 1980); Neil Postman, quoted in Erling Jorstad, *The New Christian Right, 1981–1988* (New York: Edwin Mellen Press, 1987), pp. 95–96.

4. Mel White, "The Electric Family," a "Special Advertising Section" in *Christianity Today*, April 19, 1985, p. 2; Terry Shepp, "The Media Generation," *Christian Life*, January 1986, pp. 34–36.

5. Samuel Hill, "The Shape and Shapes of Popular Southern Piety," in D. E. Harrell, ed., *Varieties of Southern Evangelicalism* (Macon, Ga.: Mercer University Press, 1981), p. 95.

6. Peter W. Williams, *Popular Religion in America: Symbolic Change and the Modernization Process in Historical Perspective*, 2d ed. (Urbana: University of Illinois Press, 1989), p. xiii.

7. Russell B. Nye, "Notes on a Rationale for Popular Culture," in C. D. Geist, ed., *The Popular Culture Reader*, 3d ed. (Bowling Green, Ohio: Bowling Green University Popular Press, 1983), pp. 24–25.

8. Robert C. Ellwood, *The History and Future of Faith: Religion Past, Present, and to Come* (New York: Crossroad, 1988), p. 123; see generally pp. 118–50.

9. Ibid., pp. 134–35.

10. News item, *Christian World Report*, June 1989, p. 8; Randall Balmer, *Mine Eyes Have Seen the Glory: A Journey into the Evangelical Subculture in America* (New York: Oxford University Press, 1989), pp. 230–31.

11. Robert Wuthnow, "The Social Significance of Religious Television," *Review of Religious Research* 29, 2 (December 1987): 134–35.

12. Peter G. Horsfield, *Religious Television: The American Experience* (New York: Longman, 1984), pp. 15–25; Richard Ostling, "Evangelical Publishing and Broadcasting," in George Marsden, ed., *Evangelicalism and Modern America* (Grand Rapids, Mich.: Wm. B. Eerdmans, 1984), pp. 51–52.

13. Horsfield, *Religious Television*, pp. 25–27.

14. *Los Angeles Times*, April 8, 1989, sec. 2, pp. 6–7; *National and International Religion Report*, May 22, 1989, p. 5; ibid., October 9, 1989, p. 5; *Washington Post*, September 17, 1988, p. B6; *Lutheran*, September 7, 1988, p. 27.

15. Razelle Frankl, *Televangelism: The Marketing of Popular Religion* (Carbondale: Southern Illinois University Press, 1987), pp. 79–90.

16. *National and International Religion Report*, January 16, 1989, p. 5; *Los Angeles Times*, February 4, 1989, sec. 2, p. 6; Quentin J. Schultze, "The Mythos of the Electronic Church," *Critical Studies in Mass Communication*, April 1987, pp. 245–61; Dan Nichols, "The Quiet Revolution in Christian Broadcasting," *Religious Broadcasting*, February 1987, pp. 20ff.

17. *Wall Street Journal*, May 18, 1987, p. 6.

18. John M. Cummuta, "Media as a Strategy," *Religious Broadcasting*, February 1987, p. 17; Bruce H. Joffe, "Junk Mail for Jesus," *Charisma*, November 1982, pp. 21–25; Perry C. Cotham, "The Electronic Church," in Allene Stuart Phy, ed., *The Bible and Popular Culture in America* (Philadelphia: Fortress Press, 1985), pp. 104–35.

19. Bruce H. Joffe, "The Ethics of Fundraising," *Religious Broadcasting*, November 1987, pp. 22–24.

20. *Time*, July 13, 1987, p. 55; *U.S. News and World Report*, March 23, 1987, p. 10; news item, *Charisma*, March 1987, pp. 71–72.

21. A Broadway play written by Tim Robbins and Adam Simon, "Carnage: A Comedy," used much the same themes; *New York Times*, September 9, 1989, p. 15; ibid., March 15, 1989, p. 20; *National Christian Reporter*, April 7, 1989, p. 4; *New Yorker*, March 7, 1988, pp. 84–87, *Harper's*, April 1989, pp. 47–56; *USA Today*, February 18, p. 3D (newspaper).

22. Editorial, *Religious Broadcasting*, December 1987, pp. 10–11.

23. Thomas Oden, "Full Disclosure," *Christianity Today*, April 18, 1988, p. 41.

24. *National Christian Reporter*, February 10, 1989, p. 3; *World*, February 11, 1989, p. 2B.

25. *Christian Century*, April 12, 1989, p. 375; *Christianity Today*, March 3, 1989, pp. 44–45; see the critical survey of religious television, ibid., March 18, 1989, pp. 28–45.

26. *Los Angeles Times*, January 31, 1987, sec. 2, pp. 4ff.; *National and International Religion Report*, January 16, 1989, p. 5; Larry Martz, *Ministry of Greed: The Inside Story of the Televangelists and Their Holy Wars* (New York: Weidenfeld and Nicolson, 1988), p. 42.

27. Charles E. Swann, "U.S. Radio Returns to the Community," *Media Development*, January 1984, pp. 40–42; *Religion Watch*, March 1989, p. 8.

28. Bob Augsburg, "Format Variety on Today's Christian Radio," *Religious Broadcasting*, September 1988, pp. 38–39.

29. Gary Crossland, "The Changing Face of Christian Radio," *Religious Broadcasting*, September 1988, pp. 12–13; idem, "How Do Various Christian Formats Compare?" ibid., November 1988, pp. 10–11.

30. Crossland, "How Do Various Christian Formats Compare?" pp. 10–11.

31. See *Religious Broadcasting*, November 1985, p. 21; ibid., July/August 1989, p. 8.

32. See KVOI's *Good News* monthly magazine; *Religious Broadcasting*, September 1987, p. 44.

33. Gary Crossland, "Where Christian Radio Excels," *Religious Broadcasting*, June 1986, p. 18.

34. *Religious Broadcasting*, April 1989, p. 44.

35. Ibid., May 1988, pp. 14, 20.

36. Summary by Walter A. Elwell, *Christianity Today*, July 17, 1981, pp. 973–74.

37. Balmer, *Mine Eyes Have Seen the Glory*, p. 159–61; news story, *Publishers Weekly*, August 18, 1989, p. 15.

38. David Hazard, "Decatrends in Christian Publishing," *Charisma*, August 1985, pp. 135–38.

39. Ibid., pp. 138–42.

40. Balmer, *Mine Eyes Have Seen the Glory*, p. 159.

41. Wayne Elzey, "Popular Culture," in Charles H. Lippy and Peter W. Williams, *Encyclopedia of the American Religious Experience*, Vol. 3 (New York: Scribner, 1988), pp. 1730–31.

42. *Christian Retailing*, December 15, 1988, pp. 1, 10; also see the periodical, *Christian Educational Computing* (Grand Rapids, Mich.).

43. Will Nixon, "Fleming Revell: A New Thrust," *Publishers Weekly*, March 4, 1988, pp. 42–45; "News," *Christianity Today*, December 12, 1986, pp. 60–62.

44. *Newsweek*, August 5, 1985, pp. 85–86; a list of all religious book clubs is in *Publishers Weekly*, March 4, 1989, n.p.; see their catalogs, and the comment in Williams, *Popular Religion in America*, p. 193.

45. *Eternity*. September 1985, p. 66; *Christian Century*, October 30, 1985, pp. 967–68; the annual reports in *Publishers Weekly*, 1981–1989; Balmer, "Bible Bazaar," in *Mine Eyes Have Seen the Glory*, pp. 155–70. *The Wittenburg Door* is now titled *The Door*.

46. See the interview by Judith Weidman of Richard Ostling in a two-part story, "Interview," *National Christian Reporter*, November 28, 1986, p. 4, and ibid., December 5, 1986, p. 4. *Wittenburg Door*, no. 61 (June/July 1981): 33–36.

47. Lisa Livingston, "Evangelicals and the Press: Are We Treated Unfairly?" *Moody Monthly*, November 1983, pp. 74, 76; *Christianity Today*, June 26, 1989, p. 58; Bill McKibben, "Why Journalists Can't Write about Religion," *Washington Monthly*, June 1988, pp. 53–56.

48. Mark Noll, "Learning the Language of Heaven," *Reformed Journal*, June 1988, pp. 14–19; a complete list of journals is in both Constant Jacquet, ed., *Yearbook of American and Canadian Churches* (annually), and the Evangelical Press Association "Membership Directory," Overland Park, Kans.

49. "Statement of Purpose," *Christianity Today*, June 13, 1986, p. 2.I.

50. See *Christian Retailing*, May 15, 1989, p. 13; *Christian Life*, March 1986, pp. 50ff.

8

Popular Religion: An Evangelical Response

The all-pervasive power of the mass media in the 1980s to reshape evangelicalism emerged within the framework of a clearly established, widely accepted set of values about the ways in which Christians should carry out their daily lives. What evangelicals achieved in these years was a vast amplification and strengthening of the leading elements of popular religion. This expression would become highly conscious of itself, especially when it was under criticism from secularists and skeptical mainliners.

Popular religion deepened its influence within several areas of daily life, too many to explore in depth here. What we do study is its intertwining with secularization, modernity, and privatization as these helped reassembled evangelical values in business, work, and attitudes toward wealth; in their involvement in sports, leisure time, and recreation; in the arts and literature; and, finally, in contemporary Christian music.

One caveat must be entered. No rigid line here separates mainliners and evangelicals. Overlap and duplication of taste and life-style preferences abound. What makes the distinction between these two groups viable is that as we have defined them, evangelicals are generally far more conscious of how they believe God works in all activities of their everyday lives; hence every part of that life, including popular culture, aims toward expressing that faith.[1]

That very relevance created a major conflict. What the American capitalist, consumer culture glorified and rewarded was, of course, maximization of profit; growth, expansion, development, and progress were measured largely in materialist terms. Hence those televangelists or radio celebrities with the largest markets and viewerships could not help but be judged to be the "best." To keep their messages alive, they needed to carry out aggressive fund-raising programs. Critics made that point in various ways during the decade. Martin E. Marty wrote, "The message is clear: come to Jesus for abundant worldly living, for success and substance more than the cross or meaning, for beauty queen cosmetics and apparel and athletes' devotion to measured self-preoccupation." Billy Graham expressed great concern over the growth of evangelicalism in this era because it showed signs of undue pride, of relying on "worldly and carnal methods" to continue growing, to perpetuate old organizations, and to "become complacent." Charles Colson told the NAE and National Religious Broadcasters that "much of the Christianity we sickly market today is nothing but a religious adaptation of the self-seeking values of secular culture."[2]

Underlying these indictments was the age-old dilemma of the extent to which believers should adapt to secular norms. One subculture within evangelicalism, known as the "simple life movement," stayed clear of choosing materialistic success as a test of virtue. This movement consisted of the separated communities of the Anabaptist tradition and its supporters in the larger society who focused on reduced consumption in clothes, housing, transportation, and entertainment. Their goal was to live free from undue care for or dependence on the material standards of the secular world.[3]

For rank-and-file evangelicals the dilemma was in deciding where any kind of satisfactory middle ground might be found. Jesus's teachings against the seductions of wealth seemed convincing enough; but austerity, even poverty, seemed a poor way to use the gifts believers had been given for abundant living. Were not believers told to "turn two talents into four, five talents into ten?"[4] Robert C. Ellwood, in examining popular religion in the 1980s, noted that few people believed "in the consistent renunciation of material or technological goods. The way of life of traditional ascetics or 'plain people' is seldom appreciated. . . . More likely wealth will be justified by church people, as it always has been, as enabling the church better to glorify God and do good in the world."[5]

The dilemma, however, involved more complexity than a simple acceptance or rejection of capitalist market values. At stake during all of evangelical life have been the implications of the work ethic. Evangelical special-purpose groups such as the Christian Ministries Management Association and Christian Financial Concepts Newsletters recognized the pitfalls of encouraging hard, disciplined work as a way of glorifying God; such encouragement could lead to neglect of one's responsibility in sharing one's earned wealth.

Yet not working up to one's full capacity posed serious problems also. Being successful as a leader meant creating more employment, providing more economic security, and providing improved educational opportunities for one's family. Yet to achieve that, the businessperson would need a great deal of inner ambition, a quality that often turned into selfishness.[6]

Throughout the 1980s evangelicals, like many Americans, wrestled with the temptations of a prospering economy, an abundance of luxury goods, and a plethora of technological wonders. The Republican party won support largely because it could provide such opportunities. Yet throughout the decade the doubts continued over whether full consumption of such goods was really the will of God. The prosperity, health/wealth preachers had their followings, to be sure, but by 1990 neither they nor those evangelicals sharply critical of capitalist values had attracted any sizeable new following.[7]

In a closely related field, the marketing of religious merchandise, both the forces of capitalism and the traits of popular religion came into view. With the vast improvement of means of reproducing great amount of materials at low cost and moving them easily to markets, evangelicals were given greater opportunity in this decade than before to purchase items expressive of their particular religious preferences. Starting actually in the 1970s, the Jesus movement caught the country by great surprise. Introducing "Christian pop culture" to the public, it embraced rock musicals, Jesus newspapers, distinctive clothes, jewelry, hairstyles, furniture, vehicles, and living accommodations.

The movement joined together teenagers and young adults looking for ways to use fundamentalist religion to deal with drugs or a sense of alienation from the straight society. They freely created their own artifacts, celebrating the gusto and freedom of the movement's merchandise. Jesus-movement goods became an instant fad across the country. Whereas religious bookstores had once stocked mainly books, plus a few other items, they became in the 1980s major outlets for an enormous variety of religious paraphernalia. Where mail-order catalog houses had once been largely the domain of the Sears, Roebuck type of entrepreneurs, in the 1980s hundreds of small firms with computers, toll-free numbers, and sophisticated marketing techniques launched a variety of both specialized and general distribution programs. Some Christian merchandise shopping malls also were built.

At this point the popular religion dimension came into view. Given their preference for the familiar and traditional, evangelicals started purchasing great amounts of religious material artifacts. Most of these were low priced, mass produced, easily identified, and aimed at witnessing to the secular world.[8] By 1989 the best estimates showed that this had become a nearly $3-billion-a-year business. That in itself raised some critical eyebrows among evangelicals.

More controversial and highly divisive was another issue: was this merely, as critics said, "Jesus junk," trivializing and secularizing the richness and depth of the Christian faith? Was it an escape from the secularized culture by moving "within a ghettoized Christian subculture . . . that offered a measure of insulation from the 'non-Christian' world?" Or was it a legitimate expression of popular taste, what its consumers wanted as their material expression of their convictions? Critics noted that by decade's end "almost anything is sacred": sweatshirts, kitchen sponges (with slogans "Keep afloat with Jesus"), fortune cookies with Bible verses inside, "Heaven Fresh" automobile deodorizer, and a beercan-shaped can retitled "Bewiser, King of Kings." One firm offered "an actual piece of the wall of the manger." A Texas firm offered "Christian clothier's shirts" with the cross and the ichthys (fish) symbol to fit the buyer's "active Christian life-style." Using the Banana Republic catalog as a model, Dunamis ("the Greek word for Power") offered in 1988 various clothing items.[9]

Such developments, while easy to exaggerate or satirize, did reflect deep divisions within the evangelical community. What unfolded in the 1980s was, of course, only an intensification of what had been a source of cleavage throughout the centuries of Christendom: the "great tradition" of the seminaries, cathedrals, and knowledge elites contesting with the "little tradition" of the everyday lives of ordinary people. Some observers saw the proliferation of artifacts as more evidence of secularization and accommodation to the lower cultural denominator. The debate and the increasing amount of merchandise showed no signs of abating by 1990.

SPORTS

Parallel to and often overlapping with popular religious expression in artifacts was the huge expansion of evangelical interest in organized athletics during the 1980s. Here, as elsewhere, evangelicalism's parachurch structure gave it opportunities to promote programs and bring together participants and fans not open to those working within denominational boundaries. In athletics, also, the values of evangelicalism were subject to sharp challenge and vigorous disputation among both leaders and participants. The full gamut of concerns of the 1980s came into play here: the adaptation of secular values, frequent uncritical acceptance of economic profits, inculcation of worldly attitudes such as winning at any price, the use of violence, and similar issues. Here we seek to outline the major contours of the debate over athletic values, summarize the pros and cons of evangelical commentary, describe the evangelical sports programs, and probe the issues of celebrity worship.

It has been well said that the United States, much like the rest of the world in the 1980s, went sports mad for athletic competition at every level, with billions of dollars annually being invested, and with politics, education, family life, and religion being among the most obvious institutions directly affected by the outburst. From its earliest expression, evangelicalism found reason to be both supportive and wary of involvement, wary because of the violence, the undue emphasis on winning, the distractions from more religious matters, and the association with less desirable characters, but favorable because at its best, organized athletics had great potential for strengthening desirable character traits such as self-discipline, team cooperation, and leadership. Billy Graham stated, "There are probably more really committed Christians in sports both collegiate and professional, than in any other occupation in America."[10] Sports offered opportunities for the participants to witness publicly, often before huge audiences, as in the case of Gary Gaetti of the Minnesota Twins, who in the All-Star Game in 1989 held up during the introductions his gloved hand, on which was printed "Jesus is Lord."

Athletes were seen as important role models, exhibiting the kind of qualities of character parents and teachers wanted to inculcate in their children. Americans generally believed that athletes were good role models; a major poll showed that 58 percent of respondents thought that big-name athletes had "a greater responsibility than the average citizen" to be a good citizen off the field.[11]

During the 1980s, especially when news of drug usage, gambling, fiscal irregularities, and undesirable social behavior among both professional and collegiate athletes became known, many evangelicals reconsidered their earlier enthusiasms. For all of the attempts during the awakening of the 1960s to replace competition with community in America, the former clearly had regained primacy by the 1980s. Yet, it was asked, what of the stress and sense of personal failure for those who lost? What of the temptations to use even a small amount of drugs such as steroids to help performance?[12]

Christianity Today provided a summary of the issue. Sports competition, first, accented winning, while Christianity "often stresses the importance of losing" ("the first shall be last"). Christianity emphasizes the need for purity of behavior, of self-abnegation. Competition encourages much the opposite conduct. Winning promotes the "spirit of self-promotion," which has little support in New Testament ethics. All this made competition for evangelical athletes extremely difficult.

As a response to the kinds of problems they faced, athletes developed what came to be called "total release performance" (TRP). It exalts intensity as the highest value, the kind of intensity that Jesus had. In competition "TRP" often is shouted by evangelical athletes in the spirit of others joyfully saying "Praise the Lord."[13]

Given the highly complex and often contradictory sets of moral values at work, evangelical athletes were admonished to accept such ambiguity, to glorify God in all that they do, and to work closely with their colleagues to do their best. That endeavor was made simpler by the appearance in the 1970s, with expansion in the next decade, of several parachurch organizations to help those determined to be both athletic and evangelical. One of the first, Athletes in Action (AIA), came out of Campus Crusade for Christ, a major pioneer parachurch ministry. Its founder, Dr. Bill Bright, had great enthusiasm for collegiate sports and established the organization to provide a means of witness and discipleship training. It evolved largely into organized teams of professional touring athletes, especially in basketball, wrestling, cross-country, track, and gymnastics, with a total staff of some 300. Its members presented witnessing speeches for civic clubs, church groups, assemblies, and youth groups. It operated some twenty sports camps for youth. A highlight for basketball came in 1986 when the AIA team defeated an all-star Russian group. That same year the American team explained their message to over 100,000 fans and received 780 individuals as converts to their born-again faith.[14] A smaller group with similar aims has been Pro Athletes Outreach, with a ministry of sponsoring Christian professional athletes.[15]

In the collegiate world, the Fellowship of Christian Athletes became a major voice for evangelical interests. Founded in 1954, by 1988 it had a staff of 175 and membership of 30,000, largely on American campuses. It has sponsored rallies, retreats, conferences, programs for high schoolers, coaches' meetings, athletic clinics, and school assemblies. It had no involvement in organized professional athletics.[16] Since 1977 a related group, Sports World Ministries, has entered the evangelical ministry. It has featured former professional athletes with a "message of deliverance from substance abuse through fundamentalist Christianity." Its speakers aimed largely at high-school audiences. Its staff by 1988 included twenty-five employees.[17]

Smaller programs within the athletic world have been SCORE International, which helps high-school athletes find a suitable Christian college and sponsors summer all-star trips overseas and summer camps and clinics for coaches to develop "strong spiritual leadership through sports."[18] Finally, the newly created World Congress on Sports offers a related ministry of coordinating efforts among local churches, denominational bodies, and parachurch groups to promote worldwide evangelism. It centers largely on education, networking of ideas, coordination of existing programs, and fellowship. It had an active ministry at the Olympic Games in Korea in 1988.[19]

On campuses, especially at the well-known Oral Roberts University and Liberty University (of which Jerry Falwell is president), organized athletics maintained a very high profile. Oral Roberts University attempted to make its way into the highly competitive NCAA Division I but found that the expenses were too high. Falwell consistently endorsed the athletes, giving prominent coverage in the *Fundamentalist Journal* to winners in collegiate competition.[20]

A central feature of evangelical popular religion centers on the use of celebrity role models as examples of righteous living. Although often criticized for being superficial or idolizing, evangelical publicity continues to give major attention to stars, including those with outstanding accomplishment records who give personal witness and testimony to a variety of audiences. Among the best known (in no particular order of importance) have been "Dr. J," Julius Erving of pro basketball, with a television program on ESPN, the late Pete Maravich, golfer Kathy Baker, baseball stars Sid Bream, Scott McGreggor, Orel Hershiser, Alvin Davis, and Al Worthington, football players such as Roosevelt Grier and Mark Mosley and coaches Joe Gibbs and Tom Landry, soccer celebrity Kyle Rote, and boxer George Foreman.[21] In the late 1980s a magazine named *Second Look*, for "athletes whose first priority is serving Christ, not winning world championships," started publication.[22] Bookstores have video programs available on these themes, as does the National Christian Network, a religious satellite network.

THE ARTS

Evangelicals in the world of the arts faced somewhat the same problem as athletes: how to witness and win conversions through a structure that has so thoroughly reflected secular values. The arts, however, presented a different dimension because the standards of excellence for centuries have exalted high culture: opera, classical music, profound and intricate fiction, including poetry and novels, and highly reflective, often abstract visual art. Evangelicals had faced this issue before the 1980s, as is outlined clearly in the writings of noted educator Frank Gaebelein and much of the Arts section of *Eternity* magazine. He and other like-minded evangelical aesthetes had attempted to infuse high culture into the much more prevalent expressions of popular religion in the arts. By decade's end it seemed that no major concessions had been made on either side.[23]

The issue emerged out of the question over whether the arts were in essence "humanistic" rather than sacred, or whether the arts should be totally and explicitly religious rather than point in earthen vessels to higher truths. Evangelical aestheticians have conceded that much of the explicitly Christian in the arts is at best mediocre but have argued that it need not remain that way. Theologian Carl F. H. Henry frequently called for a "great Christian novel" that would parallel the work of a Dostoyevsky or other nonevangelical giants.[24]

However, high aesthetic tastes were not simply inborn or easily acquired, even for those who might want to move beyond popular standards. Most fine-arts appreciation required a "trained capacity, a nurturing in a favorable social context, and a willingness to make critical judgments against inferior expression. By contrast, evangelicals see cultural expression as they do all of life, in its effectiveness in presenting a witness to the world. Art that does not do that falls short of their expectations.[25] Evangelical Jon Alexander stated the issue clearly:

Perhaps the greatest tragedy of the fundamentalist capitulation to accuracy [inerrant literalism] is that it lost for fundamentalists the power and beauty of stories and poetry. Since such things do not fit on a true or false test, fundamentalists lost interest in them. So whereas Jesus told parables, fundamentalists write systematic theology. Whereas Jesus talked of the birds of the air and the flowers of the field, fundamentalists talk of premillenialism and infralapsarianism.[26]

Despite good intentions, evangelicals have been indicted by fellow believers as failing to recognize the goodness of the arts. When Christian arts attempted to overcome this criticism, they ignored any Christian aesthetic and instead borrowed from art forms largely revolving around popular religion.[27]

Strong as the indictment has been, evangelical arts in several mediums have attempted to combine both witnessing and high cultural taste. During the 1980s this unfolded in the romantic novel, the visual arts, drama, poetry, and dance. Closely parallel to the huge market for secular writers in this form (such as Harlequin and Candlelight), evangelical presses produced Cherish Books (Thomas Nelson), Rhapsody Romances (Harvest House), Evensong Romances (Fleming Revell, later dropped), and others. Advocates claimed that evangelical women wanted to read about other people like themselves, holding the same values and ideals. Critics stated that evangelical Christianity could not produce quality literature.

Unquestionably the most popular best-selling author has been Janette Oke, who consistently ranked at the head of the best-seller lists. Acknowledged as the master of this genre, she used small-town settings, usually in the last half-century, with strong males and patient females working their way faithfully through a maze of earthly problems. Other best-selling authors, almost all using the same general format, were George MacDonald, Noreen Riols, Judith Pella, Marian Wells, Linda Heering, and Eugenia Price.[28]

Opportunities in the visual arts presented a closely allied kind of situation. Since all of life should be lived to glorify God, then, evangelicals argued, should not paintings, sculptures and other objects of art be explicit versions of traditional religious subjects? When one observes the visual arts for sale on religious television, however, she or he would conclude that the traditional view is the reigning standard among evangelicals. Some acceptance of more abstract form developed with the sculpture of Esther K. Ausburger, an acclaimed artist with explicit if muted religious symbolism.[29]

Virtually all of the leading evangelical journals carried regular arts reviews sections. The writers presented thoughtful essays attempting to carry readers beyond the popular and familiar and into new insights on both traditional painters and such contemporaries as Picasso, Mondrian, Georgia O'Keeffe, Andrew Wyeth, and Lucian Freud. Evangelical college art departments conducted summer workshops along with diversified art-major programs for their students. On the popular level, the more familiar and traditional works with explicit religious symbolism continued to fill the advertising pages of the catalogs.

A similar attempt to upgrade evangelical sensibilities about the masterpieces of literature came into prominence during these years. Readers were presented with challenging reinterpretations of such authors as Nathaniel Hawthorne, Mark Twain, Fyodor Dostoyevsky, Aleksandr Solzhenitsyn, and current writers Carl Sagan and John Updike.[30]

Along with such arts criticism, these journals gradually added to both the quality and quantity of film reviews during the 1980s. Some reviews aimed directly at helping parents or other adults know what to expect, that is, what was nonevangelical, about some films. Others reviewed movies of general cultural interest without referring explicitly to older evangelical norms. These included *Tucker, Reds, Full Metal Jacket, Ragtime* and *Agnes of God* as exemplary of this trend.[31]

In drama and the theatre evangelicals again were caught between the more academic-related critics urging them both to participate more fully in the secular world and to create their own, yet remain true to their mission to evangelize society and those who denounced the theatre. The theatre had, of course, for centuries been off limits to conservatives for its often bawdy, antireligious themes coupled with drinking and carousing. Supporters, however, pointed out that the Bible was replete with written stories, vivid pictures, and acted-out illustrations of timeless truths. If Christians failed to become involved in this medium, it would go totally by default to the secularists. Facing uphill problems such as budget, lack of managerial skills, and high production costs, some evangelical and mainline theatrical groups would stage modestly produced but sensitive dramatic productions. Some professional groups such as Artists in Christian Testimony and Christians in Visual Arts met periodically to exchange ideas, create newsletters, and keep network channels alive.[32]

Perhaps finding even more difficulty in overcoming the older resistance patterns were the evangelical artists in dance companies. Even conceding that the Old Testament did seem to approve of some kinds of dance, contemporary evangelicals believed that dancing simply was too sexual in nature and had no place in any church "with standards of righteousness."[33] But starting in 1984 out of Washington, D.C., dancers created the Christian Performing Artists' Fellowship to present the faith in that form. Their numbers included mainliners as well. Within charismatic circles religious dance was rather widely accepted as a form of worship. Some of it was spontaneous during services, and other expressions appeared in structured dance performances.[34]

MUSIC

Among the several highly emotional and angrily debated issues among evangelicals about expressing faith in a secular society, none attracted more intensity and deep feeling than that over contemporary music, especially "Christian rock." The power of music is something not easily described, nor are taste preferences in it easily changed. Hence when the kind of music that emerged out of the awakening of the 1960s found its way into evangelical circles, complete with the paraphernalia of loud amplification, flower-children-style clothes, and exuberant young adult and teen rock concerts, all in the name of religious faith, nothing but hard-core resistance and negative responses would be forthcoming from the holders fast.

In one sense, every major issue facing evangelicals during the 1980s showed up in the battle over music. The high technology so vital to modern rock music was audibly distinctive in Christian rock. Certainly many of the themes expressed by the artists were at best "secular" and often hostile to traditional morality. Finally, with the use of such new items as Walkman headsets, the opportunity to privatize the messages of the musicians was made abundantly possible for listeners. No one was arguing that Christian rock was anything higher aesthetically than one form of popular religion.

Here the work of the historian has been greatly helped by the pioneering, yet still-definitive history of Christian rock, Carol Flake's *Redemptorama*. What follows is only a brief summary of the story before her conclusion in the mid-1980s, and then a look at the issues as they developed after that. One of the permanent contributions of the Jesus movement in the 1960s was its own kind of music: informal, repeatable, loud, reaching for scriptural themes, and like nothing much ever heard before. Quickly the mass festivals for song and praise caught on, becoming in fact highly stylized in their expectations and formats. The primary emotions were enthusiasm for the goodness of God, exhilaration over being able to respond, and gratitude that this kind of music was theirs—a new cultural artifact.

At the center was Jesus, the revolutionary, the man wanted by the officials for teaching love and forgiveness, for associating with the poor, for overthrowing the old: "A new commandment I give unto you." Jesus was taken out of the nineteenth-century sentimentality genres and made a folk hero; in the words of the founder of Christian rock, Larry Norman; "Wowie, zowie, He saved my soul!" This can be interpreted to suggest that Jesus shared the life-style of youth, living communally, nomadically, and in poverty. He spoke the common idiom, rejecting materialism, and focused on personal relationships, a prototype of what adolescents thought they stood for.[35]

As the counterculture awakening unfolded, aided greatly by heavy television exposure and high-tech duplication of songs, the genre known as Christian rock gradually took a more definable form. As the hippie/free-love/drugs-for-all persona faded away in the 1970s, the music continued to exude enthusiasm, freedom, and adaptability. Evangelical choir directors, for instance, found little or no interest by the younger members in singing the old hymns; what was new was what new firms such as Maranatha! Music (originally out of Calvary Chapel, Costa Mesa, California) created by joining simple melodies to words of the Bible.[36] Similar groups such as the Fisherfolk and Integrity's Hosanna's Music contributed more of the same with enough individuality to keep their identities clear.

But the momentum for a trend of seismic dimensions among evangelical youth and young people was by the mid-1970s well under way. By 1981 contemporary gospel music was a market of nearly $100 million a year. Two years later it totaled some 5 percent of the entire market for tapes and records, compared to 4 percent for classical music and 2 percent for jazz.[37] It was attracting its own radio stations, its own magazines (especially *Contemporary Christian Music [CCM]*, and a great deal of national controversy.

Few evangelicals or other music commentators debated over the other newer forms of popular religious music: southern gospel, middle-of-the-road adult contemporary, or lite. What brought on the dispute was whether Christian rock was in fact the work of the devil or a comparable source of disaster. Were its beat, it syncopation, and its lyrics (when they could be heard and understood) actually stimulating the aficionados to rebel, to overthrow existing moral standards, and to explore the subterranean world of something like satanism?[38] Critics could not prove such charges beyond a reasonable doubt, but some insisted that Christian rock was simply too close to secular rock to be authentically religious. The profits made by the artists and record companies were too tempting to resist, the market too gullible and uninformed to know what was true gospel music.[39]

By the mid-1980s, as was true with televangelists and sports figures, Christian rock had developed its own star system of celebrities, each offering her or his own distinctive music. This satisfied the wide variety of younger customers who could become loyal fans to this or that artist, but it meant, to critics, that in the name of Christian music, bands were playing heavy metal, dance-rock, new wave, power-pop, even hardcore punk. It was simply a very big, profitable business.[40]

Leading the so-called *CCM* all-star list were superstars Amy Grant and Sandi Patti, selling well into the millions of albums annually. The statistics showed that by 1985 the four largest record companies had 300 artists under contract; they were earning some $86.5 million a year, up from $74 million a year before; 20 percent of their music was sold in mainstream record stores. To critics this was too much. The editor of *CCM* wrote, ''Amy Grant is making a lot of money, but so are Christian doctors and lawyers. If you sow spiritually, you should reap materially.''[41]

Criticism developed also of "crossing over," the trend of the famous Christian rock stars who started to use more secular lyrics and musical gimmicks to attract the secular crowd. The charge was made that one could not be both a Christian artist and at the same time a crossover success in the secular world. To this, evangelist Jimmy Swaggart preached that the music itself as well as the lyrics were simply evil. No good could come out of the heavy emphasis on love, attraction, sexuality, or most of the other themes utilized by the artists.[42]

Networking similar to that of the print media also helped carry Christian rock into the grass roots. Record clubs sprang up, offering the opportunity to purchase releases of favorite stars. The record companies also added compact discs to their long-playing and tape versions. Videos of the leading artists appeared at about the same time those for educators and parish leaders found their way to the markets.

By 1989, with fan support built up by a reward system much like the Academy Awards, Christian rock was dominated by these figures: female vocalists Sandi Patti, Amy Grant, Twila Paris, and Margaret Becker; male vocalists Carman, Michael W. Smith, Steve Green, Russ Taff, and Larnelle Harris; Christian groups Petra, Second Chapter of Acts, Mylon and Broken Heart, First Hall, and Stryper; and instrumentalists Steve Taylor, Phil Driscoll, Dino, Phil Keaggy, Michael W. Smith, and John Michael Talbot.[43]

By now Christian rock had simply taken such deep root that it had become virtually institutionalized. The evangelical Calvin College established a panel of specialists to study for a year "Youth, Electronic Media, and Popular Art." Christian music magazines and journals such as *Twin City Christian* provided networking opportunities for artists to advertise for work; the markets were abundant and reached every part of the country.

Yet the angry debates continued. Grant was frequently chided for seemingly trying to attract both the secularists and the people of faith. Her stage appearance, the "hard-edged rock" tone of new albums, and the newsiness all seemed somehow wrong. One of her songs had been used on the television program "Miami Vice," where violence and drug use seemed appropriate. In an interview with *Rolling Stone* she admitted to a skinny dip; and some of her leopard-patterned jackets seemed overly suggestive to some critics.[44] To other observers she appeared as a "vibrant modern woman and clean-living Christian. And she is neither commanding nor 'humble'. She doesn't woo the audience, nor sell to them. She just shares."[45]

Far more controversial was the hard-metal religious rock group, Stryper. Their driving music, spectacular stage outfits, and unique blend of Christianity and secular themes even attracted coverage on "CBS Evening News" with Dan Rather. Their appearance and sound led many to identify them with the more blatant glorification of the occult, sexuality, and permissiveness of other heavy-metal groups. Most of that music stood out because of its screeching lead guitars, throat-straining vocals, and throbbing power chords. But Stryper insisted, "Look, we're a rock band that sings about Jesus Christ. Call us metal missionaries or rock disciples, not a religious band. We can't sell our message, even if it's something as wonderful as the Lord's word, without being a good rock 'n roll band.''[46]

Critics were quick to make their case. Groups such as Stryper became targets for evangelical ministers such as Dave Benoit, who presented seminars on ''Occultic Tendencies in Rock Music'' and ''Violence in Rock Music'' to conservative church youth and adult audiences. The Assemblies of God at its national convention formally singled out Stryper for performances contradictory to the spirit for which the Pentecostal movement stood. ''They dress like devils and wear Spandex costumes. . . their performance contradicted everything the Gospel stands for.'' Jimmy Swaggart continued his vigorous charge that rock music simply was the ''music of Satan.''[47]

Yet Stryper and its imitators continued to attract large crowds over the next years. The Jesus-movement program out of Chicago, Cornerstone, promoted Christian rock festivals that glorified ''heavenly metal'' and ''Godarchy, not anarchy.'' Its own heavy-metal group, REZ (for ''resurrection''), found its following and continued to attract young audiences.[48]

By 1990 neither side showed indications of compromise with the other. What clearly had occurred, for the majority of evangelicals, was the widespread acceptance of contemporary worship songs both for congregations and for radio and video audiences. These songs, mostly middle-of-the-road, contained simple, attractive tunes that closely paralleled much contemporary folk-song music. The music gave audiences a sense of identifying with the age-old verities of the Christian faith but in an up-to-date, with-it informality. Among the most prominent artists here have been John Michael Talbot, Phil Driscoll, Steve Taylor, and Second Chapter of Acts.[49]

Within this ten-year period evangelicals reached positions of public privilege and acceptance only dimly dreamed of in 1980. They established in the body politic a clear identity for their social agenda, even though little of it had reached fruition in ten years. They rejoiced in the astounding growth of certain television ministries only to have two of them collapse in disgrace. They took certain older beliefs, exposed them to new evangelistic outreach via the new mass media, and came up with a distinctive form of popular religion. They were aware that secular forces were at work in every major area of their lives. By decade's end the scholars but not rank-and-file evangelicals were finding that creeping secularization would be a major threat to growth in the final decade before the millennium.

Finally, in this decade all Americans of all faiths or of no faith were by necessity brought to face the subtle but pervasive force of privatization. If the planet seemed destined for ecological decay, or if the escalating power of organized crime, drug usage, and sexual permissiveness seemed too powerful to check, if righteousness seemed absent as a commitment of public leaders, then at least the believer could take care of her or his own interests: protecting the family, holding on to traditional values in the local school, revitalizing one's inner spirituality, and keeping oneself morally acceptable before a God of judgment. Such was the major legacy of what became the third major movement of the 1980s, and the one that seems the best located (compared to mainline and evangelical movements) to take center stage in the 1990s.

NOTES

1. Robert Ellwood, *The History and Future of Faith: Religion Past, Present, and to Come* (New York: Crossroad, 1988), pp. 123–30.

2. Martin E. Marty, "How the Church Changed during the Last Ten Years," *Christian Ministry* 9–10 (November 1979): 13; Billy Graham, "The Dangers of Our Success," *Religious Broadcasting*, March 1981, pp. 32–35; Charles Colson, *Charisma*, May 1984, p. 87; David Hazard, "Holy Hype!" *Eternity*, December 1985, pp. 32–41. A sharp critique is Jon Johnston, "Materialism," in his *Will Evangelicalism Survive Its Own Popularity?* (Grand Rapids, Mich.: Zondervan, 1989), pp. 79–101.

3. David Hsi, *The Simple Life: Plain Living and High Thinking in American Culture* (New York: Oxford University Press, 1985); both *Sojourners* and *Other Side* promote this life-style also.

4. Patrick G. Coy, "Standing against the Tide," *Sojourners*, March 1986, pp. 42–43; Patrick Morley, "The Gospel Truth about Money," *Charisma and Christian Life*, October 1988, pp. 64–69.

5. Ellwood, *History and Future of Faith*, p. 136.

6. John Throop, "High Hopes: What's Wrong with Ambition?" *Christianity Today*, October 3, 1986, pp. 24–25; David and Karen Mains, "The Sacred Rhythms of Work and Play," *Moody Monthly*, June 1985, pp. 18–24; Ken L. Sarles, "A Theological Evaluation of the Prosperity Gospel," *Bibliotheca Sacra* 144 (October–December 1986): 329–53.

7. Robert Lerner et al., "Christian Religious Elites," *Public Opinion*, March/April 1989, p. 57; Dennis Voskuil, *Mountains into Goldmines: Robert Schuller and the Gospel of Success* (Grand Rapids, Mich.: Wm. B. Eerdmans, 1983).

8. Carol Flake, *Redemptorama: Culture, Politics, and the New Evangelicalism* (Garden City, N.Y.: Anchor Books, Doubleday, 1984), pp. 49–61; Richard Quebedeaux, *By What Authority: The Rise of Personality Cults in American Christianity* (San Francisco: Harper and Row, 1982), pp. 1–16

9. John W. Cook, "Material Culture and the Visual Arts," in Charles H. Lippy and Peter W. Williams, eds., *Encyclopedia of the American Religious Experience*, Vol. 3 (New York: Scribner, 1988), pp. 1364–66; news item, *Charisma*, October 1988, p. 32; *Christianity Today*, January 2, 1981, p. 59; news item, *Minneapolis Star Tribune*, July 14, 1989, p. 10E; Randall Balmer, "Bible Bazaar," in *Mine Eyes Have Seen the Glory: A Journey into the Evangelical Subculture in America* (New York: Oxford University Press, 1989), pp. 155–70. Much of this merchandise is advertised on Trinity Broadcast Network (TBN); "Commentary," *Eternity*, December 1985, pp. 56–57; ibid., May 1985, p. 16; *Charisma*, April 1987, p. 27; the 1989 Dunamis catalog.

10. Quoted in Charles D. Holsinger, "America's Sports Craze," *Eternity*, May 1987, pp. 11–15; Perry C. Cotham, *Politics, Americanism, and Christianity* (Grand Rapids, Mich.: Baker Book House, 1976), p. 272; H. Paul Chalfant, *Religion in Contemporary Society* (Sherman Oaks, Calif.: Alfred Publishing Company, 1981), p. 240–41.

11. Dennis A. Gilbert, ed., *Compendium of American Public Opinion* (New York: Facts on File Publications, 1988), pp. 347, 362.

12. See all of *Media and Values*, the theme of "Play Ball, Pay Ball," Summer 1986, pp. 3–26; Richard Lovelace, "Issues," *Charisma*, March 1983, p. 8; Truman Dollar, "After All," *Fundamentalist Journal*, February 1985, p. 66; Chris Ramsey, "Big Leagues," *Cornerstone* 12, 67 (1982): pp. 6–8; "Sports," *Twin City Christian*, October 20, 1988, p. 8A; see Steven Lawson, "God in the Big Leagues," *Charisma and Christian Life*, October 1989, p. 36–45.

13. Shirl J. Hoffman, "The Sanctification of Sport," *Christianity Today*, April 4, 1986, pp. 17–21.

14. Richard Quebedeaux, *I Found It! The Story of Bill Bright and Campus Crusade* (San Francisco: Harper and Row, 1979), pp. 142–46; Nick Dawson, "Slam Dunk Summit,"*WordWide Challenge*, February 1987, p. 46; *Encyclopedia of Associations*, Vol. 2 (Detroit: Sage Publications, 1987), no. 15,922.

15. Chalfant, *Religion in Contemporary Society*, p. 242.

16. *Encyclopedia of Associations*, Vol. 2, no. 15,923; "Sports," *Twin City Christian*, February 9, 1989, p. 8A. See the interviews in *Wittenburg Door*, no. 24, (April/May 1985): passim.

17. Rob Boston, "Quarterback Sneak," *Church and State*, June 1989, pp. 129–32.

18. Brochure, SCORE, Inc., 1989; *Fundamentalist Journal*, May 1986, p. 37.

19. Brochure, "The World Congress on Sports"; letter of David L. Birnbaum to the author, March 24, 1988.

20. David Edwin Harrell, Jr., *Oral Roberts: An American Life* (Bloomington: Indiana University Press, 1985), p. 363; issues of *Fundamentalist Journal*, 1985–1988, on sports.

21. Johnston, "Celebrityism," in *Will Evangelicalism Survive Its Own Popularity?*, pp. 123–41. A good example is "Rosey: The Gentle Giant," *Christian Reader*, May/June 1987, pp. 79–93; see also Steve Lawson, "God in the Big Leagues," *Charisma and Christian Life*, October 1989, pp. 36–45.

22. *Second Look*, Box 3566, Grand Rapids, MI 49501.

23. Roger Lundin, "Offspring of an Odd Union: Evangelical Attitudes towards the Arts," in George Marsden, ed., *Evangelicalism and Modern America* (Grand Rapids, Mich.: Wm. B. Eerdmans, 1984), pp. 135–49; Frank E. Gaebelein, *The Christian, the Arts, and Truth: Regaining the Vision of Greatness* (Portland, Oreg.: Multomah Press, 1985).

24. Frank E. Gaebelein, "The Aesthetic Problem," in *The Christian, the Arts, and Truth*, pp. 51–114; idem, "The Creator and Creativity," *Christianity Today*, October 5, 1984, pp. 33–38.

25. Paul Dimaggie and Michael Useem, "Social Class and Arts Consumption," *Theory and Society* 5, 2 (1977–78): 41–61; Leland Ryken, *The Christian Imagination: Essays on Literature and the Arts* (Grand Rapids, Mich.: Baker Book House, 1981); "Books," *Christianity Today*, August 9, 1985, pp. 62–64.

26. Jon Alexander, "Editorial," *Other Side*, December 1986, p. 38. A very different evangelical view is that of Francis Schaeffer; see Robert Booth Fowler, *A New Engagement: Evangelical Political Thought, 1966–1976* (Grand Rapids, Mich.: Wm. B. Eerdmans, 1982), pp. 61–76; Nicholas Wolterstorff, *Art in Action: Toward a Christian Aesthetic* (Grand Rapids, Mich.: Wm. B. Eerdmans, 1980); Gene Edward Veith, "Must Art Be 'Christian' to Be Good?" *Christianity Today*, February 3, 1984, p. 69; editorial, *Eternity*, July/August 1985, p. 5. A sharp criticism is found in "Claptrap Christians," *American Spectator*, December 1982, pp. 35–36.

27. James A. Zoller, "The Dilemma of the Christian Artist," *HIS*, December 1980, pp. 23ff.

28. *Newsweek*, February 20, 1984, p. 69; see reviews in *Christian Herald*, November 1985, pp. 9ff. An excellent critique of the genre is Kay J. Mussell, "Romantic Fiction," in M. Thomas Inge, ed., *Handbook of American Popular Culture*, Vol. 2 (Westport, Conn.: Greenwood Press, 1980), pp. 317–43; see also Janice A. Radway, *Reading the Romance: Women, Patriarchy, and Popular Literature* (Chapel Hill: University of North Carolina Press, 1984).

29. "Arts," *Christian Herald*, March 1985, pp. 53–55. The best overall guide is John Dillenberger, *The Visual Arts and Christianity in America* (New York: Crossroad, 1989).

30. *World*, April 29, 1989, pp. 11–12; *Eternity*, November 1985, pp. 34–35; *Christianity Today*, November 8, 1985, pp. 75–76; ibid., December 13, 1985, pp. 36–39; *Moody Monthly*, December 1985, pp. 82–85.

31. *Christianity Today*, November 4, 1988, p. 53; ibid., December 13, 1985, pp. 74–75; *Sojourners*, February 1982, pp. 34–36; *Eternity*, December 1985, p. 63; ibid., September 1987, p. 59.

32. *Christianity Today*, April 3, 1987, pp. 49–50; "Think Before You Act," *HIS*, December 1980, p. 21; *National Christian Reporter*, June 9, 1989, p. 4; *Fundamentalist Journal*, September 1987, p. 57; *Imprimis* (Hillsdale College) 24 (December 1985): 12.

33. News item, *Eternity*, July/August 1988, p. 26; Ansley Orfita, "Dancing in the Church," *Evangelist*, October 1987, pp. 5ff.

34. News item, *National Christian Reporter*, May 5, 1989, p. 3; Paul Thigpen, "Praise Him with the Dance," *Charisma and Christian Life*, March 1989, pp. 46ff.; see also the newsletters of Christians in Visual Arts, Box 10247, Arlington, VA 22210, and the forthcoming study by Professor Ann Wagner.

35. Flake, *Redemptorama*, pp. 172ff.

36. Balmer, *Mine Eyes Have Seen the Glory*, pp. 12–30. See the Calvary Chapel catalog, Box 1396, Costa Mesa, CA 92628; *Christianity Today*, November 22, 1985, p. 55.

37. Flake, *Redemptorama*, pp. 175–76.

38. Erling Jorstad, "Satanism: No Figment of the Imagination," *Lutheran*, June 11, 1989, pp. 15–17.

39. Richard Dinwiddie, "Can Gospel Music Be Saved?" *Christianity Today*, May 21, 1982, pp. 17–19.

40. Danny Collum, *Sojourners*, December 1985, pp. 50–51; "Music," *Charisma*, August 1985, p. 13.

41. *U.S. News and World Report*, August 25, 1985, p. 56.

42. Ibid.; "The Arts," *Eternity*, January 1987, pp. 50–52; Chuck Fromm, "Who Is Converting Whom?" *Charisma*, July 1987, pp. 42ff.; "Music Notes," *Christian Retailing*, April 15, 1989, pp. 9–10.

43. *Charisma and Christian Life*, July 1989, p. 37.

44. "Amy Grant Answers Her Critics," *Religious Broadcasting*, April 1986, pp. 12–14.

45. Reviews in *Christian Science Monitor*, September 3, 1986, p. 24.

46. *Minneapolis Star Tribune*, October 18, 1985, p. 4C; "Heavy Metal," *CCM*, January 1988, p. 18; Dan Peters et al., *What about Christian Rock?* (Minneapolis: Bethany House Publishers, 1986), index, "Stryper"; Paul Baker, *Contemporary Christian Music* (Westchester, Ill.: Crossway Books, 1979).

47. *National Christian Reporter*, August 21, 1987, p. 1; *National and International Religion Report*, September 1987, p. 3; *Fundamentalist Journal*, October 1986, p. 44;

Richard Stivers, "A Festival of Sex, Violence, and Drugs," *Katallagete* 11 (Winter 1979): 18–25; *Evangelist*, January 1987, p. 4.

48. *Chicago Tribune*, July 3, 1987, sec. 2, p. 10; Robert Edwin, "Rock Music: Choices for Christians," *Lutheran*, November 1987, pp. 10–12; Billy Rae Hearn, "Christian Music," *Charisma*, July 1985, pp. 69–75.

49. Bert Ghezzi, news column in *Christian Retailing*, April 15, 1988, p. 30; "Rock and Religion," *Seattle Times*, July 19, 1987, pp. L1, L5; Annie Dillard, "Singing with the Fundamentalists," *Yale Review* 74, 2 (January 1985): 312–20; *People of Destiny* 4, 3 (May/June 1989): 9–24.

PART III

PRIVATE FAITH: THE JOURNEY OF THE SELF

INTRODUCTION

Among the several reformations of religion brought about by the awakening of the 1960s, none touched the daily lives of more Americans than the spread of what can be called "private religion." Not as easily definable as mainline or evangelical religion, private religion revolved around one's immediate world: self, partner, spouse, friends, family, local community, and the realm of the personally spiritual. It found little of interest in doctrinal or governance issues but instead posited that whatever redemption or fulfillment one would attain in this life would emerge largely from one's private faith and closest relationships. If little or nothing could be done to heal the conflicts among the world's religions, superpowers, economic rivals, race, or classes, salvation was at least possible by tending carefully to that which was the closest to oneself here and now.

Private religion reflected faithfully the continually fragmenting or tribalizing quality of life in the late twentieth century. Traceable to the priorities of the awakening of the 1960s on the primacy of individual choice and moral pluralism, it offered its seekers perhaps more options over traditional social and selfhood roles than the world had known before: over courtship, marriage, family, parenthood, sexual expression, singlehood, and cohabitation, as well as over a vast variety of forms of self-discovery and self-realization. Americans had more choices for their private lives by the 1980s, choices only dimly perceived twenty years before. In Part III we seek to define, describe, and discuss these both in themselves and as they intertwined with mainline and evangelical expressions of religion.

In the first two chapters of this part we explore the major changes during this decade in the areas of private religion: that which was nondenominational (as mainline was denominational and evangelicalism was transdenominational), but integrally a part of this wider understanding of the boundaries of faith. In the final chapter we outline how the 1980s gave rise to what now seems to be a major direction of the future for religion in America, the "New Age" religion.

In all three categories we find modernity, secularization, and privatization at work. The latter especially becomes the dominant process at work. As demonstrated so compellingly in *Habits of the Heart*, much of the religious community pressed on toward a highly personalized individualism that showed little regard for the concerns of the mainline or evangelicals. It exalted the needs and interests of one's inner self and one's immediate surroundings: friends and lovers, children and spouses. It was religious but not credal, institutional, or liturgical.[1] It left behind the holding fast in the nane of pursuing that which was still to be found in the unfolding future.

Although, as we have seen, the major division during the decade within religious life was that which existed between evangelicals and mainliners, privatized religion responded to those persons and organizations who tended to "maximize self-realization and personal growth and reward primary relationships." That meant that they transformed "divine commandments into instrumental strategies for achieving personal satisfaction," thus becoming preoccupied with the immediate world of one's existence;[2] as two other observers noted, "American Christianity has its main impact on values in the domain of family life, sexuality, and personal honesty."[3]

Such a movement clearly flowed out of modernity. In a society where believers are increasingly being freed from an inherited faith, they move toward being autonomous selectors in their quest for personal satisfaction.[4] These seekers generally acted within the boundaries of the existing religious institutions. They were in no way a totally separate entity from the mainline or evangelicalism. As the decade unfolded, their presence became a matter of deep concern for the existing church communities. Both evangelicals and mainliners, pressers and holders, sought earnestly to keep this privatized religion from overwhelming their involvement in the society. In some instances they were able to at least hold the privatizers at bay; but in others the forces of secularization especially would prove to be dominant by the decade's end.

NOTES

1. Robert Bellah et al., *Habits of the Heart: Individualism and Commitment in American Life* (Berkeley: University of California Press, 1985).

2. John F. Wilson, "The Sociological Study of Religion," in Charles H. Lippy and Peter W. Williams, eds., *Encyclopedia of the American Religious Experience*, Vol. 1 (New York: Scribner, 1988), p. 28.

3. Dean Hoge and Ernesto de Zulueta, "Salience and Consequence of Religious Commitment," *Journal for the Scientific Study of Religion* 24, 1 (1985): 21–38, especially p. 34.

4. Wade Clark Roof and William McKinney, "Denominational America and New Religious Pluralism," in Wade Clark Roof, ed., *Religion in America Today*, Annals of the American Academy of Political and Social Science, Vol. 480 (Beverly Hills, Calif.: Sage Publications, 1985), pp. 33–34; Benton Johnson, "Liberal Protestantism: End of the Road?" ibid., pp. 51–52; Robert Booth Fowler, "Religion and the Escape from Liberal Individualism," in his *Unconventional Partners: Religion and Liberal Culture in the United States* (Grand Rapids, Mich.: Wm. B. Eerdmans, 1989), pp. 32–47.

9

The Self and Relationships: New Options in the 1980s

At the base of the new privatization stood the enormous transformation of sexual behavior and sexual understanding, a major legacy of the awakening. With its celebration of individual choice and freedom of expression (such as cohabitation, intercourse outside of marriage, single-parent families, and homosexual life-styles), the "sexual revolution" forced Americans to make choices many had previously been able to avoid. Whereas traditional religion had clearly upheld the sanctity of chastity before marriage, the nuclear family, and heterosexual behavior, now the privatized world of modernity and secular norms offered new opportunities and challenges.

In the view of Robert C. Ellwood, traditional religion was no longer able to enforce its age-old standards. The entire worldview, the perception of reality, had changed from "a world of shepherds, kings, and swords . . . to forest-devouring multinational agri-businesses, fragile democracy and the threat of thermonuclear war."[1] The stability and givenness of the older order had disappeared; in its place came a new world with its technology that made easier such practices as contraception and with psychological mind cures that exalted personal gratification. If the world could not be prevented from destroying itself by war or pollution, then at least individuals could enjoy and protect what was closest: their selves, their lovers and mates, their children, and their communities.

While the appearance of AIDS contributed mightily to slowing down the spread of homosexual behavior, signs at decade's end showed that the freewheeling sexual expression of earlier days was back in vogue. A few statistics: at least 50 percent of all girls had intercourse by the age of fifteen; marriage, according to specialists, had become "an optional life-style"; people were continuing to marry later in life; the remarriage rate continued to decline. Births out of wedlock increased over the ten-year span from 18 to 22 percent; divorce rates went down from 23 to 21 percent; children living with a single parent rose from 20 to 24 percent; cohabiting couples increased from 1.6 million to 2.3 million; the number of married mothers in the work force grew from 54 percent to 64 percent; and working mothers with children under three increased from 41 to 54 percent.[2]

131

Both mainliners and evangelicals understood only too well how far from the norms of the past the new sexual turnabouts had traveled. To the surprise of many outsiders, evangelicals started publicly to discuss the entire field of sexuality with greater candor and openness than ever before. Conservative book publishers started bringing out sexual manuals for married couples that included explicit, if tastefully worded, descriptions of behavioral alternatives. Church-sponsored seminars, adult forums, and weekend conferences addressed the matters of couples who were facing malfunctions of sexuality within their marriages. Women were encouraged, or at least not discouraged, to use more cosmetics, jewelry, and up-to-date hairstyles. All of this was clearly defined to be encouraged within and only within the boundaries of traditional Protestant morality through the institution of marriage. But by contrast to earlier times, when sexual matters were considered out of bounds or in bad taste or lewd, at least in public, such new developments were widely hailed by evangelicals as signs of growing maturity.[3]

Among the mainliners the issues were much the same. The major differences centered around the smaller distances they had to travel in going public with their recognition of the changes in society. Perhaps the most influential spokesperson was Professor James Nelson, whose work helped identify and carry ahead the dialogue. In brief, he argued that Christians were acknowledging the goodness of God when they acknowledged the goodness of sexual expression, seeing the traditional definition of intercourse as being but one part of a larger sense of wholeness in their personalities. The wholeness included recognizing the dangers of a purely masculinized spirituality. Rather believers should strive for "a more androgynous theology" that acknowledged the fullness that came with complete gender equality.[4]

FAMILY

The greater realism about sexual matters contributed directly to the developments in the 1980s over how religious faith should inform and guide the family. Indeed, the word "family" became something of a political shibboleth, with each major party claiming that it had better programs than its rival to strengthen the traditional family. What that meant during the 1980s, however, for religious life in America came to be something rather different than it had been in previous decades.

For many, the greater sexual freedom of the 1980s posed a direct, even immoral threat to the sanctity of the family. Viewing that social institution as God-given, as the indisputable foundation for a stable, law-abiding society, its supporters interpreted the new freedom as being inspired by Satan, encouraged by secular humanism, and destined to destroy America unless moral sanity returned quickly.[5] Other devout Americans, however, saw the changes as both inevitable responses to changing trends in economic and social life and greater opportunities to express their religious convictions.

Everyone involved agreed that religion and family matters were inseparable. Sociologist W. Lloyd Warner had written that those religious symbols that represented in a supernatural sense the real world all expressed and reinforced the family structure. In fact, the church with all its programs could not exist if the traditional family could not survive.[6] Yet that central symbol was undergoing enormous changes. The "nuclear family," father, mother (full-time homemaker), and children living under the same roof, had become a decided statistical minority. By the 1980s there were significant increases in the number of trial marriages, couples cohabiting with no intent of marrying, single-parent families, blended families, lesbian and gay families, couples without children, couples with children no longer home, permanently childless couples, families consisting of an adult and an aging parent, and families with members having no blood ties or sexual relationships but mutually agreeing to covenant as a family.[7]

With such changes came staggering problems, especially teenage single women with babies, growing numbers of such families with unmanageable poverty, and increasing amounts of child abuse, as well as traditional problems of racial and sexual discrimination.[8] Yet the family in multifarious ways continued to exist because, as Nelson suggested, it provided what no other institution could offer, "emotional and physical intimacy, nurture and support." He commented, "Those needs will never go out of style. They are absolutely vital for genuine human life."[9]

Yet, as historians had long known, the nuclear family so prized by many politically minded religious spokespersons was not truly the model described in the Scriptures and had not evolved until the Industrial Revolution came in the eighteenth century.[10] Before then, the family as such had served other functions: as an economic unit with all the children working, as a vehicle for transmitting property to the upcoming generations, and as a haven for older members. It had comparatively little to do with intimacy.

As the newer "nuclear family" emerged, it turned out to have features that fell short of its idealization by current spokespersons. It was exclusivistic in its emphasis on privacy over the good of the community; it made its own private comfort the highest good at the expense of community improvement; and it frequently replaced the organized church as a haven for nurture and inspiration.[11]

Not without considerable protest from within, those in the 1980s who viewed society and its problems through the eyes of religious faith began to suggest that the faith offered viable options to the nuclear-family model. Single mothers in the work force stated that they could not "have the relationship with the Lord" they had were they married. Couples found in their faith the motivation for taking a very active role in community building, even though it meant less time with their children and "a high level of stress." To them it was enriching to invest their talents in the life of their town as well as in their church.[12] Other parents with children became involved in such relief programs as care for the refugees to America from Southeast Asia or for retarded children. Finally, some couples chose not to have children.[13]

In the more permissive world of the 1980s the issue of adultery and infidelity attracted considerable attention. Could it not happen, some conservatives argued, that with all this freedom of choice, married couples might start choosing to have different sexual partners? Whatever else might be happening to the family, that practice remained totally forbidden on religious as well as psychological grounds. Some discussion emerged over whether a valid difference could be made between "preceremonial" sex and that occurring outside any meaningful covenant. As to the growing practice of "swinging," married couples who knowingly had sex with other couples, some Protestant writers stated that so long as fidelity was at the heart of the relationship—the bonding of trust, primary commitment, and honesty—it might not be wrong.[14]

What helped keep these kinds of issues on the front pages and in television interview shows was the increased level of political involvement in sociofamily problems. During the 1980s at every level of government, highly emotional battles occurred in city halls, county seats, state legislatures, and the nation's capital over the wide variety of issues lumped together as "welfare" or "day care." Some evangelicals created an informal network named Worldview for advocacy of their public-policy agendas. In a work by Herbert Schlossberg, E. Calvin Beisner, and others, entitled *Turning Point*, the authors spelled out their specific demands for countering the sexual/family transformations. Using a direct confrontational style (much like the rhetoric of Operation Rescue), they stated that they saw God at work in an orderly, knowable way. That "grid" of insight taught them that they must resist any liberalization by several means: holding fast to the traditional family, including for many parents the use of home or parochial schooling instead of public education; a strong commitment to the antiabortion cause; and resistance to demands by single parents for more "welfare."[15]

By contrast, mainline and liberal advocates continued to press for the prochoice position, increased federal government involvement in day-care centers for working parents, increased spending for school lunches, and expanded low-cost housing programs.[16] Congress and the White House in the late 1980s both invested great amounts of time and energy in shaping a day-care measure that would provide public funds for parents in the labor force who needed such facilities. After years of contesting over whether states or the national government should be the primary funding agencies, whether churches should be allowed to serve as places for such publicly funded programs, and related issues, Congress was not ready by early 1990 to pass a bill that would survive any presidential veto. Its position as of the writing of this work was far too volatile to allow prediction of the outcome. It does serve, however, as a superb example of how deeply political the issues of sexuality and family had become under the greater involvement of church people in public policy during the 1980s.[17]

The survival of the day-care issue, however, signifies at least one major change during the 1980s. When something like a day-care bill was passed by Congress in 1971, then President Richard M. Nixon vetoed it, calling it "the most radical" piece of legislation to come from the Ninety-second Congress. To him, it would weaken the American family and "Sovietize" its children. Since then, however, the enormous increase of women in the work force, together with growing support from certain church groups, has helped both parties realize that some such measure is indispensable, as well as politically attractive.[18] In other words, the issue signifies major changes during this decade in both policy and attitudes toward women, the family, and sexuality. As suggested earlier, much of this can be traced to the expanded definition of religion, which includes fresh evaluations of men and women and how faith informs so complex and controversial an issue.

WOMEN

Through the awakening of the 1960s the contemporary feminist movement in all its diversity and energy was born. Sharply divided internally from its beginning because of its diverse goals and the deep emotions and social values that it sought to restructure, feminism in the 1970s came to mean whether women with children should join the work force. For many, of course, there was little or no choice. Given their economic needs and long-range goals (such as college education for their children), women realized that they must find some kind of gainful employment.

In turn, this deeply affected the relationships with the family: husband and children. At that point the religious dimensions of the issue came into sharp focus. Was it in God's providence that women should leave their children, even for a few hours a day, to be cared for by others? Was it right that the husband should share headship of the household? Was it not possible that the secular values of this world were overriding what had for centuries been the proper relationships between women, men, and children?

These issues received extensive attention in the 1980s from a variety of religiously concerned individuals, both leaders and laity. What clearly had developed was a failure of the women's movement to coalesce around any single set of values or specific policy agenda. Sylvia Ann Hewlett stated, "The biggest problem has been the women's movement's attitude towards motherhood. Many feminists have alternatively ignored, reviled, and lashed out at motherhood, and in so doing the movement has alienated its main constituency."[19] Acknowledging that for the same work women were often paid considerably less than men, some feminists found that they were stymied; they needed the wages and they wanted fulfillment in a career, but they found only "jobs in the pink collar ghetto" available if they also wanted children. Their call for equal pay for equal work and related policy reforms had been from the outset strongly resisted by the religious Right, a fact noted by candidates for public office.[20]

As a result of such fragmentation, little improvement in either the economic demands or social tensions over working mothers occurred early in the decade. Within the evangelical community Billy Graham spoke for many. Although he endorsed equal pay for equal work, he stated that women's liberation would damage the family since it denied the Bible's teachings about husband/wife relationships. "God has appointed you husbands to be the head of the home. When a women opposes that order, she rebels against the will of God." So too the editors of *Christianity Today*, a group of religion teachers at Falwell's Liberty Baptist College (later renamed Liberty University in 1984), and Bill Bright, head of Campus Crusade for Christ, all taught this form of "divine order."[21]

Such resistance helped create several profeminist evangelical groups in the 1970s, notably the Evangelical Women's Caucus and the Daughters of Sarah. From these groups and some seminary sources came a response carefully worked out in Biblical terms familiar to evangelicals. First, the absolute necessity for women to work was upheld. By the mid-1980s over 50 percent of all American women were gainfully employed, and another 15 percent were actively looking for work. Only some 21 percent could be classified as "full-time homemakers."[22]

With considerable theological and scriptural research as their foundations, these groups called for more creativity in understanding what contemporary religious women should be encouraged to pursue. It was too late, spokespersons said, to hold on to the traditional role; the revolution in women's roles had already taken place. Unless major changes were forthcoming, religiously minded women would simply drop out or move to join affirming support groups. By 1986, for instance, the staunchly conservative *Moody Monthly* was calling for believers to endorse those women who wanted a good education and a good job.[23]

By the end of the decade, however, the religious Right and the more moderate evangelical women's groups were locked in disagreement. The issue had been sharply exacerbated when the Evangelical Women's Caucus (founded in 1974), with a membership by 1986 of some 650, directly addressed the issue of lesbian and gay rights. At an extended debate the delegates approved by a margin of eighty to sixteen, with twenty-three abstentions, this resolution:

Whereas homosexual people are children of God and because of the Biblical mandate of Jesus Christ that we are all created equal in God's sight, and in recognition of the presence of the lesbian minority in Evangelical Women's Caucus International, EWCI takes a firm stand in favor of civil rights protection for homosexual persons.[24]

To the minority this was too much a concession to secular standards and trends. Some withdrew from the organization, later founding the Christians for Biblical Authority (CBA), led by New Testament scholar Catherine Clark Kroeger. Two years later the division remained intact, with "more than enough pain to go around." EWCI membership had dropped some 50 percent, while CBA enrollment reached some 400 members by the summer of 1989.[25]

Two other similar groups kept programs alive during the late 1980s. The Daughters of Sarah, founded in 1974, continued its ministry as a study and network support group for women pursuing Biblical insights on women's issues.[26] A more academically oriented group, the Council on Biblical Manhood and Womanhood (CBMW) appeared first in December 1987. It offered its study programs and networking as an alternative to what it considered inadequate evangelical feminist theology. Among its Board of Reference members were Bev LaHaye, Connie Marshner of the new Child Rights and Family Protection Institute, and

Jerry Falwell and similar conservative leaders.[27] Still another group, Christians for Biblical Equality (CBE) held a national convention, claiming a membership of some 500 evangelical women and men and asserting a scriptural basis for full equality.[28]

All the while, the Concerned Women for America under Bev LaHaye continued its impressive membership growth. It found in the later 1980s, however, some competitors. Led by Anne Gimenez of Virginia, the International Women in Leadership (IWIL) program offered a national and several regional meetings annually. Largely a charismatic-Pentecostal group, it attracted such political women leaders as Secretary of Transportation Elizabeth Dole, Dee Jepson, and Carolyn Sundseth. Its National Advisory Board included something of a Who's Who, with names such as Marilyn Hickey, Rexella Van Impe, Gloria Copeland of television prominence, and Evelyn Roberts of Tulsa.[29] Such programs offered role modeling for the members, current information on women working together, and personal life management.

By contrast, women in mainline bodies worked within their own denominational groups for advancing their causes. Contrasted to the larger parachurch groups such as CWA or EWC, their organizations remained numerically small and largely out of the media spotlight. Each had its own set of publications and local, state, and national conventions. In these the issues of working mothers attracted less attention than among evangelicals, largely because a working consensus apparently had been reached in favor of such activity.

Evangelical women not in academia or leadership roles found at least two nationally prominent magazines offering advice and information on women's religious issues. These were *Today's Christian Woman* and *Virtue*; another magazine, *Partnership*, focused on issues of marriage and family. In these magazines the more systematic kinds of analysis or political concerns of CWA or EWA were supplanted by articles on personal growth, spirituality, family problems, homemaker tips, and, occasionally, job careers. No single model of Christian womanhood could be constructed from analysis of these journals. However, it seemed clear that they avoided association with any of the evangelical caucuses that seemed, correctly or not, "radical" or "separatist" from center-of-the-road wisdom.[30]

ALTERNATIVES

The growing preference for a nondenominational expression of family and gender in one's religious faith took a vividly sharp turn into more controversial areas of behavior during the 1980s. Three of these, long available but rarely discussed openly, came into greater public prominence in these years: singleness, cohabitation, and gay/lesbian expression. In each case major changes in the secular world directly affected the responses made within organized religion, and in each case the participants indicated that they were increasingly motivated by their personal life-style options rather than accepting more traditional churchly authority.

Hence these three areas illustrate the influence of privatization on personal conduct. They suggest also how deeply the conviction had grown that since political and organized church life could do little to bring happiness or alleviate the major public crises of the age, at least some measure of fulfillment was available in one's private life.

By the late 1980s statistics signified the scope of the transformation. More Americans were cohabiting than ever before; divorced and widowed persons were waiting longer to remarry; single-parent families were increasing in number; life expectancy was becoming greater. The data of the 1980s showed a record low proportion of American adult lives being spent in marriage. Further, more people were delaying the age at which they married. A remarkable rise occurred in the proportion of young adults who did not marry. In 1987 nearly 80 percent of men from twenty to twenty-four had never married, up from 55 percent in 1970. The percentage for women increased greatly, from 36 to 61 percent. Among those of both sexes between twenty-five and twenty-nine the proportion of those remaining unmarried soared upward from 19 percent in 1970 to 42 percent by 1987. For women it rose from 11 percent in 1970 to 19 percent by 1987. This suggested strongly that an increasing number of Americans were rejecting marriage altogether.[31]

Singleness, the first alternative to marriage considered here, had obviously been an option since the beginning of time. What emerged as different, especially in these years, was the extent to which singles continued heterosexual sexual behavior, achieving a "certain normative legitimacy in the society." Empirical research suggested that many single evangelicals and mainliners viewed sexuality as God-given for their enjoyment as well as existing for procreation.[32]

For traditional religious life this acceptance raised very difficult questions. As summarized by Professor James Nelson, it suggested that as a voluntary choice, singledom was preferable to marriage. It also forced churches to re-examine closely the issue of sex outside of marriage, traditionally a very sticky matter. Third, singleness suggested that its practitioners stood apart from the churches' longstanding glorification of the nuclear family, where most activities were done by the "Noah's Ark" syndrome, two by two, and sometimes with children. Finally, singledom again raised the problem of "self-love"; might not a Christian be guilty of selfish, uncharitable love by remaining in that situation?[33]

Remarkably, in the 1980s religious-minded people talked with strong conviction about the goodness and rewards of this choice. Some acknowledged that singles might be helped to "plot strategies for meeting marriageable partners, but what does that have to do with the Kingdom of God?"[34] Singles brought unique gifts and talents to the larger society. They now affirmed openly that they no longer considered themselves somehow inferior or rejected because they had not married.[35] Within congregations and in more spontaneously formed special-purpose groups, singles' organizations united by a common religious interest grew in popularity in these years.

A second alternative, obviously closely parallel to the first, was that of cohabitation. Although complete statistics remained unavailable in a situation with so many variables, its practice continued to rise in the 1980s. The Census Bureau estimated that a total increase occurred from some .5 million couples in 1970 to over 2 million in 1986. Case-study evidence points to an increase during the same period from 13 to 56 percent.[36] Evidence suggested that a major reason for the increase was the decision by partners to discover before the local complications of marriage whether in daily life they were compatible. This enlarged scope of sexual freedom undergirded their beliefs that they were acting within the bonds of accepted social norms.[37]

The implications for traditional church-related morality became obvious: increasing numbers of young people were going in other directions. The largest age group to cohabit, for both women and men, was those under twenty-three; one-half of the women and two-thirds of the men who had ever entered into a cohabiting or marital union had done so initially through cohabitation without marriage; and one-third of the women and two-fifths of the men who had married by the age of twenty-three had already cohabited without marriage. Thus, as one expert wrote, "Cohabitation without marriage has become an experience for large fractions of the population and is a life-style available to many more."[38]

Second, although empirical evidence has not become available, churches seem to have accepted cohabiting couples for marriage when application was made. Specific exceptions occurred in given localities, but generally most couples found church sanction available.[39] By 1989 courts were exploring whether cohabiting couples who claimed insurance and employment benefits that were already extended to married couples could have such claims honored.[40]

DIVORCE

Beyond singleness and cohabitation, divorce continued to grow as an acceptable, if often temporary, alternative to finding fulfillment in relationships. The statistical and attitudinal data show that during this decade the total number of divorces decreased while the ease of obtaining them through the courts apparently increased. Churches and parachurch organizations spent considerable time and energy ministering to the divorced. With the greater permissiveness and pluralism so characteristic of postawakening American society, traditional moral judgments against the divorced declined accordingly. Only a handful of denominations refused remarriage to divorced persons. Virtually every church-related service agency offered counseling and support-group outreach programs.[41]

GAYS AND LESBIANS

To suggest, as is done here, that the gay/lesbian life-style is an alternative to the nuclear family and traditional sexuality causes considerable dissent by many religious people. It seems to legitimate a sexual orientation many find unacceptable. During the 1980s, however, a significant alteration in understanding and acceptance of homosexual conduct led Americans to reconsider their attitudes.

Whether gays and lesbians were any more accepted by decade's end is a matter only they can understand. What follows here is a brief attempt to show how the search unfolded for fulfillment in private relationships undergirded by faith.

Among the several liberation movements emerging from the awakening was that for gay (including lesbians, hereafter named simply "gay") liberation. As documented by John D'Emilio and Estelle B. Freedman, it continued to expand during the 1970s. Modeling themselves after the "black is beautiful" movement, gays followed the age's wisdom of "do your own thing" by telling the world of their sexual preference. Closely allied to the radical feminists who demanded that the old patriarchal domination by males in the churches must cease, gays by the 1970s were claiming moral and social legitimacy for their cause.[42]

The movement gained momentum through conferences, newsletters, and other networking, all the while receiving extensive news media attention. Those who remained within the organized religious communities by their presence raised issues the churches had long resisted. Finding more than enough difficulty in ministering to the rank and file about the new expression of heterosexuality, women's demands, cohabitation, and divorce, now the leadership was being asked to respond to gay issues. Was this condition immoral? If so, could the participants be rehabilitated? What should be done about those who continued to remain gay and active in religious life?

Most mainline and evangelical church response emerged very slowly. Some saw in the movement an opportunity for a renewed form of ministry. James Nelson pointed to the churches as being communities rooted in the experiences of affirmation and acceptance, qualities gays were searching for their decision to go public. Second, the recent enlargement of understanding sexuality as being more than intercourse stood as another resource found within religious communities. "Christianity is a religion of incarnation, and an incarnationalist faith affirms the body as good," Nelson wrote. Finally, the expression of God's grace (unrestricted acceptance) for each person contained empowering implications for every seeker. In brief, the churches could help gays and lesbians celebrate and affirm their homosexuality.[43]

However, all through the 1980s such an affirmation seemed for most holders and seekers a remote possibility. So deeply emotional and rooted in early experiences and personal sexual identity was one's sexual preference that it defied most attempts by church people at some form of acceptance or compromise. The whole matter had burst onto prime time and front pages as early as 1977, when singer and evangelical Anita Bryant led a successful political drive to stop an amendment in Dade County, Florida, extending civil rights protection to homosexuals. From then on, churches as well as the larger society came to learn a good deal more about gay orientation and practice, and also why so many sincerely motivated believers opposed them.

By contrast to the gradual legal extension of rights to other groups of the 1960s such as blacks, gays found little or no such acceptance. Some progressive evangelical groups, such as the Other Side, called for more understanding and acceptance. On the other hand, Falwell, Robertson, and most other televangelists labeled the gay movement as the greatest possible internal threat to domestic stability in the nation's history.

What did change was the increased number of gays who publicly declared their preference and participated in the growing number of networks and associations created to further their interests. The most widely distributed religious publication was the quarterly newsletter, *Evangelicals Concerned*, located in New York City. It carried both critical and favorable news items about the movement, along with information about various local and state meetings for advancing their crusade. By 1990 gays had become more knowledgeable about such ministerial opportunities.[44]

What had not changed were the various positions on whether or not a person was born with such a preference and whether it could be permanently changed or even should be changed. For some observers, the gay/lesbian alternative story was clear evidence of secularization and modernity taking command of those church people who supported the minority's case. For others, privatization clearly meant that each person was entitled to live out her or his private sexual orientation freed from hassles and oppression. The whole matter showed every sign of continuing unabated into the last decade before the millennium.

With the evidence now clear that the awakening had transformed so much of American society, including the search for the self through relationships, a parallel set of events emerged demonstrating how dysfunctional for many that search could be. For some the transformation was little short of disastrous. Here we examine the sociomoral crises of teenage pregnancies, AIDS, and the controversies over pornography. Each issue obviously was enveloped within highly charged public attitudes toward sexual behavior and public moral conduct. In each instance some of those looking for alternatives in their closest relationships found restrictions, such as the curtailment of pornography. For others the search led to the poverty and bleak future for teenage mothers and the global epidemic of AIDS.

TEENAGE PREGNANCY

While liberating for many, the sexual revolution of the 1960s turned into an epidemic of pregnancy for unmarried teenage girls during the next decade. A major contributing factor was the lack of any systematic sex education. By the early 1980s reports showed that half the teens had learned nothing from their parents, and only six states had mandated sex-education programs. By default parents were thus turning their children loose for instruction by peers and the glamorized, often amoral sexual messages of the mass media.[45]

Contributing also were the greater mobility and personal freedom from adult supervision the young people experienced. When coupled with the attractiveness of experimenting with intercourse, this turned into a major dilemma, as explained by Victor R. Fuchs: "Most of these births are to young women from low-income families who have little education and poor employment opportunities. For young women in such circumstances motherhood appears to offer an opportunity to leave the parental home, to improve one's status, and to develop a more satisfying life.''[46] The result became a social problem of ''tragic dimensions'' reflecting sharply the contradictions of American society toward sexuality.[47]

In their impersonal manner the statistics tell the story. Between 1960 and 1980 the rate of illegitimacy had tripled. More specifically, in 1985 some 1,031,000 teenagers became pregnant, 31,000 of these fourteen or younger. The outcomes of the pregnancies included 477,710 live births and 416,170 induced abortions; the remainder were stillbirths or miscarriages. The pregnancy rate reached its highest point in 1980 and remained at that point well into the decade. The 1985 pregnancy rate for women aged fifteen to nineteen ranged from 60 per 1,000 females in North Dakota to 151 per 1,000 in California.[48]

Both the educational and religious communities searched for programs of control. The most obvious solution would be abstinence from intercourse, the action endorsed by many churches. However, within many communities nasty battles broke out over the content of sex education in both the schools and churches: the questions revolved around how best to promote abstinence, how to control venereal disease, and, most controversial of all, how or whether to teach the forms of contraception.[49]

Public schools, for the most part, advocated teaching contraception, acknowledging that sexually active teens would not practice abstinence. Many churches and certain parent groups sharply disagreed, insisting on either abstinence or no classroom instruction at all. They insisted that information about contraception and making contraceptive devices available only told the students that intercourse was permissible. Across the country in innumerable school districts the problem came to a stalemate: schools against parents, parents against churches, churches against schools. Evangelicals and fundamentalists blamed the sexual revolution and permissive liberalism for the pregnancy crisis. Mainliners often centered their energies on improving the curriculum programs.[50]

The federal government itself became involved as early as 1981. Led by religious Right–endorsed Senators Jeremiah Denton and Orrin Hatch, Congress enacted the Adolescent Family Life Act (AFL). If offered money and educational facilities to community programs, including churches, that taught abstinence and promoted adoption for out-of-wedlock babies rather than abortion.

Critics stated that the act was unconstitutional, giving public funds to sectarian groups; supporters said that it was too underfunded to ever be successful. The critics took AFL into the courts in 1987; a year later the Supreme Court upheld it, stating, in Justice Rehnquist's words, ''There is nothing inherently religious about these activities.''[51] Its limited scope of activities suggested how controversial and how difficult any kind of public involvement in the pregnancy epidemic had become.

AIDS

Unquestionably the most serious fallout from the sexual revolution came with the epidemic of the Acquired Immune Deficiency Syndrome (AIDS). In a society where the gay/lesbian alternative to traditional heterosexual behavior had taken deep root, the disease became a nightmare.[52] Medicine had no cures, and very little basic research started on any cure. Studies of AIDS in the United States show that the origins of the syndrome were known among 94 percent of those diagnosed as infected. Within that number, 73 percent had contracted it from sexual activity with other gays all of whom had multiple homosexual partners. Some 19 percent contracted it from intravenous drug use, some 2 percent from people who received blood transfusions, and 1 percent from those heterosexual contacts with someone carrying AIDS.

By 1989 AIDS had become a major epidemic on all continents for all races. By May 31, 1989, in the United States some 97,193 cases had been reported to the Centers for Disease Control, with the number climbing. Some 56,468 of these had already died. While safer sexual practices had lowered the rate among gays, AIDS was increasing among drug users and adolescents. Some observers stated that these figures were too low. By way of comparison, in San Francisco, with a total gay population of up to 69,000, more gay males of that city had died of AIDS than "from all the earthquakes and wars of the 20th century several times over."[53]

As with the teen pregnancy battle, the epidemic presented the religious community with one of its greatest domestic challenges of the decade. The questions soon appeared: How could a loving God permit so horrid a tragedy? Was it all some message from God as punishment for homosexual behavior? Was it the inevitable result of the permissiveness of the 1960s? Was the enlargement of sexual understanding and personal choice too much freedom for humans to handle?[54]

Religious Right spokepersons made their conclusions. Falwell stated, "A man reaps what he sows. If he sows seed in the field of his lower nature, he will reap from it a harvest of corruption."[55] The larger evangelical community, however, displayed a wide variety of interpretations. Asked in 1983 if AIDS were "evidence of God's punishment for homosexuals' immoral and sinful life-style," some 53.1 percent disagreed, while 30.4 agreed.[56] At the same time evangelicals, mainliners, and others spent considerable time visiting the patients in the medical facilities.

Jimmy Swaggart, a frequent critic of homosexual conduct, stated, "No, AIDS is not a plague sent by God [it] is a result of the evil, wicked, profligate life-style of the homosexual community."[57] Ron Sider of Just Life and ESA stated that all Christians should offer the stricken "our love and support, no matter how inconvenient or costly."

As the verbal battles continued, it became clear that AIDS patients were extremely bitter against church judgments on their life-styles, the homophobia of centuries-long standing. Evangelicals and mainliners pointed out that if God were passing judgment, why did heterosexuals contract the disease? They suggested also that the situation offered an opportunity for believers to demonstrate their care under very difficult circumstances.[58]

Most religious organizations, at various levels, passed resolutions calling on their constituents not to make the situation worse than it already was. The National Council of Churches Communications Commission called for responsible public advertising of preventive methods such as condoms and abstinence.[59] However, the largest Protestant body, the Southern Baptist Convention, stopped the distribution of the surgeon general's report on AIDS because it did not call for total abstinence as the only preventative for the spread of AIDS. The archdiocese of the Roman Catholic church in Boston, under Bernard Cardinal Law, told the parents of children in its jurisdiction not to allow these young people to participate in the AIDS education programs in the Boston public schools, largely because the materials there differed from the Catholic understanding of acceptable social behavior.[60] Thus the religious community itself found no clear basis for consensus on the crisis as researchers continued their search for a cure.

PORNOGRAPHY

Along with these excruciatingly difficult problems came the social, legal, and moral dilemma of pornography. Because the Constitution protected freedom of speech and expression, and because experts disagreed over what constituted pornography, its distribution through mass media such as movies, videocassettes, and printed matter became an extremely complicated matter. Further, its rapid spread throughout society turned it into an exceedingly lucrative income for its vendors, leading them to defend it as a constitutional right.[61] Sold through public outlets, sex continued its earlier record of being an ever-larger big business, a development noted by advertisers. When outraged citizens and municipal prosecutors took cases to court, they were usually overruled by judges citing free speech.

Citizens both in and outside the churches interpreted the porno industry as further evidence of freed-up sexuality gone out of control. Especially upsetting was the ease with which youngsters, especially impressionable children, could find glamorized, often violent explicit sexuality distributed as normal entertainment fare.[62]

Various school and church programs were addressed to improving the viewing and listening tastes of children, but they were no match for the economic power of explicit sexual advertising and rock music groups. As it turned out, the most successful organized effort based on religiomoral standards came out of Tupelo, Mississippi, led by a United Methodist minister, Donald Wildmon. His first tactic was to ask his parishioners to join him in turning off the objectionable fare. In 1977 he produced the first of what would become many organized boycotts of the sponsors of the objectionable materials. In February he created the National Federation for Decency (NFD) to monitor television programs. It attracted some grass root support, including that of Jerry Falwell, but was widely ridiculed by the national media as being against free speech and artistic expression. Wildmon continued his efforts, explaining (for instance, on a 1981 Phil Donahue show) that he was not a censor. He believed that he could not change the programming plans of the television network executives. They would show the materials they thought viewers would watch and support the advertisers. But the NFD could place pressure on the sponsors of such shows, acting within the law but not attempting to censor material directly. By 1982 he was attracting even more attention but met with little success.[63]

The portrayal of sexuality in the mass media failed to meet the standards of the NFD, but Wildmon continued his efforts. Within a few years he created a large National Coalition for Better Television (NCBT) consisting of both religious and secular groups, Catholics and Protestants, and feminists (who objected to the portrayal of females in the materials), as well as members of most organized religious bodies, including seventy denominations and many high-ranking church officials. Volunteer teams watched all broadcast and cable shows for incidents of sex, violence, or profanity, noting the sponsor and the amount of time sponsored. Then the leaders of the NCBT would tally the scores and announce whom they would boycott.[64]

Perhaps the most publicized success came in the summer of 1989 when PepsiCola canceled its sponsorship of the Madonna ads on television. The rock star Madonna attracted considerable attention for her video, "Like a Virgin," which Wildmon and others stated was "sacrilegious to the core." The best-known critics of the religious Right, People for the American Way, replied that Wildmon had gone "far beyond any mainstream concern about the quality of television" and was inflicting narrowly focused tastes on the public. Father Andrew Greeley found the video "utterly harmless, a PG-13 at the worst, and, by the standards of rock video, charming and chaste. More than that, it is patently a morality play."[65]

By decade's end it was not at all obvious that boycotts of sponsors were making any long-range difference. It became clear that once some viewers learned that a program was objectionable to groups such as these, they would start to watch it. The courts continued to protect freedom of expression.[66]

By 1990 the search for fulfillment through relationships reflected vividly the deep divisions among Americans over sexuality, women's rights, and the alternative expressions of singledom, cohabitation, and homosexual life-styles. The increasing complexity of teen pregnancies, AIDS, and pornography illustrated graphically how the freedom of choice and individual preferences so cherished by Americans could lead to highly unexpected results. Thus the course of private religion became exceedingly complex, as were the mainline and evangelical battles over public-policy issues and politics. What became clear was that the standards of right and wrong, of holding and pressing, were no longer what they once had been. For all the superficial prosperity of the country under President Ronald Reagan, underneath citizens were despairing that America as a nation could mend its many flaws. Yet hope still sprang eternal; if society could not be redeemed, if the search for fulfillment in relationships led to undesired results, then perhaps at least the self as such might be able to be saved and to be ready for the 1990s. That hope informs the discussion of the next chapter.

NOTES

1. Robert Ellwood, *The History and Future of Faith* (New York: Crossroad, 1988), pp. 133–45, especially p. 133.

2. Curt Suplee, "Naughty Nineties," *Minneapolis Star Tribune*, January 21, 1989, pp. 1E–2E; data in *Psychology Today*, October 1988, p. 10; see Sar Levitan et al., *What's Happening to the American Family? Tensions, Hopes, Realities*, rev. ed. (Baltimore: Johns Hopkins University Press, 1988), passim; "Sex," in Dennis Gilbert, ed., *Compendium of American Public Opinion* (New York: Facts on File Publications, 1988), pp. 321–38; statistics in *Los Angeles Times*, February 6, 1988, sec. 2, p. 7; Steve Chapple and David Talbot, *Burning Desires: Sex in America, A Report from the Field* (Garden City, N.Y.: Doubleday, 1989); news story, *U.S. News and World Report*, December 9, 1985, pp. 54–58.

3. *Washington Post*, August 13, 1988, p. B6; Tim and Beverly LaHaye, *The Act of Marriage* (New York: Bantam Books, 1978); Peter Gardella, *Innocent Ecstasy: How Christianity Gave America an Ethic of Sexual Pleasure* (New York: Oxford University Press, 1985), pp. 150–62; Donald Meyer, *The Positive Thinkers* (New York: Pantheon Books, 1980), pp. 347–50; John D'Emilio and Estelle B. Freedman, *Intimate Matters: A History of Sexuality in America* (New York: Perennial Library, Harper and Row, 1988), pp. 344–60; Barbara Ehrenreich et al., "Fundamentalist Sex: Hitting below the Bible Belt," in *The Feminization of Sex* (Garden City, N.Y.: Doubleday, 1986), pp. 134–60; Lionell Lewis and Dennis B. Brissett, "Sex as God's Work," *Society*, March/April 1987, pp. 67–75; Ernie Zimbelman, *Human Sexuality and Evangelical Christians* (Lanham, Md.: University Press of America, 1985); Christianity Today Institute, "Great Sex: Reclaiming a Christian Sex Ethic," *Christianity Today*, October 2, 1987, pp. 23–46.

4. James Nelson, *Between Two Gardens: Reflections on Sexuality and Religious Experience* (New York: Pilgrim Press, 1983), pp. 74–84; idem, "Reuniting Sexuality and Spirituality," *Christian Century*, February 25, 1987, pp. 187–90; James Moore, *Sexuality and Marriage* (Minneapolis: Augsburg Publishing House, 1987).

5. See the study in Rebecca E. Klatch, *Women of the New Right* (Philadelphia: Temple University Press, 1987), pp. 20–54, and citations in the index under "Family"; see also the study by K. Greer, "Are American Families Finding New Strength?" *Better Homes and Gardens*, January 1988, pp. 16–21.

6. W. Lloyd Warner, *The Family of God* (New Haven: Yale University Press, 1961), pp. 265–66; H. Paul Chalfant, *Religion in Contemporary Society*, 2d ed. (Sherman Oaks, Calif.: Alfred Publishing Company, 1987), pp. 223–31.

7. Levitan et al., *What's Happening to the American Family?* pp. 3–25; Nelson, *Between Two Gardens*, p. 130.

8. See the debate in Ollie Pocs, ed., *Marriage and the Family* (Guilford, Conn.: Dushkin Publishing Group, 1987), with materials on fifty-five related issues; "Family," in Gilbert, *Compendium of American Public Opinion*, pp. 137–61.

9. Nelson, *Between Two Gardens*, p. 129.

10. See the helpful bibliographical essay in Harvey J. Graff, ed., *Growing Up in America* (Detroit: Wayne State University Press, 1987), pp. 1–47.

11. An excellent discussion is Rodney Clapp, "Is the 'Traditional' Family Biblical?" *Christianity Today*, September 16, 1988, pp. 24–28.

12. Martha Stout, "Families of the 80s," *Christian Herald*, March 1985, pp. 46–47.

13. Ibid., pp. 47–51; Pamela P. Wong, "No Babies?" *Eternity*, June 1987, pp. 12–13.

14. James B. Ellens, "Infidelity," *Banner*, June 23, 1986, p. 608; see the several articles on this subject in *Fundamentalist Journal*, April 1987; ibid., May 1986, p. 12; Nelson, *Between Two Gardens*, p. 88.

15. Herbert Schlossberg et al., *Turning Point: A Christian Worldview Declaration* (Westchester, Ill.: Crossway Books, 1987). See the account in the monthly *Religion Watch*, May 1989, p. 22.

16. Laura Gellott, "Staking Claim to the Family: Will Liberals Rediscover a Heritage?" *Commonweal*, September 20, 1985, pp. 488–92; Michael Lerner, "The Politics of Moral Vision," ibid., January 11, 1985, pp. 8–12.

17. Background information is in "Child Care Legislation: Pro and Con," *Congressional Digest*, November 1988; *Congressional Quarterly*, March 18, 1989, pp. 585–87; news story, *Report from the Capital*, June 1989, pp. 7, 14.

18. News story, *Minneapolis Star Tribune*, June 16, 1989, p. 10A; news story, *New York Times*, August 21, 1989, pp. 1, 8.

19. Sylvia Ann Hewlett, "Has Feminism Hindered the Working Woman?" *Utne Reader*, May/June 1987, p. 82.

20. Ibid., pp. 91–92; see also the excellent analysis by Deborah Fallows, "The Politics of Motherhood," *Washington Monthly*, June 1985, pp. 40–49.

21. T.S. Seltte, *The Faith of Billy Graham* (Anderson, S.C.: Drake House, 1968), p. 104; *Fundamentalist Journal*, September 1984, p. 23; editorial, *Christianity Today*, February 20, 1981, p. 255; Richard Quebedeaux, *I Found It! The Story of Bill Bright and Campus Crusade* (San Francisco: Harper and Row, 1979), p. 117.

22. *New York Times*, August 21, 1989, pp. 1, 8; Mary Stewart van Leeuwan, "The End of Female Passivity," *Christianity Today*, January 18, 1986, p. 12-I; Gretchen Gaebelein Hull, *Equal to Serve* (Old Tappan, N.J.: Fleming Revell, 1989).

23. *Moody Monthly*, April 1986, p. 8; Karen Burton Mains, "It's a Mystery to Me: Struggles with Sexual Ambiguity in the Church," *Christianity Today*, July 17, 1981, pp. 953–55. A contrasting view is Patrick H. McNamara, "The New Christian Right's View of the Family and its Social Science Critics," *Journal of Marriage and the Family*, May 1985, pp. 449–58; see also Jeffrey K. Hadden, "Televangelism and the Mobilization of a New Christian Right Family Policy," in William V. D'Antonio and Joan Aldous, eds., *Families and Religion: Conflict and Change in Modern Society* (Beverly Hills, Calif.: Sage Publications, 1983), pp. 247–66.

24. *Minneapolis Star Tribune*, July 19, 1987, p. 16A; *National Christian Reporter*, August 8, 1986 p. 3; Margaret L. Bendroth, "The Search for 'Women's Role' in American Evangelicalism, 1930–1980," in George Marsden, ed., *Evangelicalism and Modern America* (Grand Rapids, Mich.: Wm. B. Eerdmans, 1984), pp. 122–34; news story, *Christianity Today*, October 3, 1986, pp. 40–43.

25. News story, *Christianity Today*, September 2, 1988, pp. 43–44; *Touchstone*, Summer/Fall 1988, p. 43; *Twin City Christian*, June 22, 1989, p. 15.

26. Daughters of Sarah, 3801 N. Keeler, Chicago, IL 60641.

27. *National Christian Reporter*, January 27, 1989, p. 4; statement in *Christianity Today*, January 13, 1989, n.p.; CBMW, P.O. Box 1173, Wheaton, IL 60189.

28. *Christian News*, July 31, 1989, pp. 1, 23; ibid., September 18, 1989, p. 11; CBE, 2832 Lower 138th St., Rosemont, MN 55068.

29. IWIL, P.O. Box 62603, Virginia Beach, VA 23462.

30. See the documentation in James Davison Hunter, *Evangelicalism: The Coming Generation* (Chicago: University of Chicago Press, 1987), pp. 61–62.

31. M. F. Riche, "The Post-marital Society," *Utne Reader*, March/April 1989, p. 50; Levitan et al., *What's Happening to the American Family?* pp. 19–35; Albert D. Klassen et al., *Sex and Morality in the United States: An Empirical Enquiry under the Auspices of the Kinsey Institute* (Middletown, Conn.: Wesleyan University Press, 1989).

32. D'Antonio and Aldous, *Families and Religion*, pp. 81–103; Jean Wulf et al., "Religiousity and Sexual Attitudes among Evangelical Christian Singles," *Review of Religious Research* 26, 2 (December 1984): 129–30.

33. Nelson, *Between Two Gardens*, pp. 100–101; see the bibliography in Deane William Ferm, *Alternative Life-Styles Confront the Church* (New York: Seabury Press, 1983), p. 132.

34. Tim Stafford, "Beyond the Stiff Upper Lip," *Christianity Today*, January 13, 1989, pp. 31–34.

35. See the issues of such magazines as the Evangelical Lutheran Church in America, *Singles Speak*; Campus Crusade, *WorldWide Challenge*, April 1987, pp. 54–69; Single Adult Ministries, *Journal*, P.O. Box 3015, Sisters, OR 97759; or magazines of specific congregations such as Church of Many Mansions, P.O. Box 9020, Van Nuys, CA 91409.

36. Arland Thornton, "Cohabitation and Marriage in the 80s," *Demography* 25, 4 (November 1988): 497.

37. Ibid.; Moore, *Sexuality and Marriage*, pp. 30–31.

38. Thornton, "Cohabitation and Marriage," p. 506; see pp. 497–508.

39. News story, *Christianity Today*, September 20, 1985, pp. 44–45.

40. *New York Times*, May 20, 1989, p. 6E; ibid., May 24, 1989, p. 13.

41. Cyril J. Barber, "Marriage, Divorce, and Remarriage: A Review of Relevant Religious Literature, 1973–1983," *Journal of Psychology and Theology* 12 (1984): 170–77; Paul E. Steele and Charles C. Ryrie, "Are Divorce and Remarriage Ever Permissible: Yes—No," *Fundamentalist Journal*, June 1984, pp. 17–19ff.; Ferm, *Alternative Life-Styles*, pp. 1–13.

42. D'Emilio and Freedman, *Intimate Matters*, pp. 318–24.

43. Nelson, *Between Two Gardens*, pp. 120–22; Ferm, *Alternative Life-Styles*, pp. 87–96.

44. Evangelicals Concerned, Suite 1403, 30 East 60th St., New York, NY 10022; see also the groups listed in Ferm, *Alternative Life-Styles*, pp. 87–96, *Encyclopedia of Associations*, Vol. 2, 23rd ed. (Detroit: Gale Research, 1989), nos. 16433–16466.

45. Steven Mintz and Susan Kellogg, *Domestic Revolution: A Social History of American Family Life*) New York: Free Press, 1988), p. 239.

46. Victor R. Fuchs, *How We Live* (Cambridge: Harvard University Press, 1983), p. 105.

47. Ibid., p. 104; D'Emilio and Freedman, *Intimate Matters*, p. 342.

48. Stanley K. Henshaw and Jennifer Van Vart, "Teen Age Abortion, Birth and Preganancy Statistics: An Update," *Family Planning Perspectives* 21, 2 (March/April 1989): 85–88; more in Eli Ginzberg et al., *Young People at Risk: Is Prevention Possible?* (Boulder, Colo.: Westview Press, 1988), pp. 72–88.

49. See "Sex Ed: Why Wait?" *Christianity Today*, September 22, 1989, pp. 19–20; Faye Wattleton, "Coming of Age: The Tragedy of Teenage Prenancy," *USA Today*, January 1989, pp. 49–50.

50. News story, *Christianity Today*, December 12, 1986, p. 45; cover story, "Sex and Schools," *Time*, November 24, 1986, pp. 54–63; "News," *Christianity Today*, April

18, 1987, p. 40; *Concerned Women*, June 1988, pp. 3–4ff.; *National and International Religion Report*, March 14, 1988, p. 2; *Liberty Report*, May 1988, pp. 10–11; interview with Josh McDowell in *Cornerstone* 10, 58 (1986): 7–9.

51. Rob Barton, "Everything You've Always Wanted to Know about the Teen Chastity Act," *Church and State*, April 1988, pp. 76–78; news story, *Report from the Capital*, September 1988, p. 10; news item, *Journal of Church and State* 30, 3 (Autumn 1988): 434; Nabers Cabaniss, "A Look at the Adolescent Family Life Act," *World and I* 4, 9 (September 1989): 604–11.

52. News story in *Eternity*, January 1986, p. 7; Robert M. Swenson, "Plagues, History, and AIDS," *American Scholar* 57, 2 (Spring 1988): 183–200; Jan Zita Grover, "Global AIDS: The Epidemic," *Christianity and Crisis*, June 12, 1989, pp. 197–200; George Gallup, Jr., and Jim Castelli, *The People's Religion: American Faith in the 90s* (New York: Macmillan, 1989), pp. 190–92.

53. *Newsweek*, July 3, 1989, p. 57. See U.S. Department of Health and Human Services, Public Health Services, PHS89-1232, pp. 1ff.; news story, *Eternity*, 1988, p. 58; *Ms.*, May 1987, p. 31.

54. D'Emilio and Freedman, *Intimate Matters*, pp. 354–60; Frances FitzGerald, *Cities on a Hill: A Journey through Contemporary American Cultures* (New York: Touchstone Book ed., Simon and Schuster, 1987), pp. 25–119.

55. D'Emilio and Freedman, *Intimate Matters*, p. 354.

56. Stuart Rothenberg and Frank Newport, *The Evangelical Voter: Religion and Politics in America* (Washington, D.C.: Institute for Government and Politics, 1984), pp. 67–70.

57. Susan J. Palmer, "AIDS as Metaphor," *Society*, January/February 1989, p. 46.

58. Ron Sider, "AIDS: An Evangelical Perspective," *Christian Century*, June 6–13, 1988, p. 11; memo, ibid., November 30, 1988, p. 1111; editorial, *Christianity Today*, March 20, 1987, pp. 16–17.

59. Paul Back, "Religious Responses to AIDS," *USA Today*, May 1989, pp. 66–68.

60. *New York Times*, May 22, 1989, p. 8; ibid., September 23, 1988, p. 11.

61. D'Emilio and Freedman, *Intimate Matters*, pp. 326–28.

62. See the NAE study on pornography in Richard Cizik, ed., *The High Cost of Indifference: Can Christians Afford Not to Act?* (Ventura, Calif.: Regal Books, 1984), pp. 121–40; news story, "What Entertainers Are Doing to Your Kids," *U.S. News and World Report*, October 28, 1985, pp. 45–49; Edward Donnersteen et al., *The Questions of Pornography: Research Findings and Policy Implications* (New York: Free Press, 1987); editorial, *Christian Century*, October 9, 1985, pp. 883–84.

63. Interview with Donald Wildmon in *Charisma*, May 1987, pp. 43–52.

64. *Christianity Today*, November 30, 1987, pp. 46–47.

65. News item, *Religious Broadcasting*, January 1983, p. 11; Donald Wildmon, "Television," ibid., April 1983, pp. 28–30; Paul A. Tanner, "How to Wage War on Pornography," *Charisma*, May 1985, pp. 72–78; Jimmy Swaggart, "Pornography: America's Dark Stain," *Evangelist*, April 1985, pp. 4–11ff.; *Time*, June 23, 1986, p. 36; news story, *Christianity Today*, June 13, 1987, pp. 74ff.; *Christian Herald*, November 1987, p. 6; *National Christian Reporter*, August 7, 1987, p. 3; *Minneapolis Star Tribune*, June 5, 1986, p. 32A; *NFD Journal*, April 1987, p. 1; ibid., July 1987, p. 1; *Twin City Christian*, March 23, 1989, p. 11A; *National Christian Reporter*, April 14, 1989, p. 1; *Time*, June 19, 1989, pp. 54–55; *Christian News*, June 5, 1989, p. 13; Andrew Greeley, "Like a Catholic: Madonna's Challenge to the Church," *America*, May 13, 1989, p. 447. A profile of Wildmon is in the *St. Paul Dispatch Pioneer Press*, June 5, 1989, p. 3B; Don

Wildmon, *The Man the Networks Love to Hate* (Wilmore, Kent, Eng.: Bristol Books, 1989), an autobiography.

66. People for the American Way, *Forum*, February 1989, n.p.; ibid., Spring 1989, p. 2; ibid., Summer 1989, p. 2; *Christianity Today*, August 18, 1989, pp. 47–49; *Christian Herald*, September/October 1989, p. 5; *Concerned Women*, September 1989, p. 19.

10

The Search for the Self

Throughout the 1980s Americans continued their religious quests through highly private, often internalized programs for self-discovery. Going beyond the search for fulfillment through social relationships, they pursued a search for religious meaning focused on their inner lives, their personal spirituality. They could draw on a very long, well-established tradition within organized religion for such a quest. Throughout the history of Christendom seekers had looked inward more than to society for nurture and direction. Christianity had embraced mystics, loners, ascetics, and contemplators as members of the larger family of believers. What came into special prominence in postawakening American life was both a resurgence of that tradition and a movement by many toward an entirely different sense of what lay beyond the everyday world of politics and church life. That sense they called a "new age."

In this chapter we examine the first of these quests, the one within organized faith. The energy for both holding fast and pressing on emerged from the continuing "thrust toward greater personal fulfillment and quest for the ideal self" so characteristic of privatized religion.[1] Although the intensity of the movement was extremely high during the 1980s, the belief that somehow religious faith and psychology (broadly defined here) were the two sides of the same coin reached far back into the American past. The first best-selling self-help book was the autobiography of Benjamin Franklin. His wryly self-deprecating account of the search for virtue and higher mortality came to be the first of an entire genre of psychoreligious quests in American society. By the time of the 1960s the two fields, religion and psychology, had in the eyes of most gone their separate ways, the latter claiming legitimation as a behavioral science subject to scholarly verification.

Yet under the umbrella of "psychology" stood the complex fields of emotions, mental processes, behavioral disorders, and personality phenomena that defied attempts to be understood only in behavioral, quantitative terms. For many seekers, those inner signs of individuality and unanswerable questions pointed to another

151

level of reality, one with supernatural origins and ultimate meanings built into its very center. The question remained: Who was correct?

During the 1980s, as had occurred earlier, pressers and holders attempted to explore the possibilities that both sides could be correct; that psychology had much to learn from religion, which in turn needed to listen carefully to what the former was saying. If somehow the self was to be better understood, then the evidence from both camps needed to be evaluated.

Signs of that decision showed up throughout the decade. In seminaries ministerial candidates continued their studies in pastoral psychology, counseling, and human relations. Churches and synagogues added outreach programs based on the combined insights of both fields, such as transactional analysis. Publishers found an enormous, ever-growing market for books on the problems central to the search for the self: depression, anxiety, stress, sexuality, self-esteem, co-optation, parenting—the subject list seemed inexhaustible.[2]

What stood out in postawakening society was the increasing acceptance of the "therapeutic" mode of ministry, as defined by Robert Bellah and his associates:

The therapeutic attitude . . . begins with the self, rather than with a set of external obligations. The individual must find and assert his or her true self because this self is the only source of genuine relationships to other people. External obligations, whether they come from religion, parents, or social conventions, can only interfere with the capacity for love and relatedness. Only by knowing and ultimately accepting one's self can one enter into valid relationships with other people.[3]

In other words, the ultimate purpose of the therapist's program "is to teach the therapeutic client to be independent of anyone else's standards."[4]

This worldview emerged because as those Americans who turned away from seeking fulfillment in public or denominational life moved into this therapeutic mind-set, they became convinced that it was in that mind-set that they achieved what had eluded them: self-realization. That in itself would become a kind of faith.[5]

The awakening contributed strongly to this search, giving the searchers reasons for changing older family and gender roles. The American consumer culture, with its vast advertising powers, also helped convince people that they now had more choices about their futures than ever before. They could by wise consumption of a plethora of leisure-time and career products become more the person they really wanted to be. What prevented even deeper fulfillment could be reduced if not eliminated by participating in the right therapy.[6]

However, as more choices appeared, so also did the search to understand why self-realization seemed so far beyond one's reach. *Habits of the Heart* and other studies demonstrated the condition of Americans remaining bewildered because their sought-after individualism had eluded them. As Bellah suggested, this had occurred because Americans were turning away from what had for centuries been the principal source of fulfillment, a sense of belonging to and participating in family, church, or community.[7] These domains obviously were at the core of religious life. Thus the response of the religious communities to the new therapeutic search illumines the deeper meaning of this phase of religion in the 1980s.

Those within the Judeo-Christian tradition had known, at least in their minds, that the searching could never achieve even a sizeable portion of self-realization apart from faith. So strong was the presence of sin—an innate quality of the self in human beings that always came between their earthborn needs and their heaven-born aspirations—that the quest must always end in stalemate. Many pressers and holders would perhaps not mean by "sin" what earlier divines such as St. Augustine or Jonathan Edwards had meant, but they would acknowledge that a permanent brokenness between people and God existed that could never be eliminated in this life.

Yet that tension, as old as the first records of humans aspiring to be with the gods, continued to haunt seekers in the 1980s. Perhaps what might be needed was to place less emphasis on shortcomings and failures and more emphasis on potential, what could be done in the here and now to help relieve if not eliminate the brokenness.[8] While the therapeutic mind-set itself might be too self-centered for the religious-minded, perhaps some other avenue might be found, some other empowering source of insight discovered to light the path for the searcher for the self.

That avenue or power took rather clear shape in this decade with the increasingly popular acceptance of using certain psychological wisdom to undergird traditional claims of religious truth. Within mainline circles, according to Benton Johnson, this amalgamation had already occurred as the educated elite accepted the truths of secular scholarship in this field at the expense of "the supernatural foundations of Christianity."[9]

During this decade, as argued by Wade Clark Roof and William McKinney, much the same mentality has permeated evangelical circles as well. Its outlook on the search for the self was highly consistent "with modern rationality and good taste" rather than with keeping alive the older holy-roller accents. "It is more instrumental, with a stress upon psychological 'needs' and the benefits of faith—joy, wholeness, happiness, health, and wealth." Salvation was being offered as the product of following specific guildlines and programs with defined procedures.[10]

This new path did not totally replace the older evangelical insistence on the instant, born-again experience, but in the 1970s and more so in the 1980s evangelicals talked less about watching and praying to avoid temptation and to be ready for Christ's imminent return to earth. Instead, the search accented the themes of self-discovery, personal growth, and fulfillment by the realization of one's potential.[11]

At the same time, however imperceptibly, mainliners moved away from earlier accommodations to secular culture to where they acknowledged the need for greater introspection, for renewed spirituality, and for acknowledging one's own shortcomings. Now the life journey was one with greater risks but also with greater opportunity or, in the key word of the times, more potential.[12]

The source of this embracing of life as a quest to meet needs, to quiet the anguish of the recognition of personal shortcomings, and to achieve a greater degree of fulfillment than traditional faith had encouraged came largely from the teachings of the school of humanistic psychology. That movement had been born out of a rejection by certain scholars of the prevailing heavy emphasis on objectivism and natural-science presuppositions in the formal study of psychology. Some researchers could not accept the going consensus that psychology, focused on human behavior, could be understood as searchers understood the fields of the natural sciences.

Scholars such as Abraham Maslow, Carl Rodgers, Rollo May, and Fritz Perls, among others, in their individual ways presented a psychology faithful to empirical observation and testing but still empathetic with deep human aspirations for greater autonomy and personal choice. Since each person had within herself or himself far greater potential for autonomy and choice, then psychology should be the avenue or the power leading each traveler to find that for autonomy for herself or himself.

The importance of this field justifies this long definition:

Humanistic psychology is not just a new brand of psychology, to set side by side on the shelves with all the old brands. It is a wholly different way of looking at psychological science. It is a way of doing science which includes love, involvement and spontaneity, instead of systematically excluding them. And the object of this science is not the prediction and control of people's behaviour [sic], but the liberation of people from the bonds of neurotic control, whether this comes from outside (in the structures of our society) or from inside.[13]

Significantly, humanistic psychology penetrated both mainline and evangelical counseling and human relations programs. Both these two groups and the psychologists, united in their search for religiously oriented psychologies, placed great importance on the experiences of everyday life. Christianity, for instance, had long emphasized the importance of Christ's responses to persons' behavior. Both systems gave attention to social justice and the rights of the oppressed. Self-realization, as taught in humanistic psychology, would lead the believer to accept many of the teachings of Christ. Both systems, finally, emphasized the importance of each person accepting responsibility for her or his own life rather than blaming misfortune on larger social or environmental causes.[14]

Humanistic psychology and Christianity differed in the worldviews of the specific spokespersons. Leaders acknowledged that they were not "value-free," as certain behavioral scientists claimed for themselves. Rather, they acknowledged personal biases and inward intuitions as contributing to their insights. These were not subject to the goals of value-free empirical research. Christians, meanwhile, argued for a more supernatural mind-set.[15]

During the 1970s church and parachurch programs freely adapted much of the programming done by the "human potential" (HP) movement, itself one adaptation of humanistic psychology. It rested on the premise that normal persons were using only a small portion of their potential for fulfilling, rewarding lives. It avoided the older model of client/therapist in favor of a model featuring leader/group as both being fellow seekers pursuing inner growth. HP also embraced a wide variety of techniques (or "training"): role playing, guided daydreams, creative body movement, sensory awareness, and similar experiences. HP allowed its followers a greater flexibility than traditional psychotherapy.[16]

All this had a marked impact in the religious world. The Christian doctrine of the Incarnation, God made person in Jesus who experienced human emotions, gave credibility to a religious person's own searchings. Christianity promised a "new life," celebrating the ordinary, everyday experiences. Such themes were widely utilized by HP programs. HP's optimistic view about coming to terms with one's inner struggles found a receptive audience in parachurch and church groups.[17]

The most widespread of these programs was "transactional analysis" (TA) with its slogan, "I'm OK, you're OK!" Created by psychiatrist Eric Berne, TA was popularized and became an enormous best-seller under the leadership of one of his students, Thomas Harris. By the late 1970s its annual sales were well over 6 million books.[18]

TA was new, trendy, and simple to understand. It embraced the everyday life experiences of all persons and offered structure and pattern to otherwise random human experiences. With its use of categories such as "parent," "child," and "adult," its use of "strokes," and its capacity to encourage people to talk in groups about unpleasant experiences or disturbed feelings added up to a program that swept the country. It showed people that by taking thought, expressing their feelings, and listening to those in their support group they could establish more self-control and self-direction in their lives, a theme not unlike much of Christianity.[19]

Well into the 1980s church groups and publishers pursued TA with considerable energy. Each person could infuse into it her or his own style of piety without damaging the author's intentions. Each church-related group welcomed the opportunity to bring families or couples into seeing more clearly the sources of their inner anxieties. Given its flexible structure, TA became a landmark for the inner search during these years. Its popularity faded during the late 1980s, but it continued to attract a variety of imitations.[20]

Alongside TA emerged another major expression of the inner search, the "healing movement." Not born from any one sacred writing or set of teachings, it drew from a variety of sources. Emerging clearly by the 1970s, it became widespread in the next decade and continues to expand. Its principal theme revolved around the conviction that healing—mental, physical, spiritual, or social—could occur through the application of certain religious beliefs by the seeker in one's daily life. As these unfolded, they contributed to the overarching motif of the age, "the therapeutic worldview."

The worlds of organized medicine and secular psychotherapy were by their own self-imposed boundaries not open to the kinds of healing that occurred when the believer trusted that God or some superhuman power was at work in that process. That believer thus could be far more empowered to direct her or his own life than by following the more traditional models and practices of healing. As searchers probed in postawakening times for understanding of the new ways their expanded definitions of religion could lead them, many concentrated on the healing ministry of Jesus. He became a model, an empowerer for those seeking inner healing and understanding, a theme strongly endorsed by the new charismatic movement.[21] For all the new enthusiasm, however, believers came to realize the potential dangers involved, largely because charlatans and nonscriptural "healers" had over the decades exploited the faithful.[22]

Evangelical psychologist Dr. Gary Collins asked, "How do we keep extremism and quackery from entering and disrupting our church, especially when some of our members appear less enthusiastic about the gospel than about the latest influential guru?"[23] The answers emerged not in any form of organized movement, but in a ground swell of involvement by seekers in "Christian healing" (as distinct from Eastern, metaphysical, psychic, and technique/manipulative programs). The charge of quackery was overcome by the religious groups following the teachings on healing in the New Testament and the early church. Within congregations and parachurch groups, healing sessions emerged using prayers, laying on of hands, reading of scripture, and song.[24]

Of central importance in this part of the search for the self was the realization that through such experiences one came to understand more clearly one's individual needs and then to trust in the miraculous powers of healing to meet those needs; it was, indeed, "faith healing." But healing embraced more than the familiar ailments, illnesses, and infirmities. It enveloped the achievement of deeper inner vision, of more tenderness and compassion for others, and of patience. Healing became equated with holiness for many, not to be achieved perfectly in this life but the goal to which one aspired. Healing became a process, an on-going search for the inner self. As one expert explained, "The healthy person is a person who is continuously becoming healthy."[25]

This form of holiness/health, believers discovered, furnished the power to deal with such human anxieties as fear, tension, stress, bitterness, broken relationships, and worries over the future. As a primary researcher discovered, the practitioners did not believe that to be healed was the same as to be cured. Healing could be temporary; it could mend one problem, while another opened. The key was to remain close to God through inner spirituality, including prayer and devotional life, and trust that God was in control.[26]

Of strong appeal for many religionists was the manner in which the healing/holiness movement incorporated both the teaching of original sin and secular psychology's explanations of illness as the source of the maladjustment. No longer was sin as depravity (in a Reformation-age sense) solely responsible for a malady. Now diagnoses showed that anger, greed, perfectionism, and even paranoia or clinical depression, to name but a few problems, helped explain in more rational terms the sources of one's inner conflicts. Thus the movement itself became attractive because of its eclectic character; it freely borrowed from a variety of sources for both diagnosis and healing.[27]

Throughout the 1980s these healing opportunities continued to appear in both mainline and evangelical circles. Most prominent in charismatic communities, they were also conducted within small groups of friends, in loosely organized prayer cells, at weekend retreats, and at area conferences. We have no reliable way in which to estimate the number of participants. It can only be inferred by anecdotal evidence and by the fact that a wide variety of numerically large and small denominations continued to furnish ministries for the seekers.

COUNSELING

Psychology and religion also came together in the related field of personal counseling. Here, despite considerable conflict between holders and pressers, searchers for the self continued to develop a long-standing partnership of pastoral ministry. The belief that helping others work through personal conflict within a religious setting, work usually done by a minister or priest, had deep roots in church life. In the 1980s this tradition both deepened and produced fresh acrimony.[28]

During the awakening ministers moved quickly to bring certain human potential programs into their counseling. At the seminaries the field of pastoral psychology became increasingly professional, drawing on current research, being responsive to higher accreditation standards, and offering field or intern experience for ministerial candidates. By the late 1970s two schools of ministerial counseling were current: pastoral care revolving around a person's needs within the community and counseling centered on one-to-one involvement.[29]

Welcome as the expanded services were for many seekers, the movement also meant that many were focusing on the realm of the inner life at the expense of community and global concerns. Also, as ministers broadened their definitions of mental health and healing, they were in essence challenging the priorities of the holders fast, who insisted on the primacy of theology, doctrine, and scriptural authority. They found great difficulty in believing that human wisdom, as expressed here in counseling, could improve on the power that scriptural teaching held for those in need. Pressers on, meanwhile, would wonder how traditional doctrine could help those clients who came for help in such matters as low self-esteem, eating disorders, sexual dysfunction, guilt, and family violence—the full range of emotional turmoil.[30]

This basic conflict also appeared in another form, the extent to which a psychotherapist's (pastor or professional) personal faith should influence her or his professional practice. Should pastors act, as did their secular counterparts, as though they were neutral, scientifically informed facilitators? Or should they bring their own ethical and theological perspectives to bear on this part of their practice? Making this issue more complicated was the debate over which form or school of psychotherapy should be implemented. Several schools, each often in conflict with the others, were flourishing in both the secular and religious world: cognitive therapy, assertiveness training, behavior therapy, time-limited dynamic psychotherapy, and client-centered therapy, to name but a few.[31]

Finally, controversy swirled over whether a counselor had the responsibility of helping bring a client to a deeper understanding of religious faith. Therapy was seen by some as an opportunity both for healing immediate concerns and for leading the person toward a stronger religious commitment. Yet for others such "ultimate concerns" were often not therapeutically appropriate. They pointed to the story of the Good Samaritan in the New Testament who simply helped a person in need without pressing for any further involvement. That was being religious in the most profound sense.[32]

Again, no reliable statistical evidence exists to illustrate the numerical strengths of each of these programs. By their nature they were largely offered for short-term therapy, with clients moving in and out with great frequency. What seems clear is that churches and parachurch groups continued to debate these and related issues and to pursue means by which religious faith and the search for the self could be brought into greater harmony.

LEADERS

As befitted the style of the 1980s, when much of popular religious life was presented through the mass media by celebrities, the various blends of psychology and religion reached the public through a variety of qualified leaders. By contrast to the single counselor working on a one-to-one basis, these personages could establish their distinctive ministries and attract millions of followers, but because they had to address mass audiences, their teachings were limited largely to areas of general concern rather than focusing on individual dilemmas.

Perhaps the best known of these media-oriented counselors were (in no particular order) Charles Swindoll, Clyde Narramore, Robert Schuller, M. Scott Peck, and James Dobson. Only a brief overview of their ministries can be presented here, but they clearly represented the larger forces and broad diversity of programs at work.

Swindoll, with a pastorate in the Evangelical Free Church in Fullerton, California, presented during the 1980s an increasingly diverse media ministry. His books, with as many as five at a time being on the evangelical ten-best-seller lists, centered on biblical messages for everyday life situations. His radio program, "Insight for Living," reached over 800 stations by late 1987. By then he had also put together a staff of 150 who published *Insights* magazine and developed and distributed Bible study guides with cassettes to coincide with the radio programs. By 1990 he had published some twenty-five books. His wife Cynthia worked closely with him as executive vice president. In 1988 he was named by the Religious Heritage of America the clergyman of the year.[33]

Swindoll became best known for down-to-earth, fatherly teachings and inspirational messages focused on everyday life—the discovery of God at work in ordinary events as well as in the great crises and turning points. He explained that when we are confronted with a dilemma where the Bible does not clearly give the solution, "we can draw upon God's power as we seek creative ways to deal with the situations we must face." On occasion he would move into the larger social implications of his kind of ministry, reminding the listener to accept personal responsibility for her or his own life. Rarely controversial, and careful to avoid committing himself to only one school of therapy, Swindoll became a major voice during the 1980s.[34]

A rather different form of inner-self ministry was that of Dr. Clyde Narramore. With headquarters in Rosemead, California, he was directing by decade's end the Narramore Christian Foundation with thirty years of experience. It concentrated on offering seminars and conferences for several audiences. He wrote for a wide readership; his staff prepared and distributed tapes and cassettes of his and others' works. His monthly magazine, *Living*, carried his message into an already heavily saturated market.

At the heart of the program was the Center, "dedicated to helping Christians navigate through the various stages of life." "The process is energized," he wrote, "by the Holy Spirit, but in practice the change takes place as we interact in a safe, secure environment with trustworthy, compassionate and wise people."[35]

Specific counseling programs were established for laity, business leaders, parish ministers, missionaries and their children, parish educators, lay counselors, and career planners. The programs included interviews and personality tests utilizing current motivational training to enrich the participant's ministries. Narramore attracted a large audience when shortly after the collapse of the PTL ministry he brought out a booklet, "Why a Christian Leader May Fail." It centered less on judgment and more on forgiveness and correction. Perhaps less prominent nationally than Swindoll, Narramore chose to define his use of media carefully and expand it in line with the range of problems and expanded public interest in new therapies.

Among the best known of all religion/psychology spokepersons has been the Reverend Robert Schuller of the Crystal Cathedral in Garden Grove, California. So well known is his story that it needs no retelling here, except to add that after the televangelist scandals his reputation remained intact. The weekly "Hour of Power" reaches some 1,215,000 households, more than the weekly telecasts of Swaggart, Roberts, Falwell, or Robertson. His appeal for his entire career has revolved around his unique blend of popular religion, mass-media usage, and motivational psychology. Despite ongoing criticism that his theology is "more Peale than Paul" (more like Norman Vincent Peale than St. Paul), he continues to attract strong support from a variety of audiences.

Schuller captured a major theme of postawakening religion, advocating that by sound mental processes, based on proven psychotherapeutic programs and rooted in the Bible, seekers could overcome their fears, doubts, and anxieties—those problems that held them back from achieving healthy self-esteem. His message focused on the self: how it could get rid of inner problems and how it could restructure the negatives and turn them into positives. He sent his message across the country by way of television, books, convention speeches, and other forms of mass media.[36]

In a different realm altogether stood the writings and lectures of M. Scott Peck, psychiatrist and mid-life convert to Christianity. His books, *People of the Lie* (1983), *The Road Less Travelled* (1978), and an audiotape *What Return Can I Make?* (1985, an audiotape of songs by Marilyn von Waldner), have remained on the best-seller lists of the *New York Times* for years, making him one of the most influential leaders of the decade in the search for the self. His audiences embraced more than the largely evangelical readership of Swindoll, Narramore, and Dobson, but his place along the theological spectrum is impossible to define with precision. Perhaps that is one clue to understanding why he became so influential: Americans have pursued the search, recognizing their individual needs but not wanting to be identified with one position on that spectrum.

Educated at Case Western Reserve and Harvard, Peck did not read the New Testament Gospels until he was thirty-nine; he was baptized two years after he wrote *The Road Less Travelled*. The term "road" well explains his concept of life as being a process of growth not always clear nor with destination precisely known. Peck discussed the need for "wholeness," a popular theme of the age, and the possibility of each seeker finding her or his own form of self-discipline for making the journey. The supreme virtue in his hierarchy is love, calling people to listen to, heed, and pay attention to those they love without considering any personal benefit for themselves. Such a course requires a good deal of courage, especially to change one's life course. The empowerment for that change comes from a higher source, which he calls "grace," the love of God for people.[37] All in all, Peck tapped into the very deep sense of personal anxiety, pointing readers to find in spiritual resources the strength to continue the search. His has been a vision markedly different from the scriptural insights of the evangelicals, but one that has found a huge audience.

Finally, perhaps the counselor with the greatest potential for direct involvement in public life has been Dr. James Dobson. Not only did he make full use of mass media in the 1980s to present his popularized psychoreligious message, but he participated directly in national public policy-making programs. His name among evangelicals, along with that of Swindoll, falls in the household-word category. By early 1989 his radio program was carried on 1,250 stations in thirty-five countries. In Pasadena the Focus on the Family operation worked out of a $12.2 million headquarters, a state-of-the-art technology center. Its staff produced a sixteen-page monthly magazine, *Citizen*; Dobson was the featured speaker on a wide variety of several series of videocassettes and audiocassettes, with themes of marriage, family, and parenthood. His books, like Swindoll's, remained steadily on the evangelical ten–best-seller lists throughout the decade. The annual budget by 1987 was nearly $33.7 million. All but 2 percent came from viewer and listener donations. His headquarters received some 150,000 letters a month. It also distributed monthly church-bulletin inserts with short, attractively worded pieces of advice. Some 700,000 American military personnel had viewed his film "Where's Dad?" adapted from "Focus on the Family" themes.[38]

His appeal emerged from his ability to address the complicated questions of applying religious faith to the problems of inner doubts and searchings and to relationships with those nearest the searcher. The teachings were conservative, traditional messages on topics such as disciplining children, sex education, sibling rivalry, and other matters, these done with common sense and humor. Always, though, the final authority was the Bible. In a world of many competing therapies and answers, Dobson's audiences chose to endorse his authoritative solutions.[39]

In the later 1980s Dobson accepted several consultation appointments from the Reagan administration for advice on pending family legislation. Early in 1988 be became directly involved in a new conservative think-tank program, the Family Research Council (FRC). Established to defend "traditional Christian Values," a code phrase for the program of the religious Right, it carried wide national prestige in these and Republican party circles. The group prepared materials to oppose many of the sex-education programs conducted in the public schools, to combat the spread of pornography, and to oppose pro–civil rights measures for homosexuals. Privately funded, the Family Research Council also provided data to Congress for pending measures such as day-care legislation. Its ties to the White House were strengthened when Reagan's director of policy development, Gary L. Bauer, was appointed president of the FRC and vice president of Focus on the Family. Aware of his critics, Dobson told reporters that he was not aiming at becoming another Jerry Falwell.[40]

As the decade ended, Dobson started to develop what came to be called "profamily" coalitions in several states, aimed at political lobbying for legislation on abortion, child care, tuition tax credits, pornography, and litigation in religious and moral court cases. By early 1989 such coalitions had appeared in Arizona, California, Minnesota, Ohio, Tennessee, Texas, Virginia, and Washington State.[41]

Obviously by now Dobson's influence in American religiopolitical life has only begun to receive wide recognition. To some observers it is conceivable that the coalitions will ally with Pat Robertson forces for greater grass roots influence. Dobson could emerge as a more visible force on Capitol Hill for the social agenda espoused by the religious Right.

In any event, the Dobson ministry stands as clear testimony of how evangelical religion, media appeal, and traditional morality can coalesce under the leadership of one celebrity. Dobson chose to move toward sociopolitical concerns more than did many of the other prominent searchers for the self. As he did so, the huge support he continued to receive demonstrated again the depth and the unpredictability of American religious life as it moved toward the approaching millennium.

CRITICS

Throughout the 1980s the inner search attracted a substantial degree of criticism by other religionists. Apart from the ongoing controversies over appropriate therapies, some critics aimed at nothing less than the entire psychology-in-religion enterprise itself. A scholar at Trinity Evangelical Divinity School, D.A. Carson, expressed concern over the "triumphalist" note he detected in much of the search. With the promise of victory over one's inner conflicts through therapy, might not the seeker ignore scriptural teachings about brokenness and sin and the need for repentance? Carson doubted that the self-esteem emphasis of Schuller could stand up well under sustained theological scrutiny; it was too optimistic about the influence of sin in all human endeavor.[42]

Jack O. Balswick considered evangelical emphasis on finding one's inner self to be based not on psychology but on traditional conversion. Evangelicals were saying that if "the best principles of counseling and psychotherapy to allow persons to become more fully healed" were utilized, the converted seeker would then go on to work for public social reform. This, Balswick charged, was much too naive a view; changed individuals would not automatically bring about more just social structures.[43]

On another level, psychologist Paul C. Vitz insisted that the differences between orthodox Christianity and mainstream psychology need always to be kept clear, lest anyone think that the two could be harmoniously blended. Fearing that many seekers had adopted the latter as their religion instead of holding to normative Christianity, Vitz became a major critic of those who failed to make the differentiation.[44]

The most sweeping denunciation of the movement embodied by the Swindolls, Narramores, Dobsons, Gary Collinses, and others was that made in 1987 by Martin and Diedre Bobgan in their work *Psychoheresy: The Psychological Seduction of Christianity.*[45] Linking evangelical concerns to New Age and secular humanist thought, and insisting that Biblical counseling that did not denounce sin as such was faulty, they maintained that only two systems of truth existed, that of God and that of the devil. Any knowledge, insight, or wisdom not inspired and informed by the traditional understanding of God was a part of the "world system" and was to be condemned. Christians, they wrote, must return to scriptural teachings or face the takeover of their domain by the new wave of occult secularists.

The mention of New Age suggested that alternative movements spreading across the country were viewed suspiciously by the holders fast. Daily involvement with people perplexed by inner anxieties, however, led local ministers and counselors to utilize a variety of therapies. What everyone concerned during the 1980s had identified as the crucial issue was whether "truth," as agreed upon by humans—scholars, specialists, experts, and laity—was also God's truth. If it were, then much of the findings of psychology could validity be utilized in the search. But what if "God's truth" was in fact truth that human beings had only now—at the start of a New Age—begun to discover? What then could be the outcome of pressing and holding?

NOTES

1. Wade Clark Roof and William McKinney, *American Mainline Religion: Its Changing Shape and Future* (New Brunswick, N.J.: Rutgers University Press, 1987), p. 8; Carl F. George, "A Tilt toward the Relational," *Christianity Today*, January 17, 1986, p. 23.

2. Joseph W. Trigg and William L. Sachs, *Of One Body: Renewal Movements in the Church* (Atlanta, Ga.: John Knox Press, 1986), pp. 22ff.

3. Robert Bellah et al., *Habits of the Heart: Individualism and Commitment in American Life* (Berkeley: University of California Press, 1985), p. 98.

4. Ibid., p. 99; Roof and McKinney, *American Mainline Religion*, pp. 47–50.

5. Benton Johnson, "A Sociological Perspective on the New Religions," in Thomas Robbins and Dick Anthony, eds., *In Gods We Trust: New Patterns of Religious Pluralism in America* (New Brunswick, N.J.: Transaction Books, 1981), pp. 52–53.

6. Laurence Shames, *The Hunger for More: Searching for Values in an Age of Greed* (New York: Times Books, 1989); John Brooks, *Showing Off in America: From Conspicuous Consumption to Parody Display* (Boston: Little, Brown, 1981); Louis Menand, "Don't Think Twice," *New Republic*, October 9, 1989, pp. 18–23.

7. Bellah et al., *Habits of the Heart*, pp. 275–96; Johnson, "Sociological Perspective," pp. 54–55; "Personal Life," in Dennis A. Gilbert, ed., *Compendium of American Public Opinon* (New York: Facts on File Publications, 1988), pp. 279ff.

8. See the insights in Elise Chase, *Healing Faith: An Annotated Bibliography of Self-Help Books* (Westport, Conn.: Greenwood Press, 1985), pp. xii–xiii.

9. Johnson, "Sociological Perspective," p. 58.

10. Roof and McKinney, *American Mainline Religion*, p. 53; James Davison Hunter, *Evangelicalism: The Coming Generation* (Chicago: University of Chicago Press, 1987), pp. 50–75.

11. See Hunter, *Evangelicalism*.

12. Obviously there were no rigid lines of demarcation between evangelicals and mainliners here.

13. John Rowan, *Ordinary Ecstasy: Humanistic Psychology in Action* (London: Routledge and Kegan Paul, 1976), p. 3.

14. Doreen J. Dodgen and Mark R. McMinn, "Humanistic Psychology and Christian Thought: A Comparative Analysis," *Journal of Psychology and Theology* 14, 3 (1986): 199–200. See the scholarly study by Don Browning, *Religious Thought and the Modern Psychologies* (Philadelphia: Fortress Press, 1987), pp. 61–93; and Gary R. Collins, *The Rebuilding of Psychology* (Wheaton, Ill.: Tyndale House, 1987), pp. 53–70.

15. Alan C. Tjeltveit, "Psychotherapeutic Triumphalism and Freedom from Mental Illness: Diverse Concepts of Mental Health," *Word and World* 9, 2 (Spring 1989); 135ff.; idem, "The Impossibility of a Psychology for the Christian Religion: A Theological Perspective," *Journal of Psychology and Theology* 17, 3 (Fall 1989): 205–12.

16. Raymond J. Corsini, ed., *Encyclopedia of Psychology* (New York: John Wiley and Sons, 1974), p. 59.

17. Donald Stone, "The Human Potential Movement," in Robert N. Bellah and Charles Y. Glock, eds., *The New Religious Consciousness* (Berkeley: University of California Press,

1976), pp. 96–115; Philip A. Anderson, "Church Administration and the Human Potential Movement," in C. L. Manschreck and B. B. Zikmund, eds., *The American Religious Experiment* (Chicago: Exposition Press, 1976), pp. 126–34.

18. Steven Starker, *Oracle at the Supermarket: The American Preoccupation with Self-Help Books* (New Brunswick, N.J.: Transaction Books, 1989), p. 115; Martin Gros, *The Psychological Society* (New York: Random House, 1978), pp. 285–89.

19. Starker, *Oracle at the Supermarket*, pp. 117–18.

20. Among the many titles, see Muriel M. James, *Born to Love: TA in the Church* (Reading, Mass.: Addison-Wesley, 1973).

21. See Mary Jo Neitz, *Charisma and Community* (New Brunswick, N.J.: Transaction Books, 1987), pp. 235–43.

22. David Edwin Harrell, Jr., *All Things Are Possible: The Healing and Charismatic Revivals in Modern America* (Bloomington: Indiana University Press, 1975).

23. Gary Collins, "Saintly Snake Oil: Weighing Church Quackery," *Leadership* 6, 2 (Spring 1985): 31.

24. Meredith B. McGuire, *Ritual Healing in Suburban America* (New Brunswick, N.J.: Rutgers University Press, 1988), pp. 19–21; see the excellent interpretive work, Robert C. Fuller, *Alternative Medicine and American Religious Life* (New York: Oxford University Press, 1989), chaps. 1 and 5.

25. McGuire, *Ritual Healing*, pp. 38–40.

26. Ibid., pp. 41–43.

27. Ibid., pp. 44–63.

28. E. Brooks Holifield, *A History of Pastoral Care in America: From Salvation to Self-Realization* (Nashville, Tenn.: Abingdon Press, 1983).

29. E. Brooks Holifield, "Pastoral Care and Counseling," in Charles H. Lippy and Peter W. Williams, *Encyclopedia of the American Religious Experience*, Vol. 3 (New York: Scribner, 1988) p. 1593; Donald Meyer, *The Positive Thinkers* (New York: Pantheon Books, 1980), pp. 361–64; see the evangelically oriented *Resources for Christian Counseling*, approximately 20 volumes (Waco, Tex.: Word Books).

30. On this general topic, see Mark R. McMinn and James D. Foster, "The Mind Doctors," *Christianity Today*, April 8, 1988, pp. 16–21; and all of *Word and World* 9, 2 (Spring 1989).

31. See the sources cited in note 30.

32. David G. Benner and Stuart A. Palmer, "Psychotherapy and Christian Faith," in L. Stanton Jones, ed., *Psychology and the Christian Faith* (Grand Rapids, Mich.: Baker Book House, 1982), pp. 172–73; interview with Gary Collins, *Wittenburg Door*, no. 47 (February/March 1979): 9–22.

33. *Los Angeles Times*, September 17, 1988, sec. 2, p. 7; past winners were Billy Graham, Jerry Falwell, and Robert Schuller, among others; "Profile," *Religious Broadcasting*, December 1987, pp. 26–28; interview in *Today's Christian Woman*, July/August 1987, pp. 26ff.

34. *Today's Christian Woman*, July/August 1987, p. 55; *Eternity*, May 1988, p. 36.

35. Newsletter from Clyde Narramore, July 1988, p. 2; *Living*, February 1988, pp. 10ff.

36. Dennis Voskuil, *Mountains into Goldmines: Robert Schuller and the Gospel of Success* (Grand Rapids, Mich.: Wm. B. Eerdmans, 1983); *Christian Century*, September 30, 1987, p. 818; *National Christian Reporter*, March 28, 1986, p. 4; David E. Wells, "Self Esteem: The New Confusion," *TSF Bulletin*, November/December 1988, p. 11; *Cornerstone* 12, 68 (1987): 16–17.

37. Trigg and Sachs, *Of One Body*, pp. 28–31; *Newsweek*, November 18, 1987, p. 79; "Book Reviews," *Christian Research Journal*, Spring 1988, pp. 28–31; Ben Patterson, "Is God a Psychiatrist?" *Christianity Today*, March 1, 1985, pp. 211–23; book review in *Religious Studies Review* 13, 2 (April 1987): 26–29.

38. *National Christian Reporter*, March 10, 1989, p. 4; a profile in *Los Angeles Times*, April 2, 1988, sec. 4, pp. 1–3; *Christianity Today*, October 5, 1984, p. 100.

39. "Books," *Eternity*, April 1988, pp. 38–39; "James Dobson," *Religious Broadcasting*, January 1986, pp. 16–18; *Fundamentalist Journal*, May 1988, p. 37.

40. Dobson newsletter, February 5, 1988, n.p.; *New York Times*, October 12, 1988, p. 13; "RNS Report," *Christian News*, March 6, 1989, p. 24; Rolf Zettersten, *Dr. Dobson: Turning Hearts towards Home* (Waco, Tex.: Word Books, 1989).

41. *National and International Religion Report*, March 13, 1989, p. 5; *National Christian Reporter*, March 10, 1989, p. 4.

42. D.A. Carson, "Whatever Happened to Humility?" *Eternity*, May 1985 p. 35.

43. Jack O. Balswick, "The Psychological Captivity of Evangelicalism," in William H. Swatos, ed., *Religious Sociology* (Westport, Conn.: Greenwood Press, 1987), pp. 147–48.

44. Paul C. Vitz, *Psychology as Religion: The Cult of Self Worship* (Grand Rapids, Mich.: Wm. B. Eerdmans, 1979); idem, "From a Secular to a Christian Psychology," in Peter Williamson and Kevin Perrota, eds., *Christianity Confronts Modernity* (Ann Arbor: Servant Books, 1981), pp. 121–42.

45. Martin Bobgan and Diedre Bobgan, *Psychoheresy: The Psychological Seduction of Christianity* (Santa Barbara, Calif.: Eastgate Publishers, 1987); much the same criticism by Dave Hunt is found in his *CIB (Christian Information Bulletin)* out of Camarillo, California; see the review in *Christian Research Journal*, Winter/Spring 1988, pp. 30ff.

11

New Age Religion: The Future Is Now

As a plausible conclusion to the decline of the mainline, the disarray of the evangelicals, and the search for the self, New Age religion offered by decade's end a viable alternative to holders and pressers. Itself an unpredictable blend of several forms of faith, New Age stood by 1990 as a rejection of both secularization and much of modernity, but a victory for privatization. Rather than find the self in church, community, or family (Robert Bellah's triumvirate), [1] New Age celebrated the private individual, "creating your own reality," as one of its slogans promised. Denying that this world and life were becoming more secularized, New Age taught that all is sacred, all is one, all is God, and God is all. Rather than reject ancient insights as outdated in the world of modernity, New Age reached back to reconnect with the wisdom of the past. [2]

Idiosyncratic as is may sound, New Age could also be understood as both a rejection of the present expression of religion and an affirmation that religious faith had indeed just at this point been born. Robert Ellwood captures the essence of this juxtaposition. The "occult" or New Age

beliefs, acted out in practices, give a sense of significance, power, and harmony with the universe on all levels. The underlying message of the occult movement is, "You belong." You are, they say, a legitimate part of the universe; in this system, this harmony, you have a proper place. If you know and enact the secrets that give you that place, the meaning and power of the entire universe also are yours. [3]

This concluding chapter explores the quest for those "secrets," as New Agers attempted to define, identify with the past, teach, defend, and convert others to their old/new faith in a rapidly changing world.

DEFINITIONS

As society continued to break into ever-smaller special-purpose groups, to tribalize, and to compete for resources and power, New Age came on the scene offering significance, harmony, and its own form of power. Rather than accept modernity's premise that the world and society were a huge aggregation of parts, each moving by its own energy, New Age linked itself to the ancients who said that the world was one, a vast interlinked organism dependent upon each part contributing to the good of the whole. It opted for a global worldview, one in which such survival issues as environmental protection, the cessation of hunger, animal rights, and gender equality took the highest priority. Since all of life was sacred, all was one, all must be protected.

At the same time New Age also taught that "social change is most effective when accompanied by efforts to transform our own consciousness and redefine our own needs. Without personal change, political action often seems to end up replacing one set of oppressive individuals or policies with another."[4] That meant the desire to create a better, even utopian world, "a new age" in which humanity lived in harmony with itself, nature, and the cosmos through both global activism and personal transformation.

Indeed, New Agers claimed that they had found the "secrets" for this transformation and stood now in the last decade before the millennium in the midst of a movement as all-powerful as the Reformation or the Renaissance. Individuals had only to realize such power to claim it. The signs pointed to it; people should learn to sense it. One could create one's own reality and expect a new age rather than believe in nothing. New Age could tap into the searcher's hopes and aspirations. With hope as its energy, its potential was limitless. Energy was, in fact, the key word. The secrets were being discovered; the energy was being defined. It was more than traditional energy (heat, light); it entered into all of existence. It had different names: the healing force or spirit or the odic force.[5]

To those caught up in its vision, New Age offered a kind of awakening, an experience that had transformed their views of the world, both physical and spiritual. They realized the truth of the wisdom of the ancients: a return to harmony with nature, to kinship with the animals and the waters and the air. The old myths of traditional revealed religions had run their course; the new myth, which was really the oldest of all, was being rediscovered.[6]

Clearly this worldview broke sharply with that of the religions of the West. It embraced a mysticism opposed to the rationalism of modernity and proclaimed that the cosmos was sacred, not secular. It followed no single sacred text, it had no revealed system of morality, it avoided any centralizing organization, and it worshipped no glorified teacher or incarnation of deity.

It spread its message through a variety of means: human potential learning centers, experiences in self-realization training, media such as books, journals, and videocassettes and audiocassettes, music, art, conferences, psychic readings, and inner meditation. At the same time its followers actively involved themselves in much the same kind of causes as mainliners and some evangelicals as well as participating in human potential self-improvement reforms. Thus from the outset New Age has been really two movements, metaphysical/new awareness and global/self reform.[7]

Such a remarkable combination seemed at best incongruous, at worst ridiculous, to outsiders. Some insisted that the two belonged in separate categories. Others, such as New Left activists of the awakening of the 1960s, saw it as deviating from the single-minded need to concentrate on social and economic issues. Still others, such as Russell Chandler, religion editor of the *Los Angeles Times* argued that it promised people that they no longer needed to separate out truth from error, that one truth was as good as another, that "one value has no greater claim on one's life or allegiance than another. Everything is up for grabs." It appealed, he claimed, to those who wanted to become wealthy without working hard, intelligent without education, and "holy without giving up any vices."[8]

What showed clearly through the controversy was that in fact by the late 1980s an alternative movement to traditional faith had appeared; whether it was "religious" or not depended upon one's definition. New Age had arrived on the scene. It moved quickly across the country through a series of both formal and informal social networks: friends, information media, conferences, and other connections.

To prove its authenticity, its spokespersons could point to a long-standing interest in metaphysical searches in the West, especially the United States. From their Puritan beginnings, colonists showed both a fascination with and fear of psychic phenomena. Arising from a belief in the satanic possession of some young women and men in Salem, Massachusetts, the "witch" trials of 1691 and 1692 stand as the first direct encounter with established religion. Among the Pennsylvania Dutch the faithful practiced spiritual healing and held psychic healings. Both hypnotism and spiritualism (speaking through mediums, often with the dead) flourished in mid–nineteenth-century America. Considerable interest developed around 1900 in certain European psychics such as Emanuel Swedenborg and Helena Petrovna Blavatsky. In brief, Americans had been at least exposed throughout their history to the reality that such activity was being carried out.[9]

Later influences included the teachings of Edgar Cayce, who founded the Association for Research and Enlightenment. This organization has continued to the present with a staff of 150 employees, a membership of some 90,000, and an annual budget of $7.5 million. The Unity School of Christianity, which offered a form of reincarnation and other expressions of metaphysical insight, emerged during the twentieth century. It continues to the present in the United States, with 437 ministries and 147 affiliated study groups.[10] Also, through the nineteenth-century writings of Ralph Waldo Emerson and later scholars in the United States of Asian religions, the worlds of Buddhism and related Eastern religions made their way onto the scene.

None of these elements in themselves would have been responsible for the outburst of enthusiasm for psychica in the 1980s. What seems likely is that the current movement had its most visible start in 1971–1972 with the publication of the first representative text of New Age, Baba Ram Dass's *Be Here Now*, the first national magazine, *East-West Journal*, and the first network directories. That blended well with the metaphysical and subjectivist ingredients in the awakening of the 1960s. In 1971 a publisher of the occult, Carl Weschcke of Llewellyn Publications (St. Paul, Minnesota), sponsored the First American Aquarian Festival of Astrology and the Occult Sciences, treated with some skepticism by the national press and with a circuslike atmosphere by the participants. The festival became an annual event.[11]

In characteristically unorganized fashion, New Age continued to grow, especially on the West Coast and in major university cities (Boulder, Madison, Cambridge, and so on). The national media took little notice of it, regarding participants as aging hippies or disgruntled yuppies (young upwardly mobile professionals) amusing themselves away from their workday grind.

But the evangelicals started watching with concern as the bookstores, training centers, music, journals, and other networking operations expanded more widely. In 1981 evangelical James Bjornstad, an alternative-religions expert, wrote that a multipronged attack by Asian gurus, human potential occultists, and pseudo-Christian cultists was spreading their faith. What was significant was Bjorstad's belief, published in the influential *Christianity Today*, that these were more than the rather quaint spiritualists of an earlier century. These seekers were at best heretics and at worst flirting with satanism.[12]

With increased attention by national media and continued expansion by New Age seekers, evangelicals decided that they must respond. In March 1985 and ad hoc conference in Denver, sponsored by Evangelical Ministries to New Religions, with some 300 in attendance, considered the movement. As became quickly evident, evangelicals brought a very wide range of interpretations to the movement, ranging from reappearances of ancient Gnostic heretics to brainwashers, Asian-religion devotees, and witchcraft. The delegates carefully rejected the earlier, sensationalist book by Constance Cumbey, an attorney who charged in the *The Hidden Dangers of the Rainbow* (Shreveport, La.: Huntington House, 1980) that a deliberate plot by anti-Christian forces was at work to overthrow the world order and substitute a one-world dictator instead. The Denver meeting did agree that the more representative works and leaders of New Age were Marilyn Ferguson and Dave Spangler, both of whom were steadily becoming best-selling authors.[13]

By about 1987, rather suddenly, New Age consciousness became a household word for the popular media, for evangelicals, and for mainliners. Already its central features, vague as they were, became identifiable. It was being popularized by show-business celebrities, it promised utopian visions of an ideal world, and it offered inspiration for producers of movies and television programs. In short, it became a staple in popular culture, and it continued to attract supporters.[14] By decade's end New Age popularity (and hostility) could be attributed to at least seven general sources: its identification with pop culture, its skillful entrepreneurship, its spread through books and other media, its penetration into major corporations seeking to improve employee health, the influence of celebrities, its wide network of conferences, and, last, because it has by 1990 found how to appeal to what became its natural social-class constituency.

As part of pop culture, New Age programs, especially those in the world of psychic phenomena, piqued the curiosity of a large portion of the population. One opinion-researcher firm found that some 42 percent of Americans believed that they had contacted someone who had died; eleven years earlier the figure had been 27 percent. By 1987 pollsters reported that two-thirds of all American adults studied astrology charts, with 36 percent believing them to be scientific. By 1984 some 67 percent thought that they "were somewhere you had been before but knew that was impossible." In that same year the same two-thirds reported that they felt that they were in touch with someone far away from them.[15]

Many of the most popular movies focused on science-fiction and outer-space themes, some carrying vague pantheistic messages. These included *Star Wars, ET, Close Encounters of the Third Kind, Raiders of the Lost Ark*, and the like. Children's cartoon shows focused on magical manifestations of Eastern mysticism. In bookstores, Chandler found, New Age gadgets and paraphernalia came into wide demand: crystals, pyramids, incense, statues, tarot and greeting cards, charms, software for personal computers, herbal teas and medicines, out-of-the-ordinary vitamins, and massage instruments, "and that's only the beginning."[16]

Behind this stood a second cause of New Age popularity, its highly aggressive sense of entrepreneurship. Noted social critic Christopher Lasch in 1987 commented on the worst of its features, "its blatant commercialization," leading him to be suspicious of large-scale fraud. With so appealing a movement being so widely diversified, the curious customer was exposed to an enormous array of options, almost all of which were expertly prepared, advertised, and distributed. Lasch included

positive thinking, meditation, faith healing, rolfing, dietary reform, environmentalism, mysticism, yoga, water cures, acupuncture, incense, astrology, Jungian psychology, biofeedback, extrasensory perception, spiritualism, vegetarianism, organic gardening, the theory of evolution, Reichian sex therapy, ancient mythologies, archaic nature cults, Sufism, Freemasonry, cabalistic lore, chiropractic, herbal medicine, hypnosis . . . a cornu-copia.[17]

Omega Watches, for example, started a new Symbol collection of timepieces in gold and steel. They featured either the ancient Egyptian symbol of the sun or the Asian yin-and-yang circle on their faces.[18]

Through the vast, often overlapping networks of correspondence, New Age salespeople were given opportunities to move into these areas for themselves. Small-sized dealers were offered ads in nationally connected computer news services. New Age Connection offered printouts on a variety of topics such as "a good health food restaurant," attorneys, body work, psychics, or other New Age thinkers to subscribers, who were invited to advertise their services for subscribers. There was a New Age Telephone Directory, and wholesalers such as First Editions of Sedona, Arizona, offered opportunities for entrepreneurs starting up.[19]

Martin E. Marty commented,

What bothers me is that the good aspects of the New Age are consistently used in egocentric, self-deifying and nearly solipsistic ways, all in the name of "connecting"—that while wimpish Christians accept admonishment against witnessing or evangelizing in a pluralistic culture, the New Age folk aggressively advertise and proselytize. *Publishers Weekly* publishes limitless bits of counsel on how to win publics and dominate markets.[20]

Both religious and commercial bookstores started carrying large numbers of New Age titles. Often placed alongside what critics called "crank literature—Bermuda Triangle stuff," these materials became a major source of income for the dealers and another vital way of spreading New Age ideas. The total number of books in print of a given title became the best quantitive statistic to help measure numerically how widespread New Age teachings were becoming. Even these totals, however, were very hard to come by.

The major trade journal, *Publishers Weekly*, started publishing an annual survey of new titles with estimated sales (September 25, 1987, December 16, 1988, and November 3, 1989). There the full panorama of titles for retail was presented alongside forecasts of what was hot or slipping in sales. What the two numbers together represented was vivid evidence of how fast and how far New Age themes had extended in a very short period of time. The success stories and the failures of specific publishers were recounted as a record of the changing tastes in public consumption. Clearly New Age book publishing was a major item and, for some firms, the only subject in total sales.

In addition, major catalogs such as Publisher's Discount House started carrying New Age titles. So also did book clubs such as Quality Paperback Book Club. The largest national chains, B. Dalton and Waldenbooks, put in large stocks of related titles. In both cases the store managers replaced the "occult" sign over the merchandise island with "New Age." In all these instances such networks helped reach audiences who otherwise might have remained uninformed. Along the same lines, by the late 1980s the annual convention of the American Booksellers Association (ABA) started holding seminars for interested dealers; the meeting was entitled "Demystifying New Age Books." Turnouts were large. Finally, some best-selling New Age titles were placed on audiocassettes.[21]

Although specific data on sales were hard to obtain, these examples suggest the national trend. After Shirley MacLaine appeared in the 1987 television miniseries, "Out on a Limb," B. Dalton reported a 90 percent increase in sales of occult and astrology books. Ingrim Book Company, a national giant in distribution, noted that its New Age sales were moving up at about 20 percent a year. New Age magazines kept proliferating, usually outselling such Christian favorites as *Moody Monthly*.[22]

Extending the book network further, a large number of catalog sales firms both old and new started adding New Age titles. These companies, using the latest desktop computer publishing technology, turned into general stores, selling most of the items associated with the movement. These attractively printed catalogs made ordering easy with toll-free numbers and credit-card opportunities. Some specialized more in crystals or in music.

But in general, the catalog firms offered both wide selection and often more specialization in esoteric titles than could retail outlets. The best known included Master of Life, Avatar Journal, New Times, Gateways Institute, and Red Rose Gallerie. Of special interest was Inner Technologies. From there seekers could purchase a dazzling array of items: audiovisual synchronizers, biofeedback items, instruments for pain management and the enhancement of learning, and flotation tanks ("the most comfortable place since your mother's womb").[23] Obviously those interested had only to send in their orders; they did not have to travel to distant locations for their needs. A few catalog firms included newsletter items, as well as photographs of the sales staff. These were aimed at building customer loyalty. Requests were filled with handwritten notes with a personal touch added. Such, for instance, was Island Pacific NW of Eastbound, Washington. Of special interest was a title on geographic sites considered sacred or regenerative to New Agers. These included mounds, mountains, earth sculptures, and Native American meeting places. For both beginners and long-time seekers, this extended the network of national special-purpose experience even further.[24]

New Age ideas also moved more into mainstream America with the adaptation of many training programs by corporations for employees. Most were products of the human potential movement to enhance productivity, reduce stress, improve interpersonal relations, and keep on-the-job morale high. Some programs were being used before human potential and New Age ideas came into popularity; others were clearly the product of the new movements. The latter aimed at more than stress management; they centered, for instance, on transformation of consciousness and inner enlightenment. These came largely from the training in meditation, self-hypnosis, guided imagery, and yoga. In these, New Age training was experienced by persons in social settings, thus helping legitimate their credibility. By 1988 estimates ran as high as $30 billion a year for psychological training of employees, much of this in inner-renewal programs.[25]

Fortune magazine gave considerable coverage to such programs in 1987, suggesting that New Age "gurus" had adapted their standard programs to suit business clients. These included Werner Erhard and the long-standing EST program, MSIA (pronounced "Messiah") from the Mystical Traveler Consciousness, and the Church of Scientology. These were selling training programs to dozens of Fortune 500 companies (the 500 wealthiest companies rated annually by that magazine). These programs listed here aimed at more than stress management, seeking "to liberate the mind . . . by breaking the chains of habit and passivity."[26]

Popular as they were, many such programs met with strong resistance from some clients. These claimed that they had been psychologically damaged, or that programs were violating their personal religious convictions. By 1990 the total number of training programs remained high, but some employers were showing greater awareness of what to keep out of such programs to avoid lawsuits.[27]

With the enormous power of the mass media to influence behavior, superstar celebrities became another potent source of leadership for New Age ideas. Easily the most influential was actress-dancer Shirley MacLaine, who became something of a guru for huge numbers of seekers. Her books and television appearances gave credibility to traditionally esoteric teachings on reincarnation and psychic intuitions. Successful by all Hollywood standards in show business, she taught followers how to be successful with their inner lives. She also offered exercise workout tapes and endorsed spiritual healing programs.[28]

So too television stars Linda Evans ("Dynasty") and Joyce DeWitt ("Three's Company") gave credence to similar programs through their participation and endorsements. Pop singer John Denver went on the lecture circuit throughout the late 1980s, attracting large crowds for his New Age messages. The famed talk-show hostess, Oprah Winfrey of Chicago, often interviewed celebrities such as MacLaine. She also spoke frequently on her own achievement of inner peace through blending Eastern and Western religions. Hers was a "triumphal" life of providing what she called a "ministry" for exploring the human spirit.

The most publicized psychic event during this period came with the disclosure in the late 1980s that First Lady Nancy Reagan regularly consulted and followed the teachings of at least one astrologer. Making her the object of considerable ridicule, the media nonetheless could confirm in some seekers' minds that they were not alone in their searchings. Finally, superstar teachers such as Marilyn Ferguson and Jean Houston attracted large crowds with frequent public presentations.[29]

The New Age spread rapidly also because it quickly utilized a widely varying network of meetings, conferences, workshops, and seminars. These could last for half a day, a weekend, a week, or longer. Some were centered around celebrities, such as the channels J.Z. Knight, Jach Pursel, or Kevin Ryerson, or focused on specific special-purpose interests such as holistic healing, exercise, or meditation. The superstars were able to present their messages coast to coast, knowing that their fame had preceded them, and their booking agents would give them maximum publicity. Doubters or cynics of, say, channeling would notice the large crowds, the enthusiasm, and the acceptance of such out-of-the-ordinary teachings as rather normal events.

At other times multispeaker conferences featuring specialists and authors were conducted on themes such as "Dreaming the New Dream: Choices for a Positive Global Future" with actor Richard Chamberlain and author Joseph Heller, among others. Promoters would sponsor "Psychic Fairs" or "Whole Life Expos" with displays, booths, seminars, and related opportunities. In June 1989 delegates gathered in Aspen, Colorado, for "World Balance: Action to Save Our Planet." It featured a clear balance between the metaphysical and the political, with speakers from Africa, Native American medicine men, healers, Asian swamis, New Age music, and environmentalists.[30]

Longer gatherings, focused on inner healing and spirituality, were available at such health centers as the Option Institute and Fellowship: A Place for Miracles in Massachusetts. Following the pattern of several church-related retreat programs, the Option Institute scheduled programs for training, group dynamics, and "Celebrating the Perfect You." During the summer programs would run from four to eight weeks.[31] Omega Institute of Rhinebeck, New York, offered much the same program.

Variations on the theme were the many alternative-university educational programs available in academic cities. Near the University of Minnesota, Minneapolis, Open U offered studies in most of the major New Age themes along with self-help, self-defense, boxing, hobbies, and recreation.[32]

Through this system of information and social networking, New Age programs found their way into every area of the country. By the late 1980s certain sociological patterns of participation were emerging. The most obvious visual conclusion was that these were attracting upper middle-class, white, usually college-educated professional adults, mostly middle-aged. In the one representative attitudinal study known to this writer, 600 answers from a total pool of 4,000 responses to a *Body Mind Spirit* questionnaire showed that 73 percent were female, 23 percent were eighteen to thirty-four, 42 percent were thirty-five to forty-nine, and 35 percent were fifty and above. Some 45 percent had some college, and 30 percent had bachelor's or higher degrees. The geographical distribution covered all areas; occupations were scattered among professional, managerial, clerical, service, sales, and retired. Some 52 percent had been raised Protestant, Catholics were 27 percent, 3 percent were Jewish, and "none" were 11 percent. Some 63 percent said that they belonged to no church, synagogue, or temple. Over 94 percent said that they considered themselves spiritual, the same percentage that believed in God. About 79 percent made a distinction between religion and spirituality; 92 percent believed in a life after death, and 81 percent believed in reincarnation.[33]

Almost half had attended a spiritual seminar or consulted a psychic or medium in the last year, with one-third seeing an astrologer, numerologist, or palm reader. Almost 30 percent had been in a spirit channeling session. Lesser numbers had been involved with psychic healers, Eastern religions, Native American practices, Western mysticism, shamanism, goddess worship, and paganism. Almost 80 percent said that they had known psychic experiences.[34]

Except for this study, evidence for sociological identity remains mostly anecdotal and impressionistic. Some communities have enough facilities to support New Age subcultures with their own shops, restaurants, social events, and professional services, even dating bureaus. In the Twin Cities of Minnesota, the full range of New Age opportunities were available by 1988: psychic readings, herb and health-food stores, training centers, and the rest; the same was true in Colorado with its attractive mountain vistas and opportunities for solitude.[35] Observers in these places concluded that New Age was indeed becoming almost mainstream in its acceptance by its adherents. Specific intentional communities appeared in Boulder and Durango, giving attention to healing, training, and environmental causes. Those interviews matched the sociological profile suggested by the *Body Mind Spirit* study. In addition, they mostly stayed out of organized church activities but showed no animosity toward those programs. Rather, as Robert Ellwood summarizes, they are people fairly well off in the world, want everyone to be happy, seem largely unbiased, and apparently take pride in their openness to new ideas and change.[36]

TEACHINGS

New Age religion, enhanced through its elaborate networks systems, would thrive or fade because it presented a compelling set of alternative beliefs to mainline and evangelical communities of faith. In this section these beliefs are described, with concentration on its worldview, crystal healing, reincarnation and channeling, and use of music. Among participants, observers, and critics, considerable differences exist about precise definitions and societal implications. But that too is an indigenous characteristic of the movement.

Little sustained disagreement exists over New Age understanding of its political and social commitments. The well-known issues of environmental protection, animal rights, holistic health care, and the like are fundamental to the movement but attract little disputation. The battles break out over the teachings on psychic and spiritual matters. A careful student, Professor Ted Peters of Pacific Lutheran Theological Seminary, Berkeley, offered an eight-point schema that in some broad sense unites the movement. These points centered around the divine reality permeating all forms of life. First would be "wholism" (or "holism"), a reblending of spirit and body, the individual and the community: unity in diversity. Second is "monism," a metaphysical, even mystical insight that one's very being blends well with the whole of existence. "Potentiality" is the third ingredient, revolving around self-help. Each person's true self has enormous potential for development, for greater integration and happiness; one needs only to find the secrets that unlock the door to walk into one's potential.

The fourth theme is "the higher self," meaning that in this cosmos there is a higher self, a transpersonal being guiding us to mystical communion with other selves; this is something akin to Ralph Waldo Emerson's "oversoul" within each person. True knowledge then comes from understanding this spark, this divine theme within homo sapiens; to know this is to know God. "Reincarnation," point five, follows from the first four. Through death and rebirth the soul travels from one body into another; each of us has had several past lives and has more such lives ahead.

The sixth point is "evolution and transformation," the confidence that as life unfolds it evolves into better, happier levels; searches become transformed. In human potential terms, we "grow" by what efforts and dedication we ourselves give to the process. The seventh point is "gnosis," much like the "secrets" discussed earlier. Such secret or esoteric knowledge opens gates previously closed, taking the soul into higher levels of awareness. Finally, there is "Jesus, sometimes." The source of Christianity, for New Age he is the source of God's energy in this life, showing us the fullness of divinity that leads us when all is complete to know that each of us is God.[37]

Under this broad umbrella is found a considerable variety of practices; those considered here, in no particular order, have received the greatest amount of publicity and criticism, largely because for so many people these seem beyond the realm of the achievable. Crystal quartz healing has dominated much New

Age insight. Believers see the physical world in feminine, nurturing imagery. The earth, like the female, brings forth and nurtures life, sustains it, and tries to protect it from destructive tendencies. Individuals have within their grasp the actual physical matter—crystal quartz rock—to achieve this. Mother Earth has brought forth over millions of years these remarkable healers, filling them with maternal love.

Users, by experimenting and study, learn that rocks do respond to human requests for help. They emit loving, healing emissions that both physically and mentally heal human ailments. By respectful, formally prescribed rituals, practitioners can overcome by crystal power both psychosomatic and physical afflictions. These rocks can also improve memory, enhance relationships, and provide better sleep. They are best used by letting them work through specific entry points, "chakras" on the body from the top of the head to the pelvis. Their potential for good is enhanced further when the ritual includes appropriate music, aromas, and colors: in brief, a total sensuous experience.[38]

Equally attractive and denounced is the age-old belief in reincarnation. What makes it so central to New Age worldviews is its appeal to experience, intuition, and feeling rather than the Western preference for secularized, rational, cognitive data. Reincarnation has fulfilled humankind's deepest desire, that of immortality. It elevates human life as being at least in its soul indestructible while all other animal and plant life passes away. If the believer has a negative or bad incarnation in one life, it is only just (some call this "karma") that she or he has the opportunity to return to this planet to make right what needs to be done.[39]

Undoubtedly what surprised nonbelieving Americans the most about New Age spirituality was the realm of channeling. Although known to ancient psychics and transmitted in occult underground circuits over the centuries, it failed until the 1980s to become a major ingredient. In this decade it came to occupy a central position, attracting more media attention than any other single practice.

At the core stood the belief (central to reincarnation) that over the centuries certain individuals had developed unusually wise, profound, and humanely inspired insights into the entire sweep of human and cosmic experience. These individuals, referred to as "paranormal entities" or "transpersonal beings" during their sojourns on this planet, have remained in existence, to the extent that humans can understand that term. Over the centuries they have been able to share their wisdom through the channels of persons living here who have the special gift of hearing these messages and transmitting them to the rest of the human race. These messages contain teachings on the conduct of life, the improvement of relationships, the road to deeper inspiration, and the path to inner peace—the full range of New Age concerns.

During the 1980s, after some experimentation in the previous decade, channeling came into its own as a major part of the movement. Certain individuals, especially J.Z. Knight, who channels the entity "Ramtha," Jach Pursel, channeler for "Lazaris," and Kevin Ryerson, became the most famous and influential channels. In a variety of settings—one to one, in small groups, at weekend conferences, in a recording studio, and elsewhere—they and the thousands of other Americans who have taken up channeling would transform themselves into a trancelike state. Then the entity would take control of their minds, spirits, and speech. The channel would talk with the entity, often asking questions and making comments but clearly allowing the entity to state what it wished to communicate to the human race.[40]

Across the country, with high density in Southern California and the Pacific Northwest, channeling became enormously popular and profitable for its practitioners. Using the best high-tech equipment, channels recorded their sessions for audiocassettes and videocassettes; books, articles, and filmstrips present this wisdom on a repeatable basis. Enthusiasts thus could find the entity they responded to most favorably and keep hearing the channel's messages as often as they chose. Through the variety of conferences described earlier, aficionados came to meet other seekers, share common experiences, and have any doubts or reservations put away.

HEALING

These three experiences—crystal healing, reincarnation, and channeling—all embraced so vast an array of psychic and occult interests as to open to believers certain opportunities previously beyond their reach. None became more popular than the dozens of forms of healing available to the searchers. In a manner parallel to the Christian ministry of healing, New Age followers explored ancient, metaphysical, human potential, and comparable forms of making themselves, others, and the world more holistic. The most definitive recent study, that of Meredith McGuire, found Americans pursuing one or more of seventy-three different forms, some of these having subdivisions within them.[41] A major leader within the medical profession, Dr. Bernie Siegal of Yale Medical School, stated that some programs simply must be viewed critically.

I think we need to keep open minds and not get addicted to beliefs. Jung said something like, Columbus, with false assumptions and inaccurate maps, nevertheless discovered America. I think that's why we should keep an open mind; we may discover something. But I tell people, "Don't die because somebody else believes in a treatment; if you are getting worse, get out of there and try something else."[42]

Thus New Age healing was highly diversified. There were quacks and unsubstantiated claims. However, at its most responsible level, such healing embraced at least three basic premises: each person was to be treated in context, with all parts of life coming to bear on her or his improvement. Second, the emphasis should be on strong health wherever possible more than on repairing what was broken. Healing came first from within each person; hence a positive attitude was essential to good all-around health. Finally, the actual treatment would include a variety of therapies and medicines, not simply what the pharmaceutical companies were producing.[43]

That emphasis led New Agers also to see that music, in its broadest dimension, was a vital part of their searches. Not only was music an artistic expression of feelings such as love, beauty, joy, and the like, it also contained specific therapeutic values. For all these reasons New Age gave considerable attention to defining and expanding its outreach. Much of the distribution took place through the retail outlets, catalogs, and learning centers. It became popular enough to be included in the music listings of Quality Paperback Book Club and International Preview Society.

By definition, New Age music could be understood first by what it was not: classical, soul, western, swing, rock, dance, almost any established genre. It did reach into the past, however, to include ingredients from established forms. It concentrated largely on synthesizing sounds from the natural environment such as the wind and water or located meditative harmonies in repetitive forms. More than "easy listening," it aimed at bringing together wholeness, spirituality, relationships, communion, self-healing, self-attunement, universal brotherhood and sisterhood, creativity, and a oneness with the universe.[44]

Its healing intentions revolved around its message that meditation through music could lead to expanded consciousness, awareness, and inner peace. It aimed at more than entertainment; it aimed at "the growth of the human spirit." Almost always performed without lyrics, it was not to be listened to "in the ordinary sense of the word." Rather it, like crystals, channeling, and other experiences, led the searcher to find the possibilities in this new age.[45]

VARIATIONS

During this rapid expansion, religionists throughout American Christendom started taking all of New Age very seriously. On several levels some of its ideas started permeating the organized life of churches as well as individuals. Some scholars, such as Father John Rossner and Father Matthew Fox, started teaching a Christian spirituality that to many listeners seemed very heavily influenced by New Age. These and comparable writers were attempting to draw out the presence of a long-standing but largely ignored tradition of inner spirituality within the faith. Rather than focus on differences among truth claims, as theologians often did, these writers probed the depths and boundaries of synthesizing the old truths and those that seemed to be springing alive in the new era.[46]

Within the Roman Catholic church leaders found the teachings of Fox in particular to be moving into "dangerous and deviant" areas. In October 1988 the pope ordered Fox, founder and director of the Institute in Culture and Creation Spirituality in Oakland, California, to remain silent about such matters for one year. Fox insisted that he was neither dangerous nor deviant but accepted the church's discipline. The national media gave the matter extensive coverage, making Fox for many New Agers and their supporters something of a cultural hero. Fox acknowledged New Age influences but also pointed to the long-standing tradition of spirituality and mysticism within European Christendom as a source of his probings. He failed to convince the Vatican, however, and spent the twelve months in travel and study.[47]

Fox had enthusiastic followers among Protestants as well as Catholics. That family, however, found by decade's end that it had other kinds of problems with New Age. Within the mainline branch concern was expressed by leaders over whether the fascination many were showing with the paranormal would in fact lead even more members out of the ranks.[48] For those who stayed, the problem was made vivid by the sudden popularity of a widely distributed study program, *A Course in Miracles*. Russell Chandler called this 1,200-page compendium of new spiritualist-psychic teachings "the biggest camel's nose to slip into the churches' tent." Starting to grow slowly in 1976, by decade's end the program had attracted over 500,000 purchasers of the work, which cost from twenty-five to forty dollars.[49]

The work of several California writers, *A Course in Miracles* sought to synthesize several spirituality themes with much of mainline Christian teaching. It evolved out of the 1960s to its first major publication in 1976. It was couched in Biblical terminology; its authors claimed that it was channeled by Jesus, at least in part. Through the networks described earlier, *A Course in Miracles* became something of a phenomenon in some liberal mainline parishes. Its popularity illustrated vividly how the battle within some mainline bodies was faring between pressers and holders.[50]

Within evangelical and mainline churches alike the response to the whole movement came in various forms. Many approved strongly of New Age concern for protecting the physical environment, global peace, and physical and mental health, among other issues. Others regarded it as simply more vague yuppie yearnings.[51] One leading scholar, Catherine L. Albanese, found that actually New Agers and fundamentalists shared several matters in common. Both insisted that "personal transformation and direct spiritual experience" were at the core of one's existence; for both, personal change must lead to changing society. Both shared a similar kind of vision, a mysticism that emerged from fundamentalist insistence on the instant-conversion "new birth" and for the New Ager from intuition and channels. Both agreed that healing is of the highest importance, with charismatics and Pentecostalists among fundamentalists finding in spiritual healing an area of common ground with New Age healers. Both insisted on a nonelitist, grass roots, do-it-yourself kind of leadership and popular religion expression.[52]

Other observers found more differences than similarities. New Age teachings reflected the earlier soft modernist doctrine fundamentalists had come to despise. Fundamentalists believed in "magic," but the magic performed by Satan and demonstrable in their view in certain New Age practices. Third, fundamentalists could not agree with New Age teaching that inner spirituality is self-generated; it must come only from God. Finally, fundamentalists put great emphasis on precise wording of pure doctrine; New Agers relied far more heavily on intuition, feelings, and hunches and less on doctrine.[53]

Another branch of evangelicalism, led by best-selling author Dave Hunt, saw only the end of Christianity with the expansion of New Age. Fearful that the End

Times were coming with millions of people still unconverted and in fact being seduced by New Age blandishments, Hunt called on true believers to purge all suspected forms of the movement from the faith. His book became something of a fad, selling over 650,000 copies by mid-1988.[54] Other conservative bodies such as the Southern Baptists and Lutheran Church–Missouri Synod published brief, scripturally based critiques of the movement. Almost every major evangelical publishing house brought out at least one and often several polemical attacks on the movement. The anticult, antimodernist research think tanks such as Cult Awareness Network of Chicago, Christian Research Institute, and Scriptural Counterfeits Project of California produced increasingly long articles of analysis by decade's end. So too, did one of evangelicalism's sharpest critics, the avowedly secular humanist Prometheus Press of Buffalo, New York. With several titles and its quarterly journal, *Skeptical Inquirer*, it joined those who found no common ground between evangelicalism and the New Age, and not much in either movement to create optimism in the future for the liberal seeker.

By 1990 New Agers could look forward with genuine optimism to the last decade before the millennium; the secrets of this cosmos were fast being discovered and turned into the truths by which they attempted to live. Mainliners, meanwhile, along with evangelicals, found little cause to welcome the appearance of the last ten-year span. As AIDS, terrorism, environmental despoilment, drug-use epidemics, implacable division over abortion, and similar matters kept their attention, they could well wonder what kind of a world would be there for what kind of a celebration of the dawn of the next millennium.

NOTES

1. Robert Bellah et al., *Habits of the Heart: Individualism and Commitment in American Life* (Berkeley: University of California Press, 1985), see the priorities of this triumvirate in part 2, "Public Life."

2. Robert Ellwood, *The History and Future of Faith* (New York: Crossroad, 1988), p. 15; Barbara Hargrove, *The Emerging New Class: Implications for Church and Society* (New York: Pilgrim Press, 1986), pp. 164–67; and the critique of New Age beliefs by Gregory Baum, *Theology and Society* (Mahwah, N.J.: Paulist Press, 1987), p. 294.

3. Robert Ellwood, "Occult Movements in America," in Charles H. Lippy and Peter W. Williams, eds., *Encyclopedia of the American Religious Experience*, Vol. 1 (New York: Scribner, 1988), p. 722.

4. Editorial in *The 1989 Guide to New Age Living* (P.O. Box 853, Farmingdale, NY, 1988), p. 103.

5. Jonathan Adolph, "What Is New Age?" *The 1988 Guide to New Age Living*, pp. 5ff.; Jean Callahan, "Cosmic Expectations," *New Age Journal*, November/December 1987, p. 82; David Toolan, "Hunting for Spiritual Gurus," *Catholic World*, May/June 1989, p. 120.

6. Jeremy P. Tarcher, "The New Age," *Master of Life*, no. 39 (1988): 17; Bill Moyers, interview with Joseph Campbell, *New Age Journal*, July/August 1988, p. 83.

7. See the dualism as shown in the best-seller lists for New Age in *Publishers Weekly*, December 16, 1988, p. 18. Also see all of the annual *New Age Catalog* (New York: Doubleday Dolphin Books); and the *New Age Yellow Pages* (Fullerton, Calif.: NAYP, 1989), Box 5978-B, Fullerton, CA 92635.

8. Interview with Russell Chandler, *Door*, March/April 1989, pp. 6ff.; Tom Athanasiou, "The Age of Aquarius," *Nation*, July 10, 1989, p. 61; Andrew Kimbrell, "The Coming Era of Activism: New Left Meets New Age," *Utne Reader*, March/April 1988, pp. 63 ff.

9. J. Gordon Melton, *Encyclopedia of American Religions*, 3d ed. (Detroit: Gale Research, 1989), pp. 115–20; Russell Chandler, *Understanding the New Age* (Waco, Tex.: Word Books, 1988), pp. 43–50.

10. Melton, *Encyclopedia of American Religion*, pp. 639–40; *National Christian Reporter*, February 17, 1989, p. 2.

11. Lawrence Sutin, "Father of the New Age," *Minnesota Monthly*, May 1989, pp. 32–39.

12. James Bjornstad, "America's Spiritual, Sometimes Satanic, Smorgasbord," *Christianity Today*, October 23, 1981, pp. 1377–78.

13. News item, *Moody Monthly*, June 1985, pp. 62–64; news item, *Christianity Today*, May 17, 1985, pp. 68–69; *Cornerstone* 14, 74 (1986): 16; Doug Groothius, "The Greening of American Politics," *Eternity*, November 1985, pp. 23–28. See Marilyn Ferguson, *The Aquarian Conspiracy: Personal and Social Transformations in the 1980s* (Los Angeles: J. P. Tarcher, 1980), and Dave Spangler, *Emergence: The Rebirth of the Sacred* (New York: Delta Books, 1984).

14. Robert J. L. Burrows, "Americans Get Religion in the New Age," *Christianity Today*, May 16, 1987, pp. 17–23.

15. Chandler, *Understanding the New Age*, pp. 20–21; George Gallup, Jr., and Jim Castelli, *The People's Religion: American Faith in the 90s* (New York: Macmillan, 1989), pp. 75–77; Andrew Greeley, *Religious Change in America* (Cambridge: Harvard University Press, 1989), pp. 58–59.

16. Chandler, *Understanding the New Age*, p. 24; Norman Geisler, "The New Age Movement," *Bibliotheca Sacra* 144, 573 (January–March 1987): 80–81; "New Age Harmonies," *Time*, December 7, 1987, p. 64; William D. Dinges, "Aquarian Spirituality: The New Age Movement in America," *Catholic World*, May/June 1989, pp. 137–42.

17. Christopher Lasch, "Soul of a New Age," *Omni* 10, 1 (October 1987): 79–81. The major periodicals are *New Age Journal* and *Body Mind Spirit*.

18. John Taylor, "Nervous about the Nineties," *New York*, June 10, 1988, p. 34.

19. P.O. Box 9408, Austin, TX 78766; letter to the author, June 7, 1989.

20. Martin E. Marty, "Memo," *Christian Century*, January 4–11, 1989, p. 31.

21. "News," *Christian Retailing*, October 15, 1988, p. 10.

22. Ibid., pp. 1, 10.

23. Catalog, Inner Technologies, Spring 1989 (51 Berry Trail, Fairfax, CA 94930).

24. Natasha Peterson, *Sacred Sites: A Traveler's Guide to North America's Most Powerful, Mystical Landmarks* (Chicago: Contemporary Books, 1988).

25. Richard Watring, "New Age Training in Business," *Eternity*, February 1988, pp. 30–34; news item, *Christianity Today*, June 17, 1988, pp. 70–74; *U.S. News and World Report*, February 9, 1987, pp. 67–69; catalog for the Robert Theobold program, "Guidebook for the 90s," Indianapolis.

26. Jeremy Main, "Trying to Bend Managers' Minds," *Fortune*, November 23, 1987, pp. 95–96; Chandler, *Understanding the New Age*, pp. 144–52.

27. Main, "Trying to Bend Managers' Minds," pp. 100–105; Spiritual Counterfeits Project, *SCP Newsletter*, 14, 1 (1988), pp. 1ff.; Karen Cook, "Scenario for a New Age," *New York Times Magazine*, September 25, 1988, pp. 26–27ff.

28. *New Age Journal*, May/June 1989, n.p.; Chandler, *Understanding the New Age*, pp. 22–23.

29. *Minneapolis Star Tribune*, June 18, 1989, p. 3A; ibid., May 15, 1988, p. 29A; Christian Research Institute, "Newsletter," June 1989, p. 1; Promotion letter, Oasis Center, Chicago, 1989; *National and International Religion Report*, September 7, 1987, p. 1; Barbara Grizziti Harrison, "The Importance of Being Oprah," *New York Times Magazine*, June 11, 1989, pp. 28–30ff.

30. *New Age Journal*, May/June 1989, n.p.

31. See the Option Institute's 1989 brochure; Rural Delivery Box 1741, Sheffield, MA 01257.

32. See Open U's 1988 catalog, Suite 102, 1313 S.E. Fifth St., Minneapolis, MN 55414.

33. *Body Mind Spirit*, May 1989, pp. 83ff.; Gallup and Castelli, *People's Religion*, pp. 75–77.

34. See again *Body Mind Spirit*, May 1989, pp. 83ff.

35. On these communities see Paul Levy, "New Age," *Minneapolis Star Tribune Magazine*, March 13, 1987; Fergus M. Bordewich, "Colorado's Thriving Cults," *New York Times Magazine*, May 1, 1988, pp. 36ff.; a series in the *Durango, Colorado, Herald*, 1989; Oliver and Cris Popenoe, *Seeds of Tomorrow: New Age Communities That Work* (San Francisco: Harper and Row, 1984).

36. Robert Ellwood, "The New Age in the New World: Social Perspectives," *Catholic World*, May/June 1989, p. 115. The connections with the "new class" are in Hargrove, *Emerging New Class*, pp. 140–68.

37. Ted Peters, "The Gospel of the New Age," *Dialog* 28, 1 (Winter 1989): 20–25; see also Marsha Sinetar, "Growing Up and Growing Whole Together," *Catholic World*, May/June, 1989, pp. 106–11.

38. A good brief summary is Edmund Harold, *Focus on Crystals* (New York: Ballantine Books, 1986); feminist themes are discussed in the interview of Lynn Andrews, *Body Mind Spirit*, September/October 1988, pp. 21ff. Almost every New Age supplier has crystal quartz collections; a critical evaluation in scientific terms is Bruce Hathaway, "Is There Anything Quartz Can't Do?" *Smithsonian* 19, 8 (1988): 82–103.

39. Melton, *Encyclopedia of American Religion*, 2d ed. (Detroit, Mich.: Gale Research, 1987), pp. 112–16; Chandler, *Understanding the New Age*, pp. 262–69.

40. Of the dozens of books on channeling, a good starting point is Chandler, *Understanding the New Age* pp. 80–88; a critical evaluation is Elliot Miller, "Channeling," *Christian Research Journal* 10, 2 (Fall 1987): pp. 8–15; 10, 3 (Winter/Spring 1988): 16–22.

41. Meredith B. McGuire, *Ritual Healing in Suburban America* (New Brunswick, N.J.: Rutgers University Press, 1988), pp. 263–65.

42. Interview in *New Age Journal*, May/June 1989, p. 37; Chandler, *Understanding the New Age*, pp. 162–70.

43. See the critical study by Dr. Paul C. Reisser et al., *The Holistic Healers: A Christian Perspective on New Age Health Care* (Downers Grove, Ill.: Inter-Varsity Press, 1983), chap. 2.

44. Louis M. Savery, "New Age Music and Spirituality," *Catholic World,* May/June 1989, p. 122.

45. Ibid., pp. 112–24. See the story on a New Age music leader, Steven Halpern, ibid., pp. 125–28. See also the Windham Hall catalogs; *St. Paul Pioneer Press Dispatch,* March 27, 1988, pp. 1D, 3D.

46. John Rossner, *In Search of the Primordial Tradition and the Cosmic Christ* (St. Paul: Llewelyn Publications, 1989).

47. *New York Times,* October 21, 1988, p. 9; Ted Peters, "Matthew Fox and the Vatican Wolves," *Dialog* 28 (Spring 1989): 137–42; *National Catholic Reporter,* November 11, 1988, pp. 1ff.; Laura Hagar, "Interview with Matthew Fox," *New Age Journal,* March/April 1989, pp. 53ff.; *Washington Post,* October 22, 1988, p. D19; Rev. James LeBar, *Cults, Sects, and the New Age* (Huntington, Ind.: Our Sunday Visitor, 1989).

48. David Toolan, *Facing West from California's Shores: A Jesuit's Journey into New Age Consciousness* (New York, Crossroad, 1987); *Los Angeles Times,* February 14, 1987, sec. 2, p. 5.

49. Chandler, *Understanding the New Age,* p. 210; catalog, Miracle Distribution Center, Fullerton, Calif.; Tara Singh, *A Course in Miracles* (Los Angeles: Life Action Press, 1976).

50. Sandra Matuschka, "A Course in Miracles: Panacea for Mankind," *Body Mind Spirit,* July/August 1989, pp. 18–22ff.; for a critical view, see the interview by Dean Halverson, "A Matter of Course: Conversation with Kenneth Wapnick," *SCP Journal* 7, 1 (1987): 8–17.

51. Chandler, *Understanding the New Age,* pp. 222–23.

52. Catherine L. Albanese, "Religion and the American Experience: A Century After," *Church History,* October 1988, pp. 337–51. Some charismatic used subliminal tapes of the Bible, parallel to New Age programs; *Charisma and Christian Life,* August 1989, p. 14.

53. Clarence Thomson, "Revelation and Response: What the New Age Can Teach Us," *Catholic World,* May/June 1989, pp. 129–33.

54. Dave Hunt and T. A. McMahon, *The Seduction of Christianity: Spiritual Discernment in the Last Days* (Eugene, Oreg.: Harvest House, 1985).

Selected Bibliography

REFERENCE WORKS

Barrett, David B. *World Christian Encyclopedia*. New York: Oxford University Press, 1982.

Burgess, Stanley M., and Gary B. McGee, eds. *Dictionary of Pentecostal and Charismatic Movements*. Grand Rapids, Mich.: Regency Reference Library, Zondervan Publishing House, 1988.

Directory of Publications: An Annual Guide to Newspapers, Magazines, Journals, and Related Publications. Detroit: Gale Research, 1989.

Eliade, Mircea, ed. *The Encyclopedia of Religion*. 16 vols. New York: Macmillan, 1987.

Encyclopedia of Associations. 3 vols. 23d ed. Detroit: Gale Research, 1989.

Forsberg, Randall, and Carl Conetta, eds. *Peace Resource Book, 1988–1989*. Cambridge, Mass.: Ballinger Publishing Company, 1988.

Hill, Samual S., ed. *Encyclopedia of Religion in the South*. Macon, Ga.: Mercer University Press, 1984.

Jacquet, Constant H., ed. *Yearbook of American and Canadian Churches*. Nashville, Tenn.: Abingdon Press, annual.

Lippy, Charles H., and Peter W. Williams, eds. *Encyclopedia of the American Religious Experience: Studies of Traditions and Movements*. 3 vols. New York: Scribner, 1988. This has extensive bibliographies on each of the many subjects.

Mead, Frank S., ed. *Handbook of Demonstrations in the United States*. 8th ed., rev. S.S. Hill. Nashville, Tenn.: Abingdon Press, 1985.

Melton, J. Gordon. *The Encyclopedia of American Religions*. 3d ed. Detroit: Gale Research, 1989.

NEWSPAPERS

National Catholic Reporter. Kansas City, Mo.

National Christian Reporter. Dallas, Tex.

National and International Religion Report. Roanoke, Va.

Religion Watch. North Bellmore, N.Y.

SCHOLARLY JOURNALS

American Theological Library Association (ATLA), Evanston, Ill., has many bibliographies, including *Religion One Index*, and annual bibliographic listing of articles in religion
journals. Most seminaries publish a scholarly journal in religious studies.

Christian Scholar's Review
Church History
Journal for the Scientific Study of Religion
Journal of Christianity and Psychology
Journal of Church and State
Journal of Ecumenical Studies
Journal of Psychology and Theology
Journal of the American Academy of Religion
Religious Research Review
Religious Studies Review
S/A. Sociological Analysis

GENERAL JOURNALS

This list is only suggestive of the dozens of relevant journals.

Body Mind Spirit
Catholic World
Charisma and Christian Life
Christian Century
Christian Herald
Christianity and Crisis
Christianity Today
Commentary
Commonweal
Cross Currents
Eternity
Fundamentalist Journal
Moody Monthly
New Age Journal
Sojourners
U.S. Catholic
Wittenburg Door (now titled *The Door*)

SECONDARY WORKS

This selective list concentrates on the most recent titles, most not in earlier bibliographies
on this general subject.

Averill, Lloyd. *Religious Right, Religious Wrong: A Critique of the Fundamentalist
    Phenomenon*. New York: Pilgrim Press, 1989.

Balmer, Randall. *Mine Eyes Have Seen the Glory: A Journey into the Evangelical Sub-culture in America*. New York: Oxford University Press, 1989.

Bellah, Robert et al. *Habits of the Heart: Individualism and Commitment in American Life*. Berkeley: University of California Press, 1985.

Carr, Anne E. *Transforming Grace: Christian Tradition and Women's Experience*. San Francisco: Harper and Row, 1988.

Castelli, Jim. *A Plea for Common Sense: Resolving the Clash between Religion and Politics*. San Francisco: Harper and Row, 1988.

Chandler, Russell. *Understanding the New Age*. Waco, Tex.: Word Books, 1988.

Corbett, Julia Mitchell. *Religion in America*. Englewood Cliffs, N.J.: Prentice-Hall, 1990.

D'Emilio, John, and Estelle B. Freedman. *Intimate Matters: A History of Sexuality in America*. New York: Perennial Library, Harper and Row, 1988.

Diamond, Sara. *Spiritual Warfare: The Politics of the Christian Right*. Boston: South End Press, 1989.

Dobson, Ed, and Ed Hindson. *The Seduction of Power: Preachers, Politics, and the Media*. Old Tappan, N.J.: Fleming H. Revell, 1988.

Fishwick, Marshall W., and Ray B. Browne, eds. *The God Pumpers: Religion in the Electronic Age*. Bowling Green, Ohio: Bowling Green State University Popular Press, 1987.

FitzGerald, Frances. *Cities on a Hill: A Journey through Contemporary American Cultures*. New York: Touchstone Book ed., Simon and Schuster, 1987.

Flake, Carol. *Redemptorama: Culture, Politics, and the New Evangelicalism*. Garden City, N.Y.: Anchor Press, Doubleday and Co., 1984.

Fowler, Robert Booth. *Unconventional Partners: Religion and Liberal Culture in the United States*. Grand Rapids, Mich.: Wm. B. Eerdmans, 1989.

Frankl, Razelle. *Televangelism: The Marketing of Popular Religion*. Carbondale: Southern Illinois University Press, 1987.

Gallup, George, Jr., and Jim Castelli. *The People's Religion: American Faith in the 90s*. New York: Macmillan, 1989.

Hertzke, Allen D. *Representing God in Washington: The Role of Religious Lobbies in the American Polity*. Knoxville: University of Tennessee Press, 1988.

Himmelstein, Jerome L. *To the Right: The Transformation of American Conservatism*. Berkeley: University of California Press, 1990.

Hoover, Stewart M. *Mass Media Religion: The Social Sources of the Electronic Church*. Los Angeles: Sage Publications, 1988.

Horsfield, Peter G. *Religious Television: The American Experience*. New York: Longman, 1984.

Hunter, James Davison. *Evangelicalism: The Coming Generation*. Chicago: University of Chicago Press, 1987.

Klatch, Rebecca E. *Women of the New Right*. Philadelphia: Temple University Press, 1987.

Lotz, David W., Donald W. Shriver, Jr., and John F. Wilson, eds. *Altered Landscapes: Christianity in America, 1935–1985*. Grand Rapids, Mich.: Wm. B. Eerdmans, 1989.

McGuire, Meredith B. *Ritual Healing in Suburban America*. New Brunswick, N.J.: Rutgers University Press, 1988.

Moen, Matthew. *The Christian Right and Congress*. Birmingham: University of Alabama Press, 1989.

Nash, Roderick Frazier. *The Rights of Nature: A History of Environmental Ethics*. Madison: University of Wisconsin Press, 1989.

Neitz, Mary Jo. *Charisma and Community: A Study of Religious Commitment within the Charismatic Renewal*. New Brunswick, N.J.: Transaction Books, 1987.

Parsons, Paul F. *Inside America's Christian Schools*. Macon, Ga.: Mercer University Press, 1988.

Peshkin, Alan. *God's Choice: The Total World of a Fundamentalist Christian School*. Chicago: University of Chicago Press, 1986.

Phy, Allene Stuart, ed. *The Bible and Popular Culture in America*. Philadelphia: Fortress Press, 1985.

Poloma, Margaret. *The Assemblies of God at the Crossroads*. Knoxville: University of Tennessee Press, 1989.

Reichley, A. James. *Religion in American Public Life*. Washington, D.C.: Brookings Institution, 1985.

Robbins, Thomas, and Dick Anthony, eds. *In God We Trust: New Patterns of Religious Pluralism in America*. New Brunswick, N.J.: 2nd ed., Transaction Publishers, 1990. This has an excellent bibliography.

Roof, Wade Clark, and William McKinney. *American Mainline Religion: Its Changing Shape and Future*. New Brunswick, N.J.: Rutgers University Press, 1987.

Rose, Susan D. *Keeping Them out of the Hands of Satan*. New York: Routledge, 1988.

Rosenberg, Ellen M. *The Southern Baptists: A Subculture in Transition*. Knoxville: University of Tennessee Press, 1989.

Rothenberg, Stuart, and Frank Newport. *The Evangelical Voter: Religion and Politics in America*. Washington, D.C.: Institute for Government and Politics, 1984.

Scanzoni, Letha, and Nancy Hardesty. *All We're Meant to Be: Biblical Feminism for Today*. Rev. ed. Nashville, Tenn.: Abingdon Press, 1986.

Shepard, Charles E. *Forgiven: The Rise and Fall of Jim Bakker and the PTL Ministry*. New York: Atlantic Monthly Press, 1989.

Wuthnow, Robert. *The Restructuring of American Religion: Society and Faith since World War II*. Princeton: Princeton University Press, 1988.

_____ . *The Struggle for America's Soul: Evangelicals, Liberals, and Secularism*. Grand Rapids, Mich.: Wm. B. Eerdmans, 1989.

Index

About the Author

ERLING JORSTAD is Professor of History and American Studies at St. Olaf College. He is the author of eight books, including *The New Christian Right*: *Prospects for the Post-Reagan Era*, and many journal articles and reviews.